THE

SECRET LANGUAGE

OF

COMPETITIVE
INTELLIGENCE

THE

SECRET LANGUAGE

OF

COMPETITIVE
INTELLIGENCE

HOW TO SEE THROUGH AND STAY AHEAD OF
BUSINESS DISRUPTIONS, DISTORTIONS, RUMORS,
AND SMOKE SCREENS

LEONARD M. FULD

CROWN
BUSINESS
NEW YORK

Published in the United States by Crown Business,
an imprint of the Crown Publishing Group,
a division of Random House, Inc., New York.
www.crownpublishing.com

Crown Business is a trademark and the Rising Sun colophon is a
registered trademark of Random House, Inc.

Library of Congress Cataloging-in-Publication Data
Fuld, Leonard M.
    The secret language of competitive intelligence : how to see
through and stay ahead of business disruptions, distortions,
rumors, and smoke screens / Leonard M. Fuld.—1st ed.
        p.   cm.
    Includes index.
    1. Business intelligence.   I. Title.
HD38.7.F865   2006
658.4'72—dc22   2005032331

ISBN-13: 978-0-609-61089-3
ISBN-10: 0-609-61089-9

Printed in the United States of America

DESIGN BY BARBARA STURMAN

10 9 8 7 6 5 4 3 2 1

First Edition

To Bert and Inge Fuld,
Stanley and Doris Domb,
my love and thanks

CONTENTS

THE

SECRET LANGUAGE

OF

COMPETITIVE
INTELLIGENCE

DISRUPTIONS, DISTORTIONS, RUMORS, AND SMOKE SCREENS

Just Another Day in the Office

The secret language of competitive intelligence is based on two building blocks. The first is the ability to find the right competitive information. The second, and most critical, is the ability to see past market disruptions and dispassionately interpret events. While I have spent nearly my entire professional life assessing and writing about competitive intelligence, I came to realize recently that it was also a major part of my father's unusual introduction to America as a new immigrant. His experience has helped me appreciate anew the framework for this book.

Along with my grandparents and his brother, my father fled Germany in 1937, barely escaping with his life. Five years later, at age eighteen, he was drafted into the United States Army, thick German accent and all.

In 1943, after my father completed basic training, an officer assigned to the army's counterintelligence group determined that this recent refugee dressed in army fatigues, with his knowledge of

Germany, its culture and language, was an asset the military could use. Dad was told to pack his bags and join hundreds of other German-speaking immigrant GIs at Camp Ritchie in Maryland, a training center for psychological warfare.

Hidden away in the Maryland hills, Camp Ritchie was designed to turn my father and other young immigrants into expert interrogators and interpreters. Ritchie's intelligence officers taught my father to read maps, memorize the Order of Battle (literally a family tree of the German command structure), understand basic cryptography, and apply methods of interrogation and translation. Toward the end of his tour of duty as a Camp Ritchie graduate, he served as a document translator for the Nuremberg trials immediately following the war.

Lots of soldiers in World War II learned how to read maps and conduct interrogations. Some had even learned German in school. German was not a secret language (except for those who could not speak German). The advantage those in Camp Ritchie had over American speakers of German was a depth of experience about Germany and its culture that allowed for interpretation. What made my father's experience different, what made the Camp Ritchie crew so effective, was the ability to apply culture and language to peer into the enemy's mind . . . and ultimately to interpret key messages.

As an example, my father tells this story: "Immediately following the war, I was sent to Cologne, Germany, as part of the military's counterintelligence group. There I interrogated a captured German soldier who claimed that he was from Hessen [a province in Germany], the same part of Germany where I grew up.

"I could tell instantly from his dialect that he was not from Hessen. It would be as if someone with a deep Southern accent in the United States claimed he was from New York or Detroit. He spoke in a way that told me he was from somewhere else altogether in Germany. I passed this information on to my officers, who interrogated him further and discovered that he was an SS officer who was attempting to escape notice."

This seemingly minor incident speaks volumes about how you develop useful intelligence. It demonstrates the importance of observation and how the appreciation of even the tiniest subtlety, such as detecting a dialect that was out of place, can yield great insight.

My father's very foreignness gave him an intelligence advantage over the many other American-born soldiers and officers at the camp, some of whom were attorneys or other highly educated professionals. Unfortunately, education alone could not unlock the information the army needed. Being able to stand outside their own culture—in this case the enemy's culture—made the Camp Ritchie graduates a priceless asset. Foreignness can be a gift in intelligence.

The interpretation and implication lessons in army intelligence my father and the U.S. military collaborated on more than half a century ago are similar in striking ways to those you will find in many of this book's business cases. You will discover, among other aspects of competitive intelligence, that being an outsider can be turned into an asset when it comes to analyzing critical competitive moves. Call these the "Camp Ritchie Rules."

The simplicity of the Camp Ritchie Rules has helped me dispel any number of misconceptions managers hold about competitive intelligence—for example, that it is impossible to develop deep insights on a rival without committing an illegal act. Or that publicly available information limits you to what you can find in an annual report or a Wall Street analyst's newsletter. Or that private companies or subsidiaries are just beyond our intelligence reach. These notions are all wrong, as this book's cases clearly prove.

Competitive intelligence—analyzed information that gives you insight and competitive advantage—is a discipline that can be taught. You and everyone else in your company, from salespeople to research scientists, can apply this discipline to improve market standing and bottom-line results.

This isn't to say that the discipline is simple and easy to learn. The biggest challenge most managers face is that they are surrounded by smoke screens, rumors, and competitive distortions. Competitors create smoke screens all the time—and the marketplace helps them out with a glut of information and misinformation. Rumors (sometimes intentionally, sometimes unintentionally placed) course through markets, prompting managers to react inappropriately or to ignore danger signs altogether.

You need to see through these smoke screens—not wait them out. If you wait until the smoke clears, you may have delayed too long. You may find that your opportunity has disappeared or the threat solidified. Either way, you lose. You need to see ahead of your competition and spot a major disruption long before it lands on your doorstep.

One thing is for certain: Competitive intelligence is both every manager's responsibility and opportunity. Corporations have begun to recognize this fact. A search on the Factiva news service (a Dow Jones–Reuters news service) reveals a meteoric rise in awareness of competitive intelligence. The number of news articles on competitive or competitor intelligence multiplied from 68 in 1990 to 157 in 1994, 751 in 1998, and 9,574 in 2003.[1] The news stories covered the need for intelligence from North America, Latin America, Europe, and throughout the Asia/Pacific region and in nearly every area of business, from R&D to sales to marketing to operations to communications.

The growth of the Society of Competitive Intelligence Professionals, based in Alexandria, Virginia, from a handful of members in 1986 to thousands today from around the globe, is another indication of the concept's acceptance within most large corporations. Yet this growth begs a question: How can even a few thousand intelligence professionals hope to meet the intelligence needs that emanate from everywhere in the corporation? As I have suggested, they can't and they shouldn't.

Competitive intelligence, as a means to see through and ahead of fast-changing rivals, has become a critical component in the business arsenal. It should be part of everyone's job. At the same time, intelligence itself has evolved into something much less neat, clean, and easy to manage. It has become more sophisticated and, for those who take full advantage of it, an ever more powerful weapon.

You must realize that there are new realities in today's competitive intelligence world. I have identified five you will need to appreciate and apply.

REALITY 1: INTELLIGENCE IS AN ART FORM

More than ever, effectively seeing through or ahead of the competition is an art form (as opposed to a totally rational and structured technique), but one that is very accessible to those willing to learn its tools, techniques, and concepts. There's a creative aspect to taking gobs of loose data and making sense out of them. Data on the competition does not come in nice, bow-wrapped, hexadecimal packages that you can digest by spreadsheet, regression analysis, or even a well-written memo. It may appear in the form of a picture, an observation of the active crowd huddled around a trade show booth, the pregnant pause of a speaker on the podium in reaction to a tough question. The observer is the artist here. He or she needs to catch the important clues, piece this image together, and create the precious intelligence.

Sometimes the artist's impression can appear in a minute; other times, it can take weeks or months of intense data collection. Just recently, for example, the CEO of an old-line U.S. textile company was concerned about an Asian competitor that was threatening to produce low-cost knockoff products out of a plant it announced it would operate in Indonesia. None of the dozen industry experts I spoke with could verify when the rival's plant would begin operation. However, an analyst from my firm visited the proposed location a couple of weeks later and sent us back a picture of a goat grazing in a field. Thinking he sent this in error, we asked him if he had made a mistake. "No," he responded, "this is the plant location. Based on what you see here, the company has not even begun to lay the foundation, let alone consider whether to begin production."

This one picture, this solid piece of data, the image of a goat grazing, led us to ask more precise questions, such as why the rival did not commission a contractor to build the plant. Was it short on funds? Did it run into a raft of government regulations? Or did a business shortfall delay the plant's construction? The goat image was a doorway through which we began to explore other intelligence options.

You need to appreciate the art, not necessarily become the artist. Nearly anyone can learn how to apply the art of intelligence. Like a painting, the competitive picture you ultimately see may not resemble the image you envisioned at the beginning. The picture at first may look disjointed. Only certain pieces of information become available, not all. In the example above, the CEO heard alarm bells sounded by his purchasing and sales groups. Weeks earlier, press reports had circulated news of the overseas plant's imminent opening, stoking the alarmist fires. Then the goat appeared on our screen.

The goat changed the CEO's decisions on increasing his own plant's output and sinking more money into an advertising campaign to bolster his product's brand and price point. The goat was not a number, not a newspaper article or an Internet blog, but it offered valuable insight nevertheless.

The art of intelligence is appreciating the information you have in whatever form it appears: as a picture, a conversation on a trade show floor, or an electronic spreadsheet. Art means you don't prejudge and you don't dismiss data out of hand, unless you have a reason, a logical argument, a structure, a discipline.

REALITY 2: THE MIND BLINDS

Sometimes people just get in the way of valid intelligence because their minds block out reality. There is a great psychological component to analyzing and convincing others of critical intelligence. For too many managers, denial, rationalization, groupthink, or not-invented-here attitudes are among the reasons why a competitive revelation never bubbles to the surface.

Groupthink strangles good intelligence. It is the term used by large organizations to describe the process of drawing conclusions based on what everyone has grown to believe is true but may or may not be accurate.

A recent vivid example of groupthink and its damage to intelligence assessment came from the U.S. government's decision to attack Iraq in early 2003. In July 2004, the *Report on the U.S. Intelligence Community's Prewar Intelligence Assessments on Iraq*[2] detailed a story of intelligence breakdowns that in many ways mirror the psychological stumbling blocks I have seen in companies over the last twenty-five years. The Senate's Select Committee on Intelligence found a long list of causes of intelligence failure, including these:

- **"THE 'GROUPTHINK' DYNAMIC LED THE INTELLIGENCE COMMUNITY . . . TO BOTH INTERPRET AMBIGUOUS EVIDENCE AS CONCLUSIVELY INDICATIVE OF A WMD (WEAPONS OF MASS DESTRUCTION) PROGRAM AS WELL AS IGNORE OR MINIMIZE EVIDENCE THAT IRAQ DID NOT HAVE ACTIVE AND EXPANDING WEAPONS OF MASS DESTRUCTION PROGRAM."** Successful users of intelligence, such as Herb Baum of Dial Corporation and Richard Branson of Virgin

Atlantic, deliberately find ways to break through the groupthink haze, as you will see later.

• **THE INTELLIGENCE COMMITTEE TENDED TO REJECT INFORMA-TION THAT CONTRADICTED THE PRESUMPTION THAT IRAQ HAD AN ACTIVE WMD.** One element that has always kept the intelligence fresh and real at the most savvy corporations is management's acceptance of minority or contrarian opinions.

Chances are that at one time or another you've been the victim of groupthink. Time and time again, I have seen a salesperson or a product manager just acquiesce to a colleague's conclusion without question, even though he or she saw a flaw. Too little time and too much politics get in the way. People are under pressure. A decision has to be made. The boss wants to move on to the next item on the agenda. The person pushing the flawed idea has political power and others are afraid to oppose him. Sometimes it's just easier to go along.

A case in point: During a recent war game I helped run (more about war games later), a group of product and marketing managers for a leading desktop applications package was convinced that their products were cutting-edge. For the last decade their sales figures were exemplary, but more recently the firm had started losing significant market share. Why was their market dominance threatened? these executives wondered. Just yesterday they were hot. Today they were nervous. Groupthink led this group to competitive inertia, then to competitive blindness. They thought they vanquished the small, specialty houses. And they did. What they didn't see, as they were congratulating themselves, was the likes of Microsoft and IBM sneaking up from behind. Groupthink allowed them to see only what they wanted to see. And when that happens, reality no longer has a place.

The surest approach to breaking through this intelligence barrier is to move all ideas and thoughts into an information laboratory of sorts. For example, when Herb Baum was head of Campbell Soup USA and launched a new pasta sauce, he encouraged creative, contrarian thinking by building a competitive laboratory in a large meeting room. He plastered the walls of this war room with advertisements, marketing data, and reports. The room was filled with specialists from purchasing, marketing, sales, and production. No one involved in the making and marketing of the product could hide. Everyone exposed his thoughts and made arguments before Baum, who constantly asked questions and tested assumptions. The analysis was real time. Groupthink did not have a chance in this fast-paced, intelligence-rich environment.

Another mind-related intelligence barrier is denial. People tend to see what they wish to see. Denial and rationalization can turn clarity into a blurred vision of the real world. Often, management would rather believe in the blurred but comforting view of the competition they think exists rather than in the real image.

For nearly a decade, Kodak, consumer photography's standard bearer, failed to acknowledge that digital cameras were a real threat to its business. It had lost sales to a number of new digital entrants in the photography business, companies such as Hewlett-Packard, Epson, and Fuji. After nearly a decade of dragging its feet, management could deny no longer. In late 2003, the company admitted it was not terrorism, a recession, or a decline in the travel business (all excuses presented to stock analysts in previous years) that put a severe crimp into film sales, but rather consumers' rapid conversion to digital cameras. Denial definitely had a strong grip on Kodak.

Contrast Kodak's denial with Visa International's willingness to explore the future and adjust its strategy to meet threatening changes brought on by the Internet, and you will see a stark difference between Visa's use of intelligence to shape strategy and tactics and sustain its brand and Kodak's deer-in-the-headlights inaction. Visa International, like Kodak, had placed a large bet on a single product. With Kodak it was chemical-based film; with Visa it was its traditional plastic credit cards. Faced with a problem, Kodak chose to sit tight and wait, despite mounting evidence of digital photography's very real threat. Visa's management felt it could not sit still. It needed to know more about alternative Internet payment systems that threatened its traditional credit card business and developed an early warning approach to track the threat if indeed it became real. Visa used intelligence to realistically examine its potential futures. For each future, Visa developed a successful counterstrategy. But more about Visa later.

REALITY 3: WITH THE RIGHT FRAMEWORK, YOU WILL CREATE X-RAY VISION

Frameworks allow you to see right through market static and information noise in an amazingly efficient way. You need to know which frameworks to use to develop intelligence and when to use them. The information itself is overwhelming—if you allow it to be—and becomes camouflage for a fast-moving competitor.

Frameworks can help you see through the camouflage by imposing informational discipline, filtering out distractions, and clarifying your vision of competitive reality.

Strategy games, such as war games or scenario analyses, are examples of frameworks that force you to confront today's real issues. The options a strategic game presents are more interesting and less scary than the images conjured up in your own mind. Wherever you face industry upheavals, price wars, or new entrants that may try to change the competitive rules, a war game is a way for you to decode a rival's cryptic moves before it's too late to do anything about it. You will see in an upcoming chapter just such a competitive decoding during a public war game event we ran between Harvard Business School and MIT's Sloan School of Management.

Salespeople can use gaming to decide on a bidding strategy. Long-term scenario games can help scientists decide whether or not to sink hundreds of millions of dollars into developing a particular compound whose market may not emerge for five or ten years. Marketing managers and strategists can apply games to understand which tactics would win their firm the best market share or strategic position—without suffering debilitating competitive attacks.

Beyond games, other types of frameworks allow vital information to rise to the surface, information often buried under argument, conjecture, and plain ignorance. Later in the book I describe a price war among companies in the pizza topping business. Price wars are vicious and often result in a company being unable to regain its former price footing. By conducting a rigorous (but not complicated) assessment of the rival's true costs, the company under assault no longer felt it was chasing ghosts and rumors. By knowing how the competitor ran its business and how it managed to stay profitable, management knew its true options. It now had the intelligence to survive a price war and win back market share.

REALITY 4: THE INTERNET HAS ITS OWN SECRET LANGUAGE

The Internet is the great intelligence hope, but lurking in its midst is overwhelming intelligence confusion. Because Internet-based information is so easily accessible, with lots of people reading largely the same news sources, the valuable information tends to become lost. You need to learn the secret language of the Internet in order to extract the precious leads and strategic gems. With the Net it is insight, not access, that's the key.

As soon as the World Wide Web threaded its way through the corporate consciousness, nearly everyone seized upon this wonderful new tool. Many even saw the Net as synonymous with intelligence itself. It's not.

"The Net is wonderful," all those millions of corporate desk jockeys declared. "Look at how we can Google all this information about our competition, and it's all available on our virtual desktop."

Tell that to Pierre Salinger, former JFK press secretary and ABC News Paris bureau chief who ruined his credibility by supporting an Internet-based conspiracy theory. Salinger claimed seven months after the July 17, 1996, explosion of TWA Flight 800 over the shores of Long Island, New York, that he had information that a supersecret navy missile actually blew the plane out of the sky in a botched test firing. It turns out that this conspiracy theory and many others had circulated on the Net for months. Salinger apparently failed to check the source of the so-called news item, instead claiming it came from an "unnamed French intelligence source."

U.S. government investigations ultimately led to a faulty fuel tank as the cause of the explosion, not an errant missile attack. Has this stopped wildly false claims from flying around the Net? No, not at all. In fact, as of this writing I found more than fifteen thousand statements on this single event within Google's discussion groups. Almost all appear unsubstantiated and take on characteristics of urban legend, broad statements made with an air of authority and factual certainty. Here is a portion of one such discussion thread written in the first-person only two months after the explosion (and some six months before Salinger's news announcement):

> I received the following information via fax. The source is a 747 Captain, but I cannot say anymore. His sources are reportedly reliable with inside information. He has transmitted the information already to ABC News. . . . TWA flight 800 was SHOT DOWN by a US NAVY AEGIS MISSILE fired from a guided missile ship which was in the area W-105 about 30 miles from where TWA flight 800 exploded . . .[3]

Salinger may have had every right to want to believe in this rumor. After all, only eight years earlier an Aegis missile did indeed accidentally shoot down an Iranian passenger plane due to an error. Many rumors such as this one begin with a grain of truth.

This kind of data murkiness occurs in business all the time. When you have tens of thousands of people contributing their views and opinions, facts are often lost. On September 20, 2000, the Securities and Exchange Commission (SEC) settled a case against fifteen-year-old New Jersey teenager Jonathan Lebed. Between September 1999 and February 2000, Lebed spread stock recommendations on stock he already owned, pumping up the trading volume and allowing him to pocket nearly $300,000 in gains. Whether or not you are on the side of the SEC or of Jonathan Lebed, he was part of the "whisper numbers" culture. These are individual investors who use the Net to announce their expectations for a particular stock before the official earnings announcement appears.

Whispers can skew market perception of a company. They can cloud a picture and even cause market chaos. The SEC chose to accuse Lebed of outright fraud. Yet companies tend to emit lots of informational static, legitimate static, into the market. For example, I have seen software companies announce product releases that end up severely delayed. In the industry they call this vaporware. This kind of news has rivals scurrying to respond, reacting to competitive ghosts. With all this informational static, how can you clearly understand a company's true intentions?

Learn the secret language of the Net. Anyone can learn the intelligence tricks known for years by professional analysts and librarians. Knowing these will help you reduce the blizzard of information to a trickle. It will help you locate true experts who can answer a question, not just some college kid posting a résumé. It can help you identify key suppliers and customers or even uncover a rival's supply chain—all normally hidden from view.

REALITY 5: INTELLIGENCE ROLE MODELS DO EXIST AND ARE GREAT TEACHERS OF THE ART

I've saved the most important piece of advice for last. Seek out an intelligence role model. These intelligence-savvy individuals can be anywhere within a company—on the factory floor, in the laboratory, or out in the field, talking to customers. You can find them in history books.

What can you learn from them? What is the discipline they exhibit that you should throw into your tool kit?

These intelligence sophisticates have developed sometimes very simple but lifelong habits that allow them to see right through and ahead of their competition. They know how to use meetings to extract information. They are expert at gathering information at the ground level. They know the most critical questions to ask each time they attack a market. They know which information is the most useful and which may be useless. And they know how to build intelligence networks.

While they may call it by different names, rosters of corporate legends from today's news as well as from the last couple of centuries have actively applied intelligence to achieve success. They've often made it a part of the corporate culture, part of the everyday conversation. This list of intelligence greats include Nathan Rothschild (the founder of Europe's investment house dynasty), Warren Buffett (Berkshire Hathaway CEO and investor), T. Boone Pickens (speculator and entrepreneur), Robert Crandall (former CEO of AMR Corporation, parent company of American Airlines), Herb Baum (president of Dial Corporation, makers of Dial

Soap), Richard Branson (chairman of Virgin Atlantic), and Sam Walton (founder of Wal-Mart).

You will see evidence throughout this book of how they and others made the active and honest collection and analysis of competitive insights part of their daily routine. No one in the above A-list of senior executives relegated competitive intelligence to a once-a-year strategic planning meeting or section III.A.1.iii of the five-year plan. Intelligence never sits on a shelf with these individuals. It is part of their decision-making lives.

This book is filled with dozens of stories about individuals and corporations that apply intelligence each and every day. Because my firm maintains the highest level of client confidentiality, I have deliberately disguised many of the stories and their details. Wherever such stories have become public through speeches, conference discussions, published papers, and other public disclosure, I have provided as much detail as possible.

I have written this book to allow anyone in business to learn how to begin using intelligence. There are no recipes, no fixed formulas for seeing through your competition. Rather, I have woven a tapestry of stories, examples, and ideas together. Each thread in this tapestry exhibits concepts you can use to see through your competition.

The first chapter or tapestry thread describes the first reality of intelligence as an art and how the perception of risk involved can change how you see your competition. Chapter 2 demonstrates how to overcome the second reality of denial and rationalization and improve the flow of useful intelligence.

Chapters 3, 4, and 5 describe the beauty and ease of using frameworks to create competitive crystal balls. If you face a new product rollout or an immediate competitive threat, then turn to chapter 3 to learn how to run a war game. Worried about an impending price war but cannot figure out how your rival can control its costs and apparent margins the way it does? Take a tour of a pepperoni manufacturing plant and the intelligence its management learned in chapter 4. Do you need to anticipate how the world may change and affect your product or service two, three, or even ten years out? If so, review chapter 5, which describes a framework for building an early warning process.

I can't discuss competitive intelligence without revealing the mysteries—and the pitfalls—of the Internet. In chapter 6, I assess how the Internet's very structure both creates strategic confusion and offers intelligence gems. This chapter explores the secret language of the Internet and shows you how to exploit it for competitive advantage.

The final chapters vividly illustrate how the famous and the not-so-famous in business have applied intelligence to succeed. I have taken an intellectual microscope and extracted the evidence of how they have very simply, but very consistently, applied critical intelligence to win markets, vanquish competition, or outfox even the cleverest of rivals.

Sure, in order to succeed you need good service, products that perform, and customers to buy from you. You also need intelligence. Intelligence helps you see both threats and opportunities to your business and your ability to sell, develop, or purchase. In short, intelligence should be part of your everyday business life.

Learn my father's lessons. Learn the value of standing outside to peer deeply inside. Clear the mind. Use the techniques. Develop the habit. Then go out and beat the competition. See *through* the competition to reap unimaginable financial and strategic rewards.

CHAPTER 1

THE ART OF SMART

How Intelligence Insight Helps Win the Game
of Risk and Reward

IT'S ALL ABOUT PERSPECTIVE

There's no better way to understand competitive perspective than to visit an art museum. Pay particular attention to the works of the impressionist painters. A school of impressionist artists known as pointillists, active in the late nineteenth century, rendered entire scenes with thousands of dabs of colored dots and brushstrokes, rather than with continuous lines. Look at any of these paintings up close and all you see are dots. Stand back ten feet and you see a field of flowers or people strolling in a city park with parasols unfurled.

One of my favorite lessons in perspective comes from a painting by the impressionist painter Georges Seurat. It is called *The Seine at the Grande Jatte,* and it hangs in the Royal Museums of Fine Arts of Belgium in Brussels. Only inches away from the canvas you cannot possibly see the image of a sailboat slowly moving through the water, the lush greenery, and the trees, bushes, and blue sky overhead. Some inches away all you see are a variety of colorful smudges. The blue, green, and yellow colors make no sense. A green brushstroke here, a yellow one there. Up close, you cannot see the story the artist is trying to tell with his canvas. Step back a few feet and suddenly the image forms.

When you view the entire painting, you marvel at how the thousands of dots have formed a coherent and easily understandable picture. You note the sailboat tilting into the breeze, the rower, trees overhanging the riverbank. As you examine the image again, you begin to see more subtle aspects, the contours, geometric shapes, proportions, a tower hidden behind some trees in the distance. You gain perspective. Seurat returned to the Grande Jatte location dozens of times. With each visit he saw different details. Staring at the painting, you even begin to imagine what the artist was thinking as he filled the canvas.

Developing intelligence on a competitor is similar to creating a pointillist painting. Your goal is not to create the perfect picture but a picture that is representative of reality (just as Seurat achieved by creating his placid scene with a minimum of brushstrokes). Walk a few feet away from Seurat's image and you feel as if you had actually sat by the riverbank on that warm, languid summer day.

Intelligence is using information efficiently, making decisions on a less-than-perfect picture. It's all about seeing your competition *clearly*, understanding its strategy, and acting *early* on that knowledge.

If you are the first to see the image clearly, you have insight that is ahead of the market and of your competitors. With this insight you've just gained competitive advantage. Intelligence—whether or not it's insight about current competitive conditions or foresight about new market opportunities about to occur—is a product of a perceptive mind. It is about seeing as much of the painting as possible, as soon as possible, and acting on this less than perfectly formed picture.

Intelligence is about making critical decisions while balancing imperfect, but reasonable, knowledge with a degree of risk. Lots of people have insight, but few act on that insight in a timely manner or with the gumption to place their own wallets on the table in a high-stakes business poker game. Intelligence means having some insight but also knowing that risk accompanies the resulting decision.

Intelligence is the art of applying imperfect knowledge. It is the art of the SWAG, the Scientific Wild-Ass Guess. No matter how much information you gather, uncertainty will always exist; still, you need to make decisions. The battle for digital photography is a perfect example of risk versus certainty. It is an example of how one company denied the changing reality and delayed taking action, while another acted on that same imperfect picture and gained competitive advantage. This is the game of digital risk played between Kodak and Fuji.

THE GAME OF RISK

Kodak and Fuji each knew that the other was approaching the digital photography battleground. Both had the insight. Fuji acted early on its imperfect knowledge. Kodak, the market leader, shelved any digital innovations for many years, denying it was a threat. Kodak's delay, supported by its own market arrogance and entrenched chemical culture, fed its denial.

When Fuji Photo Film first entered the U.S. market in the 1960s, Kodak was a well-entrenched competitor. Even into the 1980s, market analysts did not see Fuji as gaining more than 15 percent of the U.S. market (mostly at the expense of Kodak's other competitors, such as 3M, Agfa-Gevaert, and General Aniline and Film [GAF]).[1]

The amateur and professional chemical-based photographic market had not changed in any substantial way for nearly one hundred years. Kodak owned that market. It kept refining first black and white, then color film products, constantly tinkering and improving film quality and ease of use. It took the lead in roll film, then 35 mm, then cartridge easy-to-load films, such as the bestselling Instamatic cameras and film. In addition, Kodak had distribution. Nearly every retailer that carried film sold Kodak. Kodak's boxes of film with their famous gold and red logo boxes were nearly ubiquitous.

Fuji acknowledged that fact. As proof, Kodak and Fuji spent many years, during the decades of the 1970s and '80s, fighting over distribution channels, not over the product itself. Kodak accused Fuji of having an unfair competitive advantage in the Japanese market because of Fuji's participation in the tightly bound *keiretsu,* or Japanese trading circles, that Kodak claimed left it out in the cold and hurt its ability to compete fairly in Japan. In one document filed by Fuji, Fuji claimed that Kodak stated, "Fuji Photo Film is a member of the Mitsui keiretsu, a vast bank-led financial group bound together by cross shareholdings and complex lending relationships."[2] Likewise, Fuji claimed that Kodak unfairly blocked

Fuji's ability to distribute through lucrative mass-merchandise outlets in the United States.

Effectively, Fuji and Kodak had reached a stalemate. From Kodak's view of the competitive game board, it controlled most of the pieces.

A SPLOTCH OF NEW PAINT

In 1979 the canvas changed for the first time in a long time. Only the Kodak folks seemed to have missed seeing the canvas—or denied its existence altogether.

Nelson Bunker Hunt and William Herbert Hunt, members of one of America's wealthiest families at the time whose fortune began with their grandfather's stake in the oil business, decided that they wanted to corner the silver market. In part, the brothers saw silver as a hedge against inflation, as well as a buffer against any further erosion in their oil holdings. With other investors, the Hunts formed a silver pool that by 1979 had amassed more than two hundred million ounces of silver, approximately half the world's supply.

When the Hunts began their investment scheme in 1973, an ounce of silver was just under $2. By the time their plans became public in late 1979, the price skyrocketed to over $50 an ounce.[3]

The Hunt brothers' attempt to corner the silver market and the resulting meteoric rise in the price of silver sent a shiver up the spines of all film producers, Kodak included. Kodak, Fuji, Agfa, and others curtailed photographic film production. Film prices rose.

The year 1979 was a soul-searching time for film manufacturers.

How long could they sustain these high prices? What about their once fat margins? What if silver, as we know it, would be so locked up that we may not have enough to meet demand?

Fortunately for Kodak and its competition, the crisis evaporated as the market for silver collapsed, thanks in part to the steps by the Federal Reserve to raise interest rates and thus drive down inflation. Kodak's management believed that its empire was protected and life would go on as it had for so many decades.

The competitive landscape had returned to normal—or so thought the folks at Kodak. Fuji's president at the time thought otherwise. He kept wondering about the what-ifs: What if silver disappeared? What if someone found a less expensive medium other than a silver-based chemical to produce photographic images?

Around the same time, another drop or two of a new-colored paint fell onto the competitive canvas. This time Kodak's and Fuji's painting would be changed forever.

In 1984 Sony introduced its first digital camera, known as the Mavica. Kodak and Fuji management experienced both of these competitive shocks: the potential silver shortage and consumer digital photography substituting for traditional film. The data were there for everyone to see. Nothing was hidden. The image began to appear.

As soon as Minoru Ohnishi, who assumed his role as president of Fuji Photo Film in 1980, experienced these two early warning shocks, he moved very quickly. "That's when I realized film-less technology was possible," Ohnishi stated at the time. Ohnishi has invested as much as $2 billion in R&D in digital technology since the early 1980s.[4]

Kodak's management saw the same painting emerge. In response, its management had already allocated lots of resources to understanding and perfecting filmless photography. By the late 1980s Kodak, the eighth-largest patent holder in U.S. history with nearly twenty thousand patents on file, had already amassed more than a thousand patents in digital imaging alone, probably more than any other company on earth. (In 1986, Kodak announced a 1.4 megapixel CCD chip, a breakthrough years ahead of its competition and nearly fifteen years before anyone could buy a consumer digital camera with such resolution.)[5]

Despite all these patents, Kodak failed to act. By the time George Fisher arrived at Kodak as CEO from Motorola (a company that epitomized everything digital), he believed that Kodak needed to enter the digital age but instead found himself facing the managers of the chemical-based film business who considered digital a threat to traditional film. Digital technology just languished in Kodak's labs.[6] Fisher left in 1999, having failed to execute his digital strategy.

Kodak slowly began to wake up, but not before more of the painting formed and not before Fuji had taken even greater control of the digital market. Other companies—not traditional players in the century-old photographic market—began to muscle in on Kodak's lucrative turf, particularly into photo processing.

Hewlett-Packard (HP) began to run away with the color printer market for amateur digital photographers. Fuji's intelligence took it in a slightly different (but perhaps more risky) direction than that of HP. It began to attack the retail minilab market, long a stronghold for Kodak.

Minilabs are highly automated miniature photo-processing

laboratories found in retail shops worldwide and can turn around your film processing in one hour. Digital minilabs are even smaller and more automated. You simply bring in your CD-ROM or memory chip, insert it into the machine, and out comes the photo while you wait.

With a multibillion-dollar market evolving in the United States for digital processing, Fuji jumped, taking some risk—risk that apparently has begun to pay off big for this onetime Kodak wannabe.

As of March 2003, Fuji had more than five thousand digital minilabs in retail outlets such as Wal-Mart and Walgreens, giving it 60 percent of the digital minilab market. Kodak had only one hundred.[7] Considering the anchor such machines in these retail locations give Fuji, Kodak has not only lost the sale of a minilab, valued at approximately $100,000 each, but also the pass-through sales of traditional film, cameras, and other promotions. Fuji has now become the rival to beat, turning the tables (at least temporarily) on Kodak.

Once reports of Fuji's digital minilab success hit the pages of *Business Week* magazine in March 2003, the competitive advantage quickly disappeared. Kodak nearly caught up, installing thousands of minilabs the year after the *Business Week* article appeared.

The story is not over. Fuji and Kodak will likely battle each other over digital and other competitive issues for many years to come. This painting formed over years, not months or days. While both Fuji and Kodak each saw the thousands of data dots of patents and technology developments shaping this picture since the mid-1980s, only Fuji assumed the risk early into this image's formation. With the market for amateur digital photography estimated to reach $12 billion over the next few years, Fuji's early use of intelligence has allowed it to capitalize on this market while Kodak plays catch-up.

How much of a competitive landscape do you need to see before you act? Apparently Fuji, the underdog, was willing to live with less information and more risk; Kodak, on the other hand, wanted less risk and more information.

Seeing clearly does not mean seeing perfectly. Fuji understood this lesson.

FROM POINTILLISM TO THE FOUR Ps

By following the nearly mythic battle between Kodak and Fuji, you can appreciate the concept of perspective but possibly forget its practical lessons. What about all those managers who had to battle the competition each and every day at Kodak or at Fuji, the folks in purchasing, sales, R&D, marketing, packaging, and so on? How would a loss of perspective have affected them? More directly, how does a loss of perspective affect *you?*

A great deal.

Loss of perspective can confuse the information you already have in hand. It can cloud your judgment. You begin to selectively choose the data you want to work with and discard other pieces. Price, product, position, and promotion—the famous four Ps of marketing—are no longer clear. Shoot from the hip substitutes for perspective. Poor long-term, costly decisions usually result.

I experienced one vivid example of perspective loss a few years ago while running a series of intelligence workshops for managers of an online vendor of technical information (let's call it Tech-Info). TechInfo repackaged and sold scientific, patent, and other technical information to industrial and high-tech companies across the globe.

The workshop took place in a large, airy conference room, lined with blank chart paper and whiteboards. As I turned the corner and opened the door, I could see the room filled with approximately two dozen of the company's senior managers. They represented nearly every key job you could imagine—sales, development, marketing, finance—and the CEO was also in attendance. As I set down my papers for the strategy workshop that day, I looked up, noticing how familiar and comfortable all of them were with one another. They joked, made pointed arguments, and left half-finished sentences incomplete simply because everyone within earshot knew what the speaker meant.

The camaraderie belied a serious problem.

For all the industry knowledge present in the room, these executives could not see very far at all. They might just as well have been wearing competitive glasses with Coke-bottle-thick lenses. That's how bad a case of competitive myopia they had.

Their industry had changed drastically over the previous two decades. Gone were the days when online information pioneers, such as SDC ORBIT and Dialog, information aggregators, could act as critical (and sometimes sole-source) distribution centers, reselling the information for dozens of publishers all under one virtual roof. Gone were the days when the librarian was the gatekeeper, the Merlin who alone understood arcane Boolean logic and strange command terms that would provide access to these information treasure houses.

The Internet, like digital imaging for Kodak, had profoundly altered TechInfo's competitive landscape over the last six years. Ever since the World Wide Web burst onto the database scene in the mid-1990s, the Dialogs of the world lost influence since publishers could sell their wares directly to information consumers via their own Web site. More important, the onrush of free information automatically devalued the high-priced for-fee information sold by TechInfo and companies like it. (More about the Internet and its intelligence value appears in chapter 6.)

Just outside this conference room was where I witnessed evidence of this change. Standing on line in the cafeteria, walking through the halls, and just talking to others around the company, I heard lots of stories. I saw anxious salespeople phoning clients to close a deal, pricing specialists trying to figure out ways to aggressively repackage what was becoming a commodity product, and software experts attempting to add ease-of-use features that might possibly add value to their company's offering—and thereby allow the anxious salespeople to continue to sell TechInfo's product at a premium price.

Jointly owned by three partners from Asia Pacific, western Europe, and the United States, this organization had a long, successful run. For decades it sold patent data and engineering information to academia and to corporate R&D shops worldwide. Slowly but surely this long, healthy reign was showing signs of market erosion.

Then the 2001–2002 recession hit. Nearly all TechInfo's customers cut nonessential services. That included enterprise-wide database services. This was an easy decision for most companies to make. When the finance department had to choose among its options, including making payroll, pumping out product, and paying the electric company, buying database information services received lowest priority.

In addition to market erosion, one competitor in particular had placed additional pricing pressure on this firm's margins. TechInfo experienced one loss after another, mostly to this one company. Before long, everyone had begun to fixate on the rival almost to the exclusion of every other possible market factor.

Myopia had set in long before I entered the conference room. These executives could only see the rival up close, without perspective. They analyzed wins and losses but had little insight as to how or why the rival priced its product the way it did. Such win-loss analysis had been going on for a decade. Before the recession, losses did not hurt as much. There was plenty of business to go around, especially during the boom of the late '90s. All this changed after 2000.

"They will continue to low-ball us on price. They don't seem to have a bottom. How long can we chase them down that pricing rabbit hole?" asked the marketing VP.

"I heard they are planning to expand their sales organization by nearly one hundred worldwide. But how can they accomplish this, add all this cost, and continue squeezing those prices downward? I don't get it." These were the words of the global head of sales.

"We don't really know about this company's fiscal wherewithal. Who funds them, and how do they choose to spend their money?" This gutsy, candid remark came from the chief financial officer who was supposed to know the answer to this question.

I quieted the room. "Do you really know this company?" I

asked. "Sure, you live and die by each sale and head-to-head bids with this rival. When you lose, you often lose on price, sometimes on some specialty offering they have that you do not. But do you really know this rival?" No one answered.

For the next half day, I divided these managers into teams representing themselves, the rival, and a customer. I asked them to tell me what they knew and didn't know about this rival's financial capabilities, its marketing drive.

Slowly, the questions these executives began to ask became more specific, more strategic and far-reaching, than just the day-to-day win-loss analysis:

> What is this company's platform strategy?
> How does this company reinvest?
> How does the company account for this investment? Is it an expense item, or a longer-term debt item, which would imply a longer-term strategy?
> What is the parent company's commitment to this subsidiary?
> What are the company's margins, and how far is the parent willing to allow it to squeeze those margins if necessary?

By attempting to answer these broader strategic questions, the managers in my workshop exposed their intelligence myopia: They knew almost nothing about the parent company, its global aspirations, and how its portfolio of companies worked with one another.

This short exercise psychologically catapulted them out of the room. They were finally able to look beyond the win-loss sheets and see the rival in a new light. They assessed the rival's behavior as part of the media conglomerate, not as a solo entity. The questions allowed them to see the larger competitive canvas.

New insights swirled around these managers: Is the parent company going to underwrite some of these thin margins? Will the media conglomerate resell the data products sold by this subsidiary through other channels it controls, including cable news channels? How do they reinvest? Does the parent have expectations for growing this subsidiary? How do they account for the investment? Finally, how do they compensate their sales organization? Is it based on total sales volume, or based on opening up new markets or customer segments?

All eyes had opened. All the participants now saw the competitive game as a complicated interplay between subsidiary and parent. They began to see the real battle they needed to fight, and it no longer just centered on price. They could maneuver around the rival by focusing on data quality and creating products that promote ease of use. With a well-heeled parent, the managers knew they would find it difficult to win on price.

Once they knew the questions, finding the information was relatively easy. The industry was fairly small; everyone knew one another. Information access was not the problem, perspective was.

PERSPECTIVE'S FLEETING AND
VERY PERSONAL VISION

Let's take another lesson from Seurat's pointillist painting. Although Seurat produced no more than a handful of large, oversized pointillist masterpieces, he spent months sketching and painting hundreds of scenes from the same riverbank. Each time he started on another canvas, the perspective changed. The light, the people, and the activity on the river all shifted over time. Capture it once and you see one image, one impression. Turn around, and the image, the players, and their movements have changed.

Thinking about this painter has taught me two very important intelligence lessons: Intelligence is like milk or eggs and has a short shelf life; second, it is very personal, very customized, almost unique.

Even in Kodak's case, the digital landscape kept changing from year to year, from the first Sony Mavica digital camera to the very busy and competitive digital landscape of the early twenty-first century. Kodak's management was locked on the perspective of yesteryear, failing to recognize the changing landscape. Even though the digital market appeared to be slow moving—even decades in the making—Kodak needed to act quickly. Each year it waited, the opportunity cost for Kodak to enter the consumer digital market increased while the opportunity itself diminished.

At the same time, Kodak's view—its personal intelligence assessment of its competitive painting in the mid-1990s—may have been very different than it was for Hewlett-Packard, for Fuji, or for Sony. The intelligence—good or bad for Kodak—was a warning. Mistakenly, it told the film giant that it must find a way to protect a dwindling market share in the traditional film market (and not in the broader digital imaging market, as it should have realized).[8] HP and Sony saw the painting and likely imagined a new opportunity to enter the photo-finishing market through a line of cameras and printers. Fuji's intelligence directed it to construct and rapidly roll out digital minilabs, an opportunity to do an end run around Kodak's vast photo-processing franchise.

You cannot mass-market intelligence. Intelligence by its very nature is only valuable for a short time to very few individuals. Once everyone knows the "insight," it's no longer insight; it is commonly known information. Gone is the opportunity to make that killing in the market. Gone is the element of surprise.

When thousands of people know the same thing you know, you may have clarity but you've lost competitive advantage. For intelligence to be truly intelligence, it must be yours alone (even if it is for a few short days, weeks, or months).

Intelligence is also a very personal product. It is a product that helps drive the way you manage and the decisions you make. I have had the chance to speak to a number of industry leaders over the years on their use of intelligence. Here are a few examples of how they personalize its use.

Crandall and Metrics

Robert Crandall, former CEO of AMR Corporation, the parent company of American Airlines, is intensely numbers driven. Instead of colors, his painting is filled with metrics, measurements of all kinds, including utilization rate of aircraft, time on the ground, time in the air, and so on. In his own words, Bob Crandall is a man obsessed with detail.

When he became president of American in 1980, deregulation of the airline industry had just begun. Large carriers, such as American and United, were under great competitive pressures from newly formed low-cost airlines.

Bob Crandall knew that American had to understand the details of this new competitive landscape, and that meant uncovering the hidden levers of competitive advantage that lay somewhere in that painting.

Labeled by one admiring MIT professor as the Patron Saint of Operations Research, Crandall constantly needed to know what drove traffic to or away from American Airlines. "We wrote software to look with great precision at precisely what food the other guy was serving, at precisely what time of day and how that compared to our service offering on our flights . . . At the same time we were able to look with great precision at the other fellow's schedule, what time he is leaving, what is his published flight time."[9]

These numbers spoke very personally to him. They urged him forward to build the first computer reservations system, known as SABRE, which American had spent years developing. His operations research bent drove him to create the hub-and-spoke system, creating efficiencies for American. He pioneered the frequent-flyer loyalty program to retain the high-paying business travelers.

He also knew that he could overmeasure if he was not careful. Taking action was key. His investment in the SABRE system was just one example of this decisiveness. SABRE cost countless millions and took years to refine. Yet it was an investment that positioned American Airlines as industry leader for years to come.

"About half of the job of management is trying to figure out where the company is going to be five to ten years down the road, and the second half is execution." Intelligence, according to Crandall, must be applied quickly and without hesitation. "The most successful companies," he concludes, "are those whose CEOs make reasonably accurate forecasts more of the time than do their competitors."

Monster.com's Taylor and Brassy, Unconventional Competitiveness and Speed

To Jeff Taylor, founder and former chief monster (as he liked to be called) of Monster.com, arguably the world's largest Internet career and job matching service (with over fifteen million visits a month and over eight million registered members), life is about in-your-face marketing, from the oversized, very uncorporate cartoonlike monster logo to the ads that flout the old-fashioned world of traditional newspaper help-wanteds.[10]

Taylor's seemingly unbridled enthusiasm for nearly everything translates into an individual with high energy, willing to take on the world. Taylor typically attacks the world around him with his big, toothy smile. If he doesn't have the information on his competition, if his painting lacks details, well, he will go out himself to find those details.

Newspapers are Monster's direct competition for job ad placement. No problem. If Taylor wants to learn about how his competition's management is going to battle Monster, he wants to hear their plans directly. He has regularly entered the competition's lion's den and spoken at newspaper conferences. He's there to both look for coopetition opportunities and to garner publisher intentions. He wants to know where newspapers want to take their classified advertising strategy and how that strategy may have an impact on Monster.

He has learned many lessons from his slower newspaper rivals, including the need for speed, in-your-face speed. Go after employees (the sell side), not just employer ads (buy side), he learned early on. For example, when Coca-Cola announced it would lay off two thousand employees a few years ago, Taylor immediately dispatched his Monster blimp to fly over Coke's headquarters. He was intent to remind all buyers and sellers that Monster.com was the place to go, no matter on which side of the table you sat.[11] He left the Atlanta newspapers in the dust.

Gut instinct and fast action drive him in the same way that numbers shape Crandall's thinking. He seems to assemble odd bits and pieces of information, then quickly and intuitively build a better whole. Monster itself was born from just such a confluence of insights.

Early in 1994 Taylor, out of college and running his own ad agency, was told by one of his clients, "I don't want any more big ideas. I want a monster idea." That was ingredient number one. At the same time he had been tooling around the nascent World Wide Web, trolling through BBS (bulletin board systems), noting how people often posted jobs on these primitive sites. That was ingredient number two. That's all he needed.

In the middle of the night, some days after this client's remark, Taylor woke up at 4:30 A.M. with the concept of the first Monster board rattling around in his head. Not wanting to wait until the morning, he got dressed and sat in a coffee shop where he sketched out the interface that represents the Monster board today. As evidence of his finely tuned instinct combined with speed, his Monster.com site was only the 454th dot-com on the

Web. Many other career-hunting sites followed, but Monster, with over tens of thousands of prospective job seekers, remains the Web brand to beat.

The perspective on his painting changes too fast. Taylor thinks in hypermoving Internet years. "You snooze for an hour, you snooze for a day." He spits out this homespun platitude like so much quick, staccato advertising copy he used to write. In Taylor-speak he is intently telling you never to relax, never stop absorbing ideas that may in some way, small or large, affect your success.

"Once you see the signals of change on the horizon, it's too late."

Herb Baum and Signals

If Taylor uses signals, then Herb Baum is always looking for them. Whether as president of toy company Hasbro, or chief executive of the soap manufacturer Dial, Baum tries to anticipate those seemingly quiet dots of change making their way onto the painting.

Alan Hassenfeld, Hasbro's chair, CEO, and chief of the next-big-thing idea, always pounds the pavement, speaking to customers and reading newspapers from around the world. Herb Baum, at the time, felt it was his job to help Hassenfeld tease out the best of the ideas and measure the risk each would present to the company. "The first thing I asked Alan Hassenfeld when I walked in the door was 'Where's the son of Furby?'" recalled Baum. "What are some of the ways you try to see into the not-too-distant future? With the relatively high-risk position of following a trend, you need to make sure you make the right investments at the right time. What signals do you look for in the market before committing resources?"[12]

Similarly at Campbell Soup, as you will see in chapter 8, Baum believed his goal was to identify new opportunities just slightly ahead of the market's embracing them. He did so at Campbell with the spectacularly successful launch of an upscale line of pasta sauce. He knew that if he did not act quickly, Campbell's rivals would beat it to market, making it more difficult to gain the market share for this relatively high-value, high-margin product.

Herb Baum has made a career of identifying and acting on signals before everyone else in the marketplace sees the same picture.

Novartis CEO Daniel Vasella and Culture

Daniel Vasella is very sensitive to cultural nuance. Not all actions have demarcated bright lines around them. He knows this, and it informs his life, the way he uses information (see chapter 6 for his view of the Internet), and the way he makes decisions.

He realizes that the messenger who carries the information can be as important as the information itself. Almost as an illustration of the value of culture and delivering the message, he recalled an experience at a recent basketball game. "Hans, one of my colleagues (a German living in the U.S.), went with another colleague, Jim, to the game. Jim was coaching. His son was shooting the ball and couldn't score. My colleague thought, 'What a poor shot!' while the American said, 'Great try, Johnny!' I felt that this was an example of the difference in attitude: One focuses on the effort and the possibilities for the next time, while the other thinks first about critique."

Similarly, Vasella appreciates that data are not just data, pure and neutral. Human beings need to interpret it and by doing so will overlay their own backgrounds, cultures, and opinions on it. Marketeer versus scientist, American versus German, each may unconsciously place a different spin on the same piece of information. Background and education can make all the difference in intelligence, Vasella realizes.[13]

Vasella has used this cultural sensitivity to help him negotiate the successful merger of Ciba-Geigy and Sandoz, the two Swiss companies that became Novartis. According to Vasella, even though these two companies coexisted in the same city, separated only by a river, they were two very different cultures.

He understands the minds of the researchers in his labs and frequently visits them, chatting with the scientists to understand their view of the research—as opposed to relying on a sanitized version read only through a memo or e-mail report. Part of the reason Novartis has achieved a highly competitive pipeline is attributed to Vasella's digging into the R&D trenches and hearing the assessments from his scientists working at the lab bench.

Just as pointillist paintings contain many shades of color, some more significant than others, so, too, does information contain cultural overtones. Vasella is a very astute reader of these.

T. Boone Pickens and Ground-Level Intelligence

Like Vasella wandering through the labs, T. Boone Pickens, the oil and gas entrepreneur, sometimes corporate raider, and trained engineer, probably realizes more than anyone else I have spoken with that you need to escape your desk if you truly want to see the competitive landscape (see more about Pickens in chapter 8). Any business he has ever run demanded he pay attention to what was going on in the ground itself to stay competitive. Whether he was operating an oil drilling business, buying and selling water rights, owning a quail farm, or operating natural gas fueling stations, he always paid attention to natural canvas—the ground around him.

Recalling his early days in the oil and gas business, he describes how he learned about a rival's drilling activity long before everyone else in the market. "We would have someone who would watch [the rival's] drilling floor from a half mile away with field glasses," recalls Pickens. "Our competitor didn't like it, but there wasn't anything they could do about it. Our spotters would watch the joints and drill pipe. They would count them; each [drill] joint was thirty feet long. By adding up all the joints, you would be able to tally the depth of the well."[14]

Pickens understood that the deeper the well, the more costly it is to bring the oil or the gas to the surface. It was a simple equation but one that provided him with competitive advantage.

For Pickens, seeing your competitive landscape in perspective meant watching and observing activity at the ground level. Leave the confines of your office and go outside where the market takes shape. What's happening outside is real. You can see it.

DEVELOPING intelligence seems so simple, not unlike teaching someone how to dance. Step 1: Stand back from the painting, find your intelligence perspective. Step 2: Take the advice of one great CEO after another, such as Crandall, Taylor, Vasella, Baum, and Pickens. Measure your metrics; appreciate the cultural overtones, read the signals, and always look for ground-level information. It's all so straightforward—until human nature gets in the way.

As simple as collecting intelligence may appear, there is one obstacle to its effectiveness: the human mind. The same brain that can accept less-than-perfect information and still deduce what a competitor will do next can distort and twist that same reality.

The managers at TechInfo at first saw only what they wanted to see, a competitor that seemingly low-balled its prices to gain share, but upon further poking away at the same information, they discovered that the picture was more complicated than they first thought. They needed to include the strategic goals of the rival's parent company as well as reexamine their own customer's market signals.

Lots of airlines have come and gone during Robert Crandall's reign at American. They had the same public data on the market that he did. One of the differences between Crandall and his competitors was the way he coldly and decisively read that pointillist painting. He drew a different set of conclusions, a different intelligence reading, then changed the way American did business.

What we take for granted today was a bold move on Crandall's part. He gambled on a very expensive and initially money-losing SABRE reservations system; he gave away free seats in the form of airline miles to passengers; he reconfigured the routing system to hub and spoke instead of point to point. He read his painting's metrics and decisively acted upon them. As a result, American rose from a $1 billion loss position when he took over to more than tripling its revenue, finding itself $1 billion in the black when he left.

In the meantime, TWA, Pan Am, Eastern, Braniff, and a host of other domestic U.S. and international carriers closed their doors.

Crandall, Taylor, Baum, Vasella, and Pickens, as well as nearly a dozen other non-CEO types you will read about, have found ways to overcome the mental blinders that block intelligence reality. So, before I show you how to assess your rival's costs, develop early warning on your market, or even mine the Internet for critical intelligence, you need to ask yourself if you have ever been blind to a changing market reality. Have you ever encountered informational silos or walls within your company? Are you in denial about a threat? Do you simply shut down from information overload?

The mind can blind you to reality. Blinders, the second intelligence reality, can distort good intelligence, or at the least delay the decisions you must make. As you have already seen in Kodak's case, any delay in the use of intelligence can lose you a market. You need to take off your blinders to use intelligence when it is still valuable. As Yogi Berra, one of baseball's famous—and most quotable—personalities once said, "It gets late early out there."

Don't let blinders make you late.

CHAPTER 2

REALITY BITES

Remove the Blinders

How could phones and beer clash in the minds and wallets of the consumer? If you played a game trying to find words most closely associated with *beer,* you might say "sports," "sex appeal," or "youth." Try this same word game when thinking of mobile phones and you will likely come up with the same associations. Why then was a famous beer company surprised when it lost sales to cell phones?

Sometimes managers just become stuck. They can only see the market from one vantage point and then seek to collect on the data that conforms to that viewpoint. In effect, they develop biased, myopic assessments. They become blind to vital intelligence knocking right outside their doors.

"We didn't see it coming," a marketer for Guinness, the world-famous Irish beer brewer, told me when recalling a market surprise that temporarily hurt sales in Africa. She then recounted how Guinness's seemingly unending rise in sales throughout

45

Africa had suddenly hit a wall in the 2000 to 2001 time frame. When Guinness did finally identify the cause of the sales drop—a sharp rise in the use of mobile phones—it seemed to come out of nowhere. In truth, it did not.[1]

Guinness, a historically strong and savvy competitor, was blind to the intelligence around it. It was a blindness that had set in over many decades.

There are two types of competitive blindness: one that results from a strong belief that can mask reality and one that is caused by pure information overload, an inability to see reality because you are simply overwhelmed by information—good and bad, valuable data and pure static. Guinness's blindness was the former. It was blinded by a belief in its own myth, a myth so strong that it may have ignored the changes around it.

MIRROR EFFECT:
SEXY MIRROR ON THE WALL,
WHO'S THE FAIREST OF THEM ALL?

Guinness had been the leading brewer throughout most of the African continent since the early nineteenth century. European merchants trading in Africa during the 1800s preferred Guinness because of its higher, 7.5 percent alcohol content, which also gave the brew a long shelf life. Over time, Guinness became known as an aphrodisiac, and the myth eventually grew and spread throughout the continent.

Nigerians, in particular, began calling Guinness "black power" or "Viagra," referring to Pfizer's male virility drug. Guinness had emerged as a status symbol, as a lifestyle statement for many young Africans in Nigeria, Kenya, Cameroon, Ivory Coast, and South Africa. Advertisements with slogans such as "Guinness Is Good for You" promoted the product's supposed health benefits since the early part of the twentieth century. African countries, unlike those in the European Union, have historically been relatively lax in their regulation of advertising messages.[2]

So when Guinness's management asked itself about competitive threats, it tended to ask the wrong questions. The mirror effect kept them within their own world. Management appeared much more interested in the other brewers, especially Heineken, which owns Nigerian Breweries and other brands, and SABMiller (South African Breweries). A beer war had emerged throughout Africa in the 1990s with SAB moving into Tanzania, Mozambique, and Zambia, and BGI, a French brewer, advancing rapidly into French-speaking Africa.

The Guinness-sex syllogism had cemented itself firmly in place: If all beers have sex appeal and Guinness is the best among beers, then Guinness has the greatest sex appeal. This was a perfect formula for the blindness of denial.

Believing in the Wrong Mirror

Results in the marketplace, both close up and from afar, were hypnotic. Any marketer for any product group would drool over these numbers.[3] The data all indicated nearly straight-line growth in all categories traditionally important to the beer industry.

BASIC BEER INDUSTRY STATISTICS: NIGERIA

	2001	2002	2003 (projected)
Nigeria's total beer consumption requirement	9.4 mm hectoliters	10.0 mm hectoliters	10.7 mm hectoliters
Overall national beer production	7.8 mm hectoliters	8.0 mm hectoliters	9.5 mm hectoliters
Per capita beer consumption	6.5 liters	7.0 liters	7.3 liters
Imports	180,000 hectoliters	195,000 hectoliters	N/A

Increasingly, Guinness and other brewers serving the African continent, such as Heineken NV, became reliant on sale volumes there to boost profits for the corporate parent. In 2003, sales of Guinness in Africa accounted for nearly 17 percent of Diageo (Guinness's parent company) profit worldwide, and this dependence caused concern to stock analysts who monitor the industry.

Any derailing of the African consumer's thirst for beer consumption—whatever the reason—could do tremendous harm to Guinness's bottom line. What if Guinness and other brewers were blind to subtle shifts in their competitive canvas? Just such a blindness did occur—albeit briefly. Nevertheless it rattled Guinness's confidence.

Retail beer sales in South Africa for a period during 2000–2001 for all brands suddenly fell off by as much as 6 percent.[4] Was the allure of this supposed aphrodisiac suddenly tarnished?

Entranced by its own sales numbers, Guinness managers may have failed to ask the real question: Mirror, mirror, on the wall, what other product could offer the same sex appeal, the same thrill as a glass of Guinness? In fact, the evidence was all around them:

- **RAPID ADOPTION OF MOBILE PHONES WAS PROJECTED.** The African market for mobile phone buyers during 2001–2002 was expected to grow by 60 percent. This translated into nine thousand new phone customers signing up each day, spending money they would otherwise have used on beer or other status symbols.

- **SOUTH AFRICA HIT THE SEX-APPEAL TRIFECTA.** In addition to the mobile phone, two other services brought with them their own allure: a state-run lottery (introduced in South Africa in 2000) and gambling (legalized in 1994), both of which distracted the Guinness consumer and stole some sexual market share.

- **MOBILE PHONE PRICES PLUMMETED.** With prices falling more than 50 percent in just a few short years in the late 1990s, Africa and the Middle East experienced the sharpest drop worldwide and threw open the door for consumers under age thirty to buy this newest status symbol.

- **AGGRESSIVE INCENTIVES WERE OFFERED TO PHONE RETAILERS.** Vodacom, South Africa's largest cellular network, allowed retailers to keep a share of the revenues of any mobile phone they sold. In effect, Vodacom co-opted the South African retailer to subsidize phones. This revenue sharing encouraged all kinds of retailers (even food and grocery stores that sell Guinness beer) to sell phones.[5]

Intelligence demands clarity as well as perspective. By staring into its own mirror, Guinness only believed the myth that it had cultivated for so long. Thankfully for Guinness and its other rivals, the demand for beer continued to rise, albeit with a slight mobile phone hiccup along the way. In fact before long, Guinness's management recognized the mobile phone's own unique sex appeal and began to co-opt its market power. Perhaps phones could sell beer, not just compete with it. Most recently, the brewer has cut deals with mobile phone carriers to send Guinness advertisements across their networks. "Win free Guinness beer and other prizes," the ads declare in short text messages.[6]

The damage could have been worse than a short dip in sales. But Guinness executives were not only inquisitive enough to assess the intelligence, they were open-minded enough to accept its verdict.

It's certainly easy enough for me to recommend that you just pull back and look away from the mirror, but it's more important to be able to show you how to change the way your company behaves given existing market pressures. You may need to contend with an ingrained mirror culture and a management team that doesn't want to see other perspectives. Most large companies tend to change their direction rather slowly. How then can you pull away from the mirror? How do you force management to take off its blinders?

This next tale, the tale of Corning, helps answer such questions. Corning, known for its various industrial ceramic, fiberglass, and other glass products, also looked too intensely into its mirror. Like Guinness, it was a superpower in its own market. Also like Guinness, it tended to believe in itself so intensely that it miscalculated a rival's approach so that the rival appeared to magically change the market rules. The following story shows how Corning managed to remove its blinders and develop the critical intelligence necessary to win the market back.

CORNING'S METAMORPHOSIS

Harry Houdini, the nineteenth-century escape artist and illusionist, spellbound audiences with an escape act he called metamorphosis. During this trick, members from the audience would tie Houdini up, place him in a sack, and lock him into a trunk. Seconds later he would appear in front of the audience untied and out of the sack, while his assistant was now found in the trunk, in the sealed sack. Audiences marveled at the mysterious, nearly instantaneous escape-and-switch illusion.

In this story, Corning is the audience, mystified at how one of its chief rivals, Schott Glas of Germany, performed its own metamorphosis on Corning. Schott's apparent plan was to enter a market just after Corning and with irrationally low prices relative to Corning; surprisingly, Schott appeared able to sustain the low, unprofitable prices and still stay in the market.

Gary Roush is the corporate marketing manager at Corning who helped remove his company's internal blinders. Gary is a savvy, soft-spoken individual with a background that does not instantly conjure up the image of a change agent. He grew up in southern Ohio on a small tobacco farm and graduated from Ohio University with a BS in industrial technology. Before joining Corning, he had served in Vietnam as a helicopter pilot.

Corning moves around within its organization smart people well schooled in the company's manufacturing processes to help fix process or help grow a new products group. Roush was one of those people. Now retired, he held many positions during his career at Corning, but one of the most challenging was his time spent in uncovering the Schott mystery. Management appointed him to head a small team of people from Corning's marketing department to sort out the Schott dilemma.

The Corning company is one of the great American success stories. Hidden away in upstate New York, it's in a quiet, industrial town and is one of the most innovative glass and ceramics technology companies in the world. In the mid-1960s, Corning's engineers invented a process to make large flat pieces of Pyroceram, a glass ceramic material used to make Corning Ware, the popular consumer cooking dishes found in many American homes at the time.

With this new flat-glass technology, Corning created the first glass ceramic cooktop. Spotting an opportunity in the consumer market, Corning took its design and started manufacturing entire stovetops with this new high-tech glass. The company featured this product as the "counter that cooks." Corning eventually extended Pyroceram's applications to kitchen countertops, trivets, and elevator panels. The Brooklyn Battery Tunnel, linking Manhattan and Brooklyn, was even tiled with a version of this glass.

Corning Ware was such a success that by the early 1970s, Corning eventually stopped producing entire stove units and just focused on manufacturing and selling the stovetop ceramic.

Schott Glas, a multinational company based in Mainz, Germany, and a producer of advanced optical materials and optoelectronics, was one of Corning's major rivals in the glass and ceramics business during this same period. According to Roush, Schott would lower its prices in specific product categories to the point where Corning could not successfully compete. Corning's product managers were mystified. How could Schott offer such low prices and still be profitable? In a number of instances, Schott appeared to have targeted one or another of Corning's major product groups. It seemed that Schott's goal was to sell its competing product at far below that of Corning in order to drive Corning out of a selected market or product category.

In this instance, Schott chose to zero in on Corning's glass cooktops. Even though Corning had left the retail stove and oven markets, it was still selling its product to stove manufacturers. By the late 1970s Schott introduced a similar ceramic cooktop and began to lower its prices, tightly squeezing Corning's profit margins.

Corning, acting in a way that it thought was very rational, stuck it out for a period of time. Then in the early 1980s, Corning abandoned the product category to Schott. As soon as Schott saw Corning withdraw, it pushed prices up once again and effectively owned the market.

Revealing the Illusion: Take Another Vantage Point

Schott's cooktop maneuverings did not smell right. It didn't make sense to Roush or anyone else at Corning that a relatively high-cost operation such as Schott's could have consistently undersold Corning.

"My primary objective was to figure out a way to compete

more effectively with Schott," states Roush. "The way I did that was to prepare others who reported to me to act as if they were a Schott employee."

Roush broke down the Schott knowledge silos that had formed among various Corning product groups by playing competitive games. He instructed his analysts and product managers to immerse themselves in Schott's culture, its operations, and its financial details. As a group, they became Schott. This shadow competitor approach proved very effective.

By the end of the exercise, Roush's team had amassed a great deal of information, some coming from within Corning's ranks and other pieces collected from outside sources. Team members collected annual reports, product literature, and articles on Schott. They would make phone calls, ask questions, and keep their eyes and ears open during trade shows and conferences. Corning's people, many of whom are trained mechanical and chemical engineers, were also very good at assessing plant drawings and manufacturing processes, where available through public filings.

Brainstorming with his shadow Schott team and others, Roush analyzed and presented his conclusions to management. "We briefed Roger Ackerman, the president of the company, and his chief advisers two or three times a year," he recalls. Through a series of these face-to-face briefings, Roush built the case for Schott's pricing strategy, one assessment after another.

By the second round of presentations to Roger Ackerman, Roush understood the shell game that Schott had played with Corning. Schott realized that Corning evaluated the success or failure of each of Corning's product lines based on its own financial performance, almost as if each product group became its own stand-alone company. This is not unusual. Most large corporations operate with specific and distinct profit centers. From an intelligence point of view, this proved unfortunate for Corning. The firm essentially knew bits and pieces of Schott's pricing game but failed to share it among the various Corning business units. Hence, Schott's strategy remained a mystery at the business-unit level. Each unit saw only its own numbers and compared those numbers with the Schott business-unit equivalent. Schott was aware of Corning's information silos and used Corning's own rules against itself.

The German rival, whose margins were likely no better than Corning's, decided very consciously to lower the prices dramatically in one product class and fund the resulting loss from another end of the Schott operation. Its goal was to force Corning out of a particular product class—without Corning understanding how Schott managed to do so.

"During the normal business review, Corning's management would focus on the [individual Schott] product and not its revenue or profitability across all of Schott," says Roush. Therefore, if Corning found its product line lost money over some sustained period of time, that was enough to convince Corning to leave the business.

"We in corporate marketing were the first to compare Schott across all business units, and we discovered that Schott would use the higher margins to beat down the prices in other areas, using Corning's money to make more money."

It was not until the late 1980s that Corning finally understood

Schott's strategy, some half-dozen years after Corning was forced to exit the cooktop market because of Schott's price pressures. By comparing Schott's own overheads for the cooktop group with other Schott business units, Roush discovered that Schott had grown the cooktop business into a very profitable operation, achieving as much as a 45 percent profit margin. Following Roush's decoding of Schott's strategy, Corning's president, Roger Ackerman, decided to reenter the "counter that cooks" market, selling exclusively to companies manufacturing stoves. In 1991, Corning formed a joint venture with St. Gobain Vitrage SA, the French glass producer, to produce ceramic cooktops in Greenville, South Carolina.

Ackerman decided to act on Roush's recommendations, in part to remedy Corning's earlier strategic mistakes. It entered the market with far lower prices and successfully forced Schott to lower its prices, hence squeezing Schott's profit margins and halting the domino effect Corning had experienced in past years.

You will read more about war gaming and strategic role-playing in the next chapter. While Gary Roush did not run a formal game, his deployment of competitive teams allowed Corning to see the entire beast and make sense of Schott's seemingly irrational competitive behavior. Because of Roush's discovery, Corning now observed all of Schott, not just its cooktop business unit. By doing so, Roush and Corning stripped away the competitive illusion.[7]

NUMBERS: A ONE-DIMENSIONAL BLINDNESS

When business historians decide to write about the last two decades of the twentieth century, they very well may label it the era of the spreadsheet. No matter what the decision, business cannot seem to function without it. Seemingly every piece of data has to fit within a cell. If it does not, it is not a fact.

No doubt, business needs numbers. Yet reality dictates that much more soft information find its way into critical negotiations, corporate acquisitions, investment decisions, and product rollouts than most would like to imagine.[8]

Soft, qualitative information can be as critical to an acquisition for a CEO as any hard numbers you might insert into a spreadsheet. Nearly every merger or acquisition assignment we have completed over the years for a company's executives are either driven by the soft data or heavily influenced by it.

Think of the many disappointing acquisitions in recent years that were driven by the numbers and in the name of enhancing shareholder value—AOL Time Warner and Daimler Benz Chrysler prime among them. Grant Thornton LLP, the British-based international accounting and consulting firm, studied merger failures and concluded that beyond the numbers, three important soft intelligence criteria dominated: (1) accountability for postmerger integration plans and implementation, (2) the strategic rationale for approving the merger in the first place, and (3) whether the culture and the people of the firm with whom you merge fit or are polar opposites.[9]

Consider the AOL Time Warner $165 billion merger (a situation explored more deeply in the next chapter on war games). At the time, in January 2000, it appeared to be a merger based solely on hubris and pure valuation. Immediately after the announcement, Wall Street analysts began mumbling their complaints. Why, they asked, should AOL, with a stock price to earnings ratio of 188, consider the merger? Content (Time Warner's publications) and broadband (its cable division) was the answer AOL gave. AOL needed to ensure growth, and Time Warner was the ticket to its future. However, as the next few years rolled on, the weaknesses underlying the merger became evident—all weaknesses highlighted in the Grant Thornton report. Integration plans were unclear, details underlying the strategic rationale appeared highly flawed, and the cultures never seemed to mesh.

At the time, David Shook, a *Business Week* writer, asked a few simple but revealing questions that underscored the opaqueness behind AOL's and Time Warner's thinking: "But how will these combinations work?" asked Shook. "Will *Fortune* publish its 500 list first on an AOL Web site? And how does that kind of cross-promotion add to revenue growth?"[10]

The AOL Time Warner merger was most definitely a combination blindly driven by numbers, astronomical numbers that soon began to collapse under numerous false assumptions. The synergies never seemed to happen. Management, represented by Gerald Levin, CEO, and Steve Case, former head of AOL and then chair of the combined AOL Time Warner, battled each other during the postmerger until both were eventually forced out. This megamerger had turned into a megamess, and it all started because of the entrancing numbers.

How can you account for the unquantifiable? How can you measure the softer aspects of due diligence and avoid the numbers blinder?

The education industry provides one case in point. The burgeoning market for educational services comprises three main segments: K–12, higher education, and professional licensure and certification. EduCo, a leading firm in the field, was active in two of these segments but had virtually no business in the K–12 arena, which it felt would provide a logical pathway to exploit core competencies and investments in infrastructure. A half-dozen other firms, some with an international customer base, had managed to grow this part of the educational market, while EduCo had remained largely on the sidelines, despite the apparent synergies with its existing business units.

EduCo's senior management very much wanted to capture some of the revenue in the K–12 segment but felt that it would cost too much to build its own service. The fear that EduCo's management had was that several other players were most likely engaging in the same types of discussions; if EduCo didn't act quickly, it was very possible that one of these competitors would beat EduCo to the punch. To address this acute concern, EduCo's management made it a strategic imperative to enter the attractive K–12 segment within six to nine months. Having resolved that both the opportunity and the timing were right, one key question remained: Form an alliance or make an acquisition?

Generally, all those involved at EduCo—the vice president of strategy, the chief financial officer, and the vice president of marketing—understood the numbers involved in the buy or ally decision. Revenues for all the major players were fairly well known among the firms. Everyone also had a sense of profitability. What management lacked was the softer aspects of due diligence, exactly the issues cited in the Grant Thornton report that pointed to merger failure if left unrecognized. EduCo's executives knew the importance of removing the blinders blocking the clear vision needed for this type of decision making. Because the market was on a dramatic growth trajectory, if EduCo relied on numbers alone, there was a strong chance management would miss the best prospects. The management team knew they needed intelligence on the potential candidates' management style, operating approach, and *their* views of the future in education markets.

In combing through the most important due diligence criteria, EduCo's executives decided that strategic or cultural fit was the most important gap in their understanding of potential partners. So, in addition to that aspect, EduCo engaged Fuld & Company's help to examine a host of other "soft" issues that could make or break a strategic or cultural fit. Does the sales force follow an approach that would mesh with EduCo's approach? How committed is the potential partner to this sought-after niche? Does that commitment reflect a long-term set of objectives or just a strategic experiment? Has the prospect successfully delivered on its promises? How deep is its intellectual bench? How well does it use the Internet to attract and retain customers? What unique technological capabilities does it possess? What other alliances or partnerships does it have that could be advantageous or problematic to EduCo?

After conducting dozens of key interviews with industry insiders, we were able to present EduCo management with subtleties in the interplay among the ally-or-buy candidates—subtleties often missed in the general and trade press. Each criterion received a weighting factor; some criteria had a greater impact than others on the list. Each softer acquisition characteristic received a score.

The ranking system was straightforward. Though subjective, it was relatively easy to apply given all the interviews and other data collected from online sources. It went as follows:

Ranking System

1 = limited capability or fit with EduCo
2 = moderate capability or fit with EduCo
3 = good fit with EduCo's goals
4 = excellent fit/strong synergies anticipated

We then applied the rankings to each of the criteria. The chart looked like this:

Candidate	Cultural Fit	Sales Force	Commit-ment	Service Delivery	Web Capability	Total
A	4	4	3	3	4	18
B	3	2	4	2	4	15
C	2	3	3	3	1	12
D	2	3	2	1	1	9
E	1	1	4	2	1	9
F	4	1	1	1	1	8

After tallying the scores for all criteria, one company rose to the top of the pile. The scoring placed the "winner" well above the next closest candidate.

But that alone was not enough. We also worked with EduCo management to develop a series of scenarios to assess the potential future outcomes for the other players. The what-if story lines examined the competitive market were our client to ally with each of the players. As you will see in chapter 5 on early warning, scenarios are a powerful and eye-opening intelligence tool. In EduCo's case, playing the scenario game allowed us to test the various alliance or merger combinations, almost akin to the way a grade school student would cross-check an addition-subtraction or division-multiplication problem. The cross-check in this instance did confirm the original recommendation. That is, candidate A, which received the highest composite score in our rankings, also made the most sense when the scenario was fully played out to incorporate the likely reactions and combinations of other industry players.

The company now knew what made this likely candidate such a good fit with its own strategy and its management culture. Undeniably, the numbers—sales, profitability, and cash flow, among other factors—remain in the forefront of any acquisition or alliance strategy. Yet so many so-called deals fail for reasons that fall outside the margins of the spreadsheet. The ones that succeed seem to do so because those in the deal match both fiscally and culturally.

DEER-IN-THE-HEADLIGHTS BLINDNESS:
INTELLIGENCE OVERLOAD

Rumors, news sound bites, and stock market speculation swirling around a company all can create a deer-in-the-headlights effect as paralyzing as even the worst case of denial. The California energy market of the mid- and late 1990s had exactly that effect on energy companies in this regional market.

In 1994 California's public utilities commission announced it would deregulate the retail energy market by 1997. While the plan did not play out according to the original timetable, it did stamp California as the laboratory petri dish for the new energy experiment. Everyone—every energy company, every investment house—had their eyes on California.

California had a new gold rush on its hands, but in this case it was energy. Who was going to buy which power generator or gas distributor was one of the hot questions of the day. Along with the rumors and speculation came a great deal of confusion, confusion caused by too much information. Too much data can create distortions and freeze decisions just as effectively as overreliance on spreadsheets, a bad case of denial, or the silo effect.

Chuck Rooney, former strategic planning director at Pacific Enterprises, a gas distribution company that has since become Sempra Energy, believed his company was at the very center of the competitive storm.

The market had become extremely complex. No longer were California energy companies only looking in their own backyards. Suddenly, the world was looking at the state, and it had to look at the world. Everyone was predicting a great flurry of merger and acquisition activity, as well as severe price competition. For a formerly insulated, somewhat isolated, monopolistic marketplace, this hyperbolic rise in competitive activity both excited and unnerved local utilities. Rooney's company found itself in a new world with an extremely uncertain future. No doubt, Pacific Enterprises' management needed early warning.

"I had convinced management of the transmission unit that we had a need to implement an early warning system to understand what the customers of our transmission services were doing . . . The customers are major customers that would be taking pipeline or transmission service [e.g., big corporations and municipalities]," Rooney told me.[11]

Rooney expected a relatively simple, rational process. Make a list and then whittle it down to a reasonable number of companies to watch. Unfortunately, that was not the case. "What should have been something simple turned out to be a tremendously complex exercise that wound up burying itself under its own weight," Rooney stated in hindsight. "The variables became so numerous that we could not clearly weave a thread through even one of these variables—from competitor to regulator to government. By the time you got through it all, you were buried."

Acquisition fever had taken hold in the energy business and in California energy companies specifically. You could open any issue of *Public Utilities Fortnightly,* one of the leading industry trade journals, and locate literally hundreds of deals—domestic and international. Many of the suitors came from outside the confines of the traditional energy producer or utility marketplace.

It was no wonder Rooney's managers feared it was ripe for acquisition. What they didn't know was how to anticipate the most likely suitor. The initial list of potential predator-acquirers numbered into the hundreds and ranged from AT&T to Duke Energy to Enron to Time Warner and Walt Disney. The range was dizzying, the number of candidates numbing.

Filter Out Blindness

The answer to the informational blizzard was to employ filters. Rooney wanted to look at his company the way the predator might. For example, does the potential suitor have an explicit energy strategy? He weighted each filter according to its importance to the final analysis. What characteristics, he asked himself, would a true acquirer need in order to enter our market?

The first few passes found Rooney and his executives playing with too many filters, perhaps a dozen or more. After a few more edits, he was able to eliminate all but a half-dozen critical filters. Like a noise filter in a stereo, these intelligence filters rapidly eliminated the informational noise created by the merger and deal-making mania swirling around the company.

Financial capability was one filter. If the candidate demonstrated the fiscal wherewithal to purchase a small to midsized utility, it received a weighted score of 2 instead of a 1, which Rooney scored for anyone just demonstrating interest in the California energy market. Interest in the retail energy segment was another filter. A candidate that demonstrated an interest in the retail (not wholesale) energy market received 1½ points. If a company had invested in the West Coast energy market, it received another point, and so on. The highest total score any potential suitor could receive was a 9.

By running all the candidates through these filters, Rooney was able to rank the would-be suitors. The curiosities on his original list, such as Walt Disney, QVC, Johnson Controls, and Time Warner, dropped out. Companies such as PacifiCorp and Enron remained at the top.

As it turned out, Enron, one of the five finalists on this far more rational list, wound up acquiring Portland General, its neighbor to the north, rather than Pacific Enterprises. Yet the process of using filters eliminated the blinding effect of the intelligence blizzard in this overheated marketplace. Filters helped management get on with business and analyze the true predators rather than being distracted by background noise.

You have now witnessed how sometimes very simple devices, such as Chuck Rooney's information filters or Gary Roush's competitive role-playing, reduced the informational noise or demystified a competitor's supposedly amazing, gravity-defying strategy. Both Rooney's and Roush's approaches to removing the intelligence blinders worked for them at the time, but their efforts don't begin to exhaust the alternatives. If true intelligence is the ability to anticipate a competitor's next move, you need to do more than just remove blinders and examine a rival. You need to build a framework that helps you see through or ahead of the competition.

Frameworks enable you to examine every aspect of that rival and how it tends to behave in a variety of competitive settings.

Frameworks sharpen your competitive vision by helping you anticipate a company's tactics and strategies.

Can you imagine building a competitive laboratory to test the strategy of your rivals, new entrants, customers, or suppliers? Can you imagine building a framework that would prepare you for likely and potentially surprising competitive upheavals? The intelligence clarity a framework delivers is like X-ray vision, and it is the subject of the next chapter.

CHAPTER 3

WILL GOOGLE BEAT MICROSOFT?

Using War Games to See Three Moves Ahead

When a rival broadsides you with a price cut, a new technology disrupts your plans, all your traditional tactics appear to be failing, or your market is about to undergo a major change, just play. Play a war game, the tool of choice to help you gain strategic transparency of your marketplace and your competition.

A war game is not about outright victory or defeat. It is about yanking you out of your comfort zone and helping you gain a fresh, realistic view of the competitive landscape. It allows you to test the true tensile strength of your own strategy and peer inside that of your rival's. It can demonstrate whether or not your strategy can truly withstand a rival's onslaughts, or guerilla tactics.

A war game is a live simulation reflecting the real industrial world, forcing competitors, customers, and possible new entrants to act out their strategies. Working through a set of rules, executives articulate and argue tactics in hopes of developing a strategy that will allow a company to grow as its customer base grows, even as its rivals grow, or even if new entrants begin their competitive march, attempting to steal market share.

The following example helps explain what I mean. In a recent pharmaceutical industry war game my firm organized, XYZ was severely behind schedule in its development of a new product. This future gee-whiz product was designed as the successor to XYZ's current cash-cow product whose patent was about to expire. XYZ expected generic manufacturers to swoop in and take most of the profit in this category, leaving the client with a dying, older brand, a common occurrence in the pharmaceuticals industry.

Before the game, XYZ was going to dutifully forge ahead with the new product, thinking it had the better mousetrap, arrogantly believing customers would wait for its next-generation product. The game, however, quickly revealed that at least one of its rivals was ahead in development of a similar new product and would likely beat it to market. Based on the market push-back it received from customers in the game, as well as industry partners, XYZ decided that the only course was to either sell this division to a rival (not a desirable option) or to form a cross-licensing deal that would use the client's extensive sales network to market the rival's product. The rival did not have an adequate sales force to do the job—but it did have the product ready to launch in the next year. Coopetition, not competition, was the major lesson from this game. No battlefield deaths. Everyone would win in this game.

CAN you anticipate changes from the dark corners of your market, such as an upheaval brought about by unexpected mergers, surprising new entrants, or sudden regulatory shifts? The pharmaceutical, telecom, software, and other industries have recently seen such upheavals. Google must worry about all these questions. It may be fighting today's ultimate business war, a war in which nearly all competitive options and threats are in play.

Google, the Web's premier search engine, first sold its shares to the public in 2004. Now the threat it poses to Microsoft is even greater than the one Microsoft faced a decade ago from Netscape for control of the desktop market.

Is Google about to fight the last war, one similar to the Microsoft-Netscape battle? Will it be vanquished—as Netscape was a decade earlier—by an oversized competitor, Microsoft? With billions in revenue, Google is still young and moving very quickly across a competitive landscape that is largely unknown. The stakes are high for Google, and it needs to see its rival's strategy very clearly.

Google is more than a portal, more than a mere access road to the World Wide Web. For many users it is the source for tapping into all knowledge. With Google Desktop, for example, you can index every single file, e-mail, and graphic on your own computer, allowing you to retrieve all of this information in the blink of an eye. You can almost hear a collective "Wow!" from all those early adopters who had loaded Google Desktop onto their PCs.

Contrast this to Windows Explorer, a filing and search device long present on the Microsoft operating system. Everyone who has ever used Windows Explorer knows how slow, awkward, and difficult it is to find any file or piece of information hidden in your hard drive. Use the wrong phrase or point it to the wrong sub-folder on your computer, and you won't find your file at all. Not so with Google Desktop, where your entire hard drive becomes transparent. You wait a split second, not minutes, to find a specific reference, and you don't have to know in which folder you originally buried the information. Wherever it is, Google Desktop will find it.

From Microsoft's point of view, Google has tried to hijack the desktop as well as the operating system. It's war again, and this time the enemy is much tougher. What's next? Microsoft's management may wonder. What will Google do to supplant us? The Google crew is generally a secretive bunch with lots of good ideas. Everyone knows that, including Microsoft.

Microsoft was chastened in the Netscape battle and unlikely to use the same tactics. Since its run-in with the Justice Department, as well as its ongoing antitrust dispute with the European Union not yet settled, it hesitates to take obvious, heavy-handed moves to marginalize rivals. No longer can it simply add packages to its Windows platform without first thinking of antitrust implications. Even with $60 billion of cash in its treasury, it can't go on a shopping spree to solve its competitive threats.

Other changes have occurred since Netscape's early days to change the Internet battlefield. Yes, many of the dot-coms have come and gone. Pets.com, Petstore.com, Petopia.com are examples of businesses with high "burn rates" of capital but no revenue. They were ideas without profit and have mostly disappeared.

Google poses a different type of threat to Microsoft and to other traditional media and publishing companies because it's a powerful search engine that drinks in advertising revenue. Every time you search, you find an ad related to your search. The ads, set to the side of the screen, are present and readable but discreet. Unlike Netscape, Google has real revenue, over $3.2 billion in

2004, and real profits. Given enough time, Google may figure out how to grab the hundreds of billions of dollars of advertising revenue in the far larger off-line, traditional publishing and media markets.

Internet Explorer's purpose is to keep Microsoft's customers buying and using Windows. Explorer represents Microsoft's past, not its future. MSN, the Internet news and search division of Microsoft, and its emerging software technology, are among the business services that the Redmond, Washington, company believes is its future—and in part the answer to Google's challenge.

Google's early success has also invited other rivals to the table. It's no longer just Microsoft's game alone, a chess game between two opponents with a clear winner and loser. This is a world war, not a regional war, with the likes of Yahoo!, Time Warner (and its AOL subsidiary), and other traditional publishers and media companies wondering how to cash in. Time Warner and its AOL division in effect shaped the Web advertising space. Yahoo!'s revenues currently surpass Google's. Each come from a different pedigree—Time Warner from traditional publishing; Yahoo! from a blend of Hollywood and Internet multimedia—that reflect their current positions in the market. In the end, they all want a piece of the consumer's wallet. How they get there will likely vary widely.

America Online began its life as an all-encompassing online Web service, replete with click-through advertising that would direct you to products, movies, and a variety of services. In the mid-1990s it was the darling of the Internet boom. But as you have already read in the last chapter, AOL's eventual 2001 merger with Time Warner was overpriced and judged by many as a poorly thought-out strategic move. The synergies between the two companies did not evolve as predicted. Added to this problem, AOL was bleeding subscribers, a key source of revenue. In 2004 alone, two million subscribers (roughly 9 percent of its subscriber base) defected to rival high-speed and discount Internet services.

The 2000–2001 recession and the resulting advertising slump did not help matters for AOL either. It began using a nontraditional approach of charging advertisers based on how many telephone calls (not just clicks) are generated by its ads. It is also positioned for strong advertising and revenue growth through its AIM (AOL Instant Messenger) service, highly appealing to the younger range of its customer base.

At the same time, AOL decided to shore up its weakness in generating advertising revenue through customer searches by forming a partnership with Google. The relationship is valuable for both companies. Google gives AOL a majority of the advertising revenue generated by AOL customer searches, and AOL in turn is Google's largest outside revenue source (as of 2004), generating 13 percent of the company's sales, when the ad commissions paid to AOL are included.[1] As of this writing, AOL is therefore connected at the hip with Google, a relationship that could stunt its competitiveness against Google, Microsoft, Yahoo!, and others.

Yahoo!, while having a spotty track record since its founding, has come back strong in recent years, an able rival to Google. David Filo and Jerry Yang developed the Yahoo! search engine while they were students at Stanford (also the birthplace of Google) in 1994.[2] Within a few years, it found itself on an acquisition tear, including $3.7 billion for GeoCities and more than $5 billion for Broadcast.com. With a recession starting in 2000, Yahoo!'s management felt it needed a new source of revenue and began charging users for listing products on its auction sites. The result: 90 percent of its users abandoned the site.

Terry Semel, formerly of Warner Brothers, joined Yahoo! as president in 2001 and quickly reshaped its revenue base. Under Semel, Yahoo! regained its momentum and direction. It entered the digital music world, won an unsolicited bid for HotJobs.com, redesigned and uncluttered its home page in a Google-like approach, and acquired Inktomi and Overture Services to give it full search capabilities, allowing it to compete on Google's playing field. By the beginning of 2005, Yahoo! was drawing 220 million visitors each month. Most important, it manages to retain each visitor to its site for longer periods of time than does Google—a fact that advertisers find attractive.

Google can clearly hear the competition scratching at its door. When Sergey Brin and Larry Page, two Stanford University PhDs, created Google in the late 1990s, they developed its search product quietly, using its diminutive size and near-stealth penchant for secrecy as its best competitive weapon.

Now classified by many observers as a media company, Google is currently being traded by investors at $300 a share, many times the value of its earnings. Its market capitalization (the trading value of a share of stock multiplied by the number of shares outstanding) effectively places Google alongside corporate behemoths such as Abbott Labs with revenues of $24 billion and UPS with revenues of $44 billion. By the same measure, it's one-fifth the value of General Electric.

No longer can it hide from the global market. Money trumps secrecy when it comes to attracting competitive interests. As John

Hussman, owner of Hussman Strategic Growth Fund, commented on Google's soaring stock price, "When you value a company at 20 times revenues and over 100 times earning, you're going to invite competition from some very, very intelligent people."[3]

Google knows this. It realizes competition is out there, as does Microsoft. It's a tumultuous marketplace with some rivals clearly outlined and others still hidden in the shadows. Knowing this, how can Microsoft or Google play their strategies—and win? How can either of these companies avoid being blindsided? How can they see through their rivals' plans by making moves that place them closer to the competitive finish line? If neither Google nor Microsoft can win it all, how can they at least win at the margins?

Allowing you to see and test the tensile strength of your own strategy and anticipate those of your rivals is what makes a war game such a useful tool. It allows management to articulate and argue over the intelligence it has collected on its rivals. Most important, it teaches you the implications of your decisions.

Google and Microsoft both need such a game—so urgently that I along with my colleagues staged one on April 10, 2005. We called it the Battle for Clicks, the battle for Internet advertising. The flyer promoted it as the "techno-battle of the 21st century." The planning for this game began in September 2004.

In most war games, company management wants to challenge its thinking by introducing other critical players into the mix. These include rivals, key customers, and even government agencies. In this instance, we felt that the best way to challenge Google's strategic plans and actions was by pitting it against its three key rivals: Microsoft (and its MSN subsidiary), Time Warner (through its AOL division), and Yahoo!

IT'S THE YANKEES VERSUS THE RED SOX
ALL OVER AGAIN!

This war game fulfilled a second purpose. Instead of corporate executives, our "players" were top business school students. In effect we pitted two great business schools against each other: MIT's Sloan School of Management and the Harvard Business School.

The two schools were fighting for more than the winning team's $5,000 cash prize. One of the MIT students compared the impending competition to the perennial highly competitive baseball contest between the New York Yankees and the Boston Red Sox. A lot of pride was on the line.

On April 10, 2005, we established the global battleground in a hotel in Cambridge, Massachusetts. Representatives for each school walked up to the front of the room and drew their assignments, four teams in all. Harvard got Microsoft and Time Warner; MIT got Yahoo! and Google.

THE FRAMEWORK IS EVERYTHING:
PORTER'S ECOSYSTEM

A mere half-dozen years ago, the marketplace was flooded with Internet buzz. It was an irrational, nearly inebriated reaction based on wild jumps in stock prices and companies being given millions of dollars in venture capital based on high-concept PowerPoint presentations to investors eager for a logarithmic return.

Now it seemed that the battle for Internet advertising revenue was déjà vu all over again. In the highly competitive atmosphere in which Microsoft, Google, Time Warner, and Yahoo! find themselves, a strategic clarifier was needed. A war game done effectively accomplishes this. The rules are simple.

1. **ASSIGN TEAMS.** Assign teams to represent competitors, key customer groups, vital suppliers, or even government regulatory bodies.
2. **ANALYZE AND PRESENT YOUR FIRST STRATEGIC RESPONSE.** Each team analyzes and presents its strategic response to the market around it; at the same time each team is allowed to critique its rival teams.
3. **REVISE STRATEGY.** Revise your strategy based on critique.
4. **INTRODUCE A MARKET-SHIFTING SCENARIO.** Introduce one or two surprising but plausible events into the game that will cause all the companies to review and possibly rethink their strategies. Such an event may also create a deal-making atmosphere among the players in the room, causing mergers or other massive corporate changes.
5. **REGROUP AND ASSESS YOUR OWN STRATEGY.** Regroup as one company pooling the lessons learned from viewing and acting out other strategies.

The framework is everything in a war game. It is the means by which you analyze intelligence and the strategic thrust of your rivals. The framework we find ideal for war games is Michael Porter's five forces and four corners models.[4]

What is useful about Porter's models is that they are based on the idea that every company is part of a larger industrial ecosystem and must play within it. Before Porter—that is, before the late

1970s—a strategist might outline a company's strengths, weaknesses, opportunities, and threats (otherwise known by the acronym SWOT) and compare the information in these four boxes with similar information drafted on its rivals. But these were all one-off scenarios, making it difficult to truly see the effect that one SWOT description would have on another. It gave you no assurance that you included all the factors pressing on you and your competitors, such as regulatory changes, new technologies, and growing strength of customers. (Think, for example, how Wal-Mart has dramatically changed the strategic future of consumer powerhouses such as Procter & Gamble. Before Wal-Mart, P&G was such a force in the marketplace that it could virtually dictate how much shelf space it wanted. Today, Wal-Mart *tells* P&G how much it can have!)

With SWOT you might indeed list P&G's marketing strength as well as its growing inability to control its shelf space. You might also see the threat that big box store buying power would place on P&G's margins. Maybe. SWOT is just a neatly arrayed series of lists, and no more. Sometimes interpreting a SWOT matrix is like reading tea leaves; you interpret them any way you want. Porter's five forces and four corners models tie all the pieces together, leaving you with greater insights and less guesswork.

The principle behind the five forces model is that five forces affect all industries. The first and most obvious force is competition between the current players. We sometimes think that strategy is only about dealing with the competitors. However, there are also four *external* forces:

> The threat of new entrants
> The threat of substitutes

> The power of buyers
> The power of suppliers

The relative power of each of these external forces affects the behavior of the players in the industry. If one or more of the external forces are important, the strategy of the companies in the industry must deal with that force just as it deals with the competitors.

The impact of each of these forces changes over time. The changes can result from a shift in industry structure, such as the consolidation of buyers, or from changes in technology, consumer preferences, regulations, or mergers.

No longer will a simple list of competitor strengths and weaknesses suffice to explain success or failure. In Porter's world, the most successful companies are the ones that can best navigate among the five forces using the most effective strategy.

This is the competitive ecosystem in which both Harvard and MIT students had to survive for the next eight hours. These future entrepreneurs and executives were about to face an industry still in formation, one with almost no history to speak of. Each team's survival or race to victory would depend on how well it navigated the many issues it would face, including the following:

> Can Google, whose stock price has soared to $300 a share, continue to defy the laws of competitive gravity?
> Google at the moment depends on its search engine advertising approach. It's a one-note company with 95 percent of the company's sales coming from this one revenue source. How can it diversify or build on this base

before its market share erodes from new entrants in the Internet search business?

> How can AOL, Time Warner's division, slow down the rapid loss of subscribers? Can it find a way to truly leverage Time Warner's valuable content, in the form of its rich family of magazines, broadcast group, and cable network?

> What can Microsoft do to prevent or at least slow down Google's hijacking of the desktop through such ingenious tools as Google Desktop? Will Microsoft's MSN search engine be powerful enough to grab a share of the click-for-advertising away from Google?

> How can Yahoo! break out of the pack? Despite its expanded search capabilities and revenues that equal that of Google, it can very easily lose its focus as it moves in many directions at once.

YEAH, YEAH, BUT WHAT ABOUT OUR STICKINESS?

Many of the players in the Battle for Clicks war game were too young to remember the strategic insanity of ten years ago. Much as Netscape once did, Google has captured the imagination not only of people in business, but also the media and general public, as evidenced by the following headlines:[5]

GOOGLE SAID TO PLAN RIVAL TO PAYPAL

LIVING BY GOOGLE RULES

GOOGLE ATTEMPTS TO BREACH THE
GREAT FIREWALL OF CHINA

With this kind of buzz, how can Google's management not think that customers will just flock to its doorstep and stay there, forever loyal?

Beware of the buzz, warns Porter. Too many dot-coms in the late 1990s believed their own hype about customer loyalty. They falsely relied upon what they felt were rock-solid barriers to what they called "stickiness" and Porter labels as switching costs. Switching costs are the costs the customer will incur to move to a new vendor (or to a new Internet address or information platform, in Internet jargon). No Internet company should believe its customers have invested so much emotion, time, and expense that they would not switch to another vendor at the drop of a hat (or a click of a mouse). All a customer need do is type a new address into a browser and the stickiness disappears.

BUILDING BARRIERS WITH STRATEGY

In theory, the combined effects of the five forces, including the level of competition among the players, determine whether an industry as a whole is profitable. However, companies that succeed in differentiating themselves from their peers can often build barriers against existing competitors and the outside forces. For example, Time Warner is a broad media and entertainment company with interests in broadcast networks, publishing, film, and cable systems. It could use its combined market power to bundle advertising products across its range of media businesses. Wouldn't that forestall Google?

According to Porter, there are three "generic" strategies that companies can use to be more profitable than the average company in the industry: (1) They can differentiate themselves and thereby get a higher profit for their products, (2) they can be low cost, or (3) they can focus on a particular market segment or geographic niche where there is less pressure from competitors and external forces.

Which of the three broad strategies do the four teams in this war game follow and how might the strategy change in response to the other players and dynamics in the industry as a whole?

WHAT'S HIDING IN THE FOUR CORNERS: HOW TO SHAPE YOUR STRATEGY

The secret to winning in the real marketplace is having the best strategy and then executing it. Porter's five forces model describes industry behavior. His four corners model helps you assess how companies shape their individual strategy within that industry. It further shows how companies respond when their core goals and assumptions are challenged.

1. **A DRIVER** is what motivates management; it is the thing that makes executives get up in the morning and go to work. For example, Pfizer's management wants to run the world's largest pharmaceutical company. The *New York Times* wants to be the national "newspaper of record." Apple seeks to be a leader in high-technology product innovation.

2. **ASSUMPTIONS** are the beliefs a company has about its industry, how competitors behave in that industry, and beliefs a company has about itself and what motivates it. Companies in the same industry may have different and contradictory assumptions. Traditional music publishers had assumed for years that the consumer would buy entire albums of their favorite artist, despite the fact that he or she likes only half of the music on a twelve-song album. Apple Computer assumed differently and had the iTunes technology to deliver individual songs on demand. Almost overnight Apple's iTunes business was worth hundreds of millions of dollars. The record companies are working with Apple and others to catch up and to counteract the loss in album sales. Assumptions are the darkest and often most misjudged part of the Porter model. Assumptions are where companies often know the least about their competitors and trip up the most.

3. **STRATEGY**, as described above, is the road map a company has chosen to achieve profitability and real economic value. A company, according to Porter, must decide on one of these three general strategic paths: differentiation, low cost, or focus. A management that tries to take its corporation in two or three different directions, instead of one, often fails.

4. **CAPABILITY**, the fourth corner, is the resources the firm brings to the party. Does a company have the cash, personnel, global distribution or information systems infrastructure, and a well-integrated product line to achieve its goals?

WHO IS THAT MYSTERIOUS FACILITATOR
AND WHY IS HE BOTHERING ME?

All war games need a facilitator. A facilitator's role can be described as a guide, someone who keeps the teams on track and the strategic thinking moving forward to a successful conclusion.

Games without a facilitator tend to wander into chaos and their players into brainstorming sessions without direction. The result of facilitatorless games are a lot of "attaboys" and backslapping; that, or a series of unconstructive arguments. Either way, a game without a facilitator usually fails to move a company's strategic thinking forward.

Facilitators are supposed to be neutral but do not confuse neutrality with consolation and empathy. Facilitators play a number of roles during the game itself: They challenge poor logic, point out issues that teams have omitted, inject facts where emotion can tend to overtake an argument, and challenge entrenched assumptions.

Like an iceberg, most of the work that goes into preparing for a war game is invisible to participants. It takes place months or weeks ahead of the game itself. Typically, a facilitator should interview the principal players in the game, trying to understand key issues or concerns, as well as prepare a briefing book for participants. The briefing book is critical. It presents both the inside knowledge gleaned from the interviews and the positions of each of the key industry players.

Finally, the facilitator prepares a series of what-if "shock" scenarios to confront the teams with during the latter half of the game. You will see just such a scenario upset the strategic balance in the Battle for Clicks event.

For this event, we appointed a lead facilitator and a group of four judges. The judges, not ordinarily part of a typical corporate war game, were Internet advertising market watchers selected from leading investment houses and technology forecasting firms. We appointed them to ensure accuracy of the strategic statements each team would make and to offset any lack of expertise on the part of the students.

SURVIVING A FIRST ENCOUNTER WITH THE ENEMY . . . BUT FIRST YOU HAVE TO SURVIVE YOURSELF

Following a short discussion of the Porter models with the entire audience, the facilitator instructed each of the four teams to separate and huddle, each in its own breakout room. There, each team began its work.

The first assignment for each team was to explain its company's four corners and describe how the team was shaping its strategy to win—even if winning meant winning at the margins, and not outright victory.

As it turned out, understanding the four corners model initially was the easiest part of the exercise. Every one of the students easily grasped the meaning of drivers, assumptions, strategy, and capability. Students had more than enough data from the briefing book research provided to them and could also draw on their own knowledge as consumers of these Internet products. It was easy because no one had yet challenged anything.

The most difficult aspect of the game involved leaving one's own view of the market (and its many biases) behind. These very smart, very savvy business school students needed to do more than play the role of the enemy or opposing company: They needed to *become* that company.

The Google team at the start of the game hadn't quite made the transition. They were still MIT students playing the role of Google, not becoming Google. Google felt like a foreign entity you addressed in the third person. It was not "us"; it was "them," resulting in comments such as "I think that *these* guys wake up each morning, living and breathing the coolest technology on the planet" and "I don't think *they* wake up thinking about market share. *They* are just a bunch of guys having a great time."

Harvard's Time Warner–AOL team was stuck on more than just psychology. The AOL team felt it was mired strategically and had been dealt a very poor hand with which to play the game. AOL, the students observed, had evolved into no more than a clunky distribution channel for Time Warner's content, content that most would find elsewhere on the open Internet—for free! Dial-up, formerly AOL's key to gaining and locking in subscribers, was antiquated in this day of widely available Internet access via cable TV broadband and telephone company DSL (digital subscriber lines).

The AOL team had become so pessimistic about its future after only the first hour and a half of the eight-hour game that it nearly stopped generating ideas altogether. The entire discussion had begun to circle back on itself and was going nowhere. Team members felt they entered the game as losers and effectively began writing AOL's eulogy.

One of the facilitators, standing at the side of the room, had to step in and point out the team's myopic view. "Why not turn AOL's strategy away from pursuing dial-up revenue," the facilitator commented, injecting a ray of hope into the room. "Find ways to attract online advertising, much as Google has done so successfully through its search engine."

His prodding energized the team. The students began thinking about ways AOL could mine the rich resources within Time Warner's media empire.

The Harvard-staffed Microsoft players considered deal making as a way to crack into the Internet advertising market. After all, here is a company with $60 billion of cash burning a hole in its pocket. As long as the Justice Department or the European Union does not get in the way, there are deals to be struck.

Two hours had come and gone. The judges and facilitators had circulated and listened to all the developing responses in this Battle for Clicks marketplace. It was now time for the first presentations—or should I say first confrontations.

No battle plan has ever survived contact with the enemy, said Heinz Guderian, a German World War II panzer general and one of the architects of the Blitzkrieg. As all the teams learned early in the game, winning in a strategy exercise is not solely a matter of having the right facts and thorough analysis. Success is in large part based on finding the ability to articulate the message, build credibility, and fundamentally believe in your strategy. Yes, you still needed rational, executable strategies. Sure. But you also needed to be able to sell and convince.

Yahoo! presented first. Yahoo!'s presenters exuded confidence. Without hesitation they offered up their main driver as their reason for being: Make Yahoo! the "first stop, one stop, all stop" place to go on the Internet. Yahoo!'s presenters then expanded on their slogan.

> First stop: They wanted the consumer to consider Yahoo! the first place to go on the Internet.
> One stop: They wanted the consumer to feel there is no need to go anywhere else; everything the consumer wants is here.
> All stop: They wanted the consumer to feel comfortable staying on the site for long periods of time.

The Yahoo! team was justified in staking out this "first stop, one stop, all stop" position. A Nielsen Net ratings survey in February 2005 reported that consumers stayed on Yahoo!'s site for nearly three hours each month, more than five times that of Google. Their positioning statement made some sense.

The fundamental assumption Yahoo! believed would make its portal extremely valuable to advertisers is that more eyeballs equals more revenue. Therefore, any new function would be a new way it could capture a new pair of eyeballs.

This all sounded like an unassailable argument. Then Yahoo! stumbled. "All I have to be is good enough for the consumer," stated a Yahoo! presenter. But good enough doesn't cut it. In this world of differentiated strategies, how can Yahoo! capture an advertiser's interest if it is just "good enough"? The audience quickly latched on to this strategic flaw.

Microsoft attacked first. The strategy was too generic, too much like everyone else's, claimed Microsoft. Besides, added Microsoft, how can Yahoo! claim this if Time Warner (through its AOL division) owns more customers than Yahoo!? The objector was correct. According to the Nielsen survey, AOL retains customers for nearly twice as long (six minutes) as Yahoo!, each and every month. "Good enough" won't work when Yahoo! is trying to climb to the top of the competitive heap.

Yahoo! needed to respond. It needed to clarify its strategy if it was to convince its rivals as well as the judges. It did so—by back stepping a bit. By "good enough," they referred to the search engine. In this area, Yahoo! conceded its position to Google. But in every other way, the Yahoo! team believed it provided the most fertile venue for advertisers. When it comes to online advertising, Yahoo! saw its future as a superb integrator of advertising and advertising services. Advertisers do not just place ads, they can target their advertisements and receive analysis that will further allow them to zero in on their market. The result will be consumers who stay on their site longer and remain loyal and advertisers who will wish to come back over and over again. *First stop, all stop, one stop.*

As the first guinea pig in the experiment, how did Yahoo! do? So-so. The judges felt that the presentation was too generic, lacked evidence, and contained a lot of positioning statements without much substance. The Yahoo! team needed to do a better job identifying who they were. Was it a media company or a tech company? They did not describe what they would do with all their pieces other than their search engine. They focused too much on search, allowing Google's strategy to subconsciously drive theirs.

This was little more than a B− presentation by all accounts. Upon sitting down, all the team members held their collective breath knowing other presentations lay ahead. Their rivals would certainly learn from Yahoo!'s pummeling.

Ah, the fate of the first presenter.

It was now Microsoft's turn. You could almost see the other three teams readying their barrage of questions. Everyone wanted to take a swipe at the evil empire.

The entire room knew that Microsoft owned a very large $60 billion war chest from which it could acquire its way into a market or wear down the competition. The technical and fiscal capabilities were there somewhere within the Microsoft empire. No doubt about it.

It jumped out of its corner, spewing forth daunting statistics in Gatling gun–like fashion:

> Aside from the $60 billion cash hoard, Microsoft generates $14 billion in cash annually from operations.
> Microsoft has fifty-seven thousand full-time employees.
> Microsoft has a strong brand name.
> Microsoft has a broad assortment of Internet properties.
> The MSN home page is the number-one portal with 350,000 users per month.
> MSN has an AOL-like business with over eight million subscribers.
> MSN has 135,000 active instant messenger accounts of its own.
> MSN offers hundreds of communities of interest on its site, much like Yahoo! or Google.
> Microsoft provides desktop leadership through its Windows platform and Office software suite.
> Microsoft has strong existing relationships with industry channels.

> Microsoft has a history of coming from behind and capturing the market, as it did with Netscape ten years earlier.

The capabilities list was numbing and irritating to the audience at the same time.

Microsoft's strategy was simple: Keep building its MSN search capabilities and follow closely on the heels of Google, until—through a combination of acquisitions and product improvements—it overtakes and overcomes Google. Netscape redux.

But even Microsoft can stumble—at least in a war game. In this instance, Microsoft had a dark corner lurking among its assumptions.

The first assumption made sense: You don't have to be the first to market to become the ultimate winner. No one could argue with this. After all, Microsoft had proven this time and again in its word processing, spreadsheet, and Internet browser businesses, and even with the Windows platform itself. It was not first to market in any of these businesses.

The second assumption, however, revealed its Achilles' heel. "Windows PC will continue to be the center of the IT world: We can submerge search into our complete platform," the Microsoft team declared on a PowerPoint slide.

Members of rival teams throughout the room shot up their hands. No one saw the world the way Microsoft did. All the Internet planets did not revolve in the least around the PC.

A Yahoo! objector chose to lecture the Microsoft team about its blatant blind spot: "You do keep in mind," she chided Microsoft, "that what we are talking about here is Webcentric. You have applications such as Salesforce.com that keep showing that applications can be Web hosted very successfully and that the PC may become the commodity. So keep that in mind with your assumption."

What this encounter reveals is how assumptions are indeed the dark corner of Porter's four corners model. You can adjust strategy, but if your assumptions are proven wrong you will find yourself fighting the wrong battle or the last battle. You may even discover you are fighting in the wrong arena altogether, in this case the PC instead of the Web arena. Microsoft would just not let go of its PC-centric viewpoint.

This chiding did not deter Microsoft. If anything, the team became more stubborn, more resistant to altering its strategy. Unlike Yahoo!, it felt no need to step back.

We are going to be a gorilla, a Microsoft presenter said. Yes, it understood the market changes currently taking place but still believed that the Windows platform (or its successor) will remain the dominant one.

Microsoft outlined a high-investment strategy that would stubbornly and persistently snatch away market share from Yahoo! and Google bit by bit. This was a war of attrition, not of innovation. It would build market share by paying its online partners to preinstall Microsoft's Search Toolbar, pay content sites to use its search engine, and build an advertising center to eventually replace Yahoo! on all MSN properties. It would do all this even if it meant sacrificing short-term profits.

Still wearing its gorilla suit, Microsoft declared that if all else failed, it would acquire technologies and work them into the Microsoft strategy.

The Microsoft argument was accurate and well articulated.

Any arrogance and attitude displayed did not seem to bother the judges as much as it did the rivals. Its facts all seemed in line with reality.

Where Microsoft lost points was in its failure to acknowledge that its PC-centric assumptions were wrong (most of the judges believed they were in the long run), the lack of details on how it was going to execute its strategy, and general lack of foresight. How will Microsoft build its advertising center to replace the one run by Yahoo!? That is just one example of a statement made without supplying the details to support its execution. The Microsoft plan was too here-and-now and did not paint a picture of how it would handle the market shifts over the coming few years. B+ overall.

Hats in hand, Time Warner's AOL team shuffled to the front of the room. You could see the team had metamorphosed. This was no longer a group of bright, ambitious Harvard Business School students; they had become lackluster AOL.

Despite the fact that AOL still claims more paid subscribers than any other company in the room, it saw a struggle ahead. It wasn't rich enough to buy its way into a market like Microsoft. It wasn't as hip and as tech-savvy as Google, the perceived leader. It wasn't plugged into the world of Hollywood as was Yahoo!. The AOL team members felt a bit like a relic, despite the facilitator's earlier pep talk.

Still they marched on, taking the facilitator's advice and playing on their strengths. Their assumptions made sense and were notably underscored by Time Warner's key strength: Content is king, particularly content combined with detailed demographic information on its customers. Unlike Microsoft, it realized the inevitability of a market shift that was not in its favor. It knew its precious subscriber base was disappearing and needed to be recaptured so that it could grow advertising revenues. Finally, it also believed that search technology is a commodity; whatever Google has, AOL can possibly replicate.

Based on these assumptions, AOL outlined its strategy: It would leverage the potential advertising revenues by exploiting its base of twenty-two million instant messaging users. First and foremost, it would continue to follow its family-oriented approach, specifically investing in Internet security and eliminating e-mail spam.

Moving forward, it realized that customizing its advertising to consumers was a priority. Customizing ads would provide it with a powerful incentive for advertisers who desire the teenage market, the core group of AOL instant messaging users. To support its strategy, AOL offered a number of realistic proposals, including bundling its ad placements across all of Time Warner's media properties and tapping into existing relationships that the Time Warner parent already has with advertising agencies.

Microsoft tripped up on its assumptions. Yahoo! lacked specificity in its strategy. For AOL, its weakness was in its very strategy. Saying you are going to push targeted advertising to each of your instant messaging customers is one thing; making it happen is another. AOL was strategically inconsistent on this point. All of its proclamations discussed AOL and Time Warner's leveraging mass market ads through mass media, not targeting the advertising in a Google-like way. Pushing ads shaped to match a single consumer's need is Google's strength, not AOL's. AOL needed to clarify how it was going to make its wishes a reality. In this one aspect it failed the first time around.

Overall, however, the judges felt that the AOL team played its hand as well as it could. The panel (and even its rivals in the audience) appreciated the way AOL exploited its instant messaging strength as well as its family-oriented approach. Grade: A−.

Finally, it was Google's turn. It was the rabbit all the dogs were chasing. Google had invented a very real, revenue-generating market for search. It had in effect created its own competition.

After briefly acknowledging its partnership with AOL and the vast content Time Warner has to offer, it immediately set off on a different course. The entire fabric of its presentation positioned itself as genetically very different from any of the other players in the room.

That content is plentiful on the Web was the first of Google's assumptions—a slap in the face to Time Warner, the king of content. Information in the Internet age is a commodity, plain and simple, asserted Google. As for advertising revenue, contextual advertising is a powerful source for revenue generation and an area Google feels it manages better than anyone else. "Standards matter" was its last and possibly most audacious assumption.

Standards? You mean Google feels it can impose standards on the free-ranging Web? That sounded a bit arrogant, not unlike Google's rival at the other end of the room, Microsoft. Standards matter to Google, and with this assumption it declared its intention to become the platform everybody uses for everything—off-line (for finding files on your own computer, for example) or online (in the hunt for information).

Arrogant or not, the Google team also believed it had the wherewithal to act on these assumptions. Among its capabilities is its ability to place and manage these ads for every advertiser. With a $56 billion market capitalization, it also has the money for acquisitions or other investments. Most important, it benefits from the Internet's network effect. Because it is the search engine of choice for so many millions of users, Google has a critical mass of information about the demographics of its users that no one else can yet match.

Always looking to the future but not wanting to toss away its valuable revenue-producing relationship with AOL, the Google team spent the first few minutes of its presentation acknowledging the importance of its AOL partnership. AOL, which provides Internet access to more than twenty-two million U.S. subscribers, currently relies on Google to provide most of its search results. The relationship has been valuable for both companies. Google gives AOL a majority of the advertising revenue generated by AOL customer searches. AOL is also Google's largest outside revenue source, generating 13 percent of the company's sales, when the ad commissions paid to AOL are included.

AOL intends to reduce its dependence on Google as it tries to stake out its own piece of the search-advertising arena. The Google team appreciated this fact. For instance, AOL is expanding its geographically targeted searches where users can look for organizations or services in a specific area. Google offers a similar service, but AOL decided instead to work with a Norwegian-based concern, Fast Search & Transfer Inc. AOL says its expanded search functions don't jeopardize its relationship with Google and that AOL is continuing down the path of what it views search should be, which is a little bit different from Google's vision.

Google wishes to look forward, not backward. AOL is history. That's just the way it is. Google's stated strategy was intended to put a lot of distance between it and everyone else, primarily by creating a lot of value for the customer, and it would do this in ways the other rivals could not approach. It has customized its search engine to work in over one hundred languages and cultures with a goal of being in 198 countries; its free news service skims forty-five hundred information sources; and its desktop search tool is by far the best in class, and again free.

Someone from the AOL team feebly objected by asking why Google thought it had the best search engine. Amazon or other sites and tools on the Net already have powerful search capability. The Google team's response: We have "uniqueness protection." Translated, that means that Google has gone to great lengths to patent its search technology and continue to drill down more deeply into that technology. This is something that neither AOL nor any of the other rivals in the room could claim. Whatever Google is doing technologically seems to work.

No more objections came from the floor.

Google felt it had clear and direct purpose in its strategy and marched through the rest of the presentation without hesitation: It is not about ruling the desktop (like Microsoft) or owning the world (another Microsoft put-down). Google very simply and clearly wanted to help people find the information they need. If Google could accomplish this, it felt it too could gain the most revenue and growth.

This strategy was consistent with everything Google has grown to become, before and after its intial public offering. One of

Porter's key principles of strategic positioning states that a company's strategy must deliver clear benefits that are different and distinct from its rivals. This is exactly the razor-sharp strategic position the Google team drove home to its audience.

The judges reviewed each of the rivals based on four criteria: insight into their strategic position, accuracy in presenting the facts, creativity in proposing a new strategy, and foresight into the near future. Based on these four criteria, Google, along with AOL, received high marks.

Was the game over? Not quite.

MARKET UPHEAVAL: TEST YOUR STRATEGY'S TENSILE STRENGTH

The world is not quite so simple. How many of us would like to execute our PowerPoint-designed strategy, devised in the isolation of a boardroom, and then march ahead without encountering resistance? All of us would. The world usually does not allow us this luxury. That is why a war game needs someone to inject an unexpected shock or two into the event.

Shocks test limits. They test your ability to respond. They test the depth and consistency of your strategy altogether.

The resiliency and survivability of your strategy can be tested by fashioning an extreme but plausible event. Such an event will force rivals, customers, suppliers, government regulatory bodies to react, thus potentially showing you how to design a better strategy that anticipates changing conditions.

In the Battle for Clicks, we did just that. We concocted a surprising incident. The result: Microsoft and Time Warner dramatically altered their paths; Google and Yahoo! did not. All were better informed as a result and learned lessons about their strategic strengths and weaknesses—lessons that would have been far more costly were they forced to play them out in the real world.

The shock was an economic one. It began as a political clash that mushroomed. In the fictional scenario we devised, the Bush administration warned the People's Republic of China not to interfere in Taiwan, which has been making louder noises in its desire for independence from China. The Chinese government responded to the Bush administration's threat by decoupling its currency, the huan, from the U.S. dollar, allowing it to float, and selling U.S. dollars onto the global currency market. The dollar went into a tailspin, triggering an economic slowdown.

Congress, wanting to close the rapidly widening federal deficit, partly as a result of the Chinese action, advocated a series of new taxes and tax hikes. One of the new tax measures was aimed at Internet service providers (ISPs). The current communications tax would rise from 3 percent of revenues to 4.5 percent and extend to ISPs. The average dial-up customer would see Internet charges rise $.67 a month and broadband subscribers jumping as much as $1.98 per month. The Congressional Budget Office estimated that the increase in the tax rate and the extension to ISPs would raise $2.3 billion a year.

This was only the beginning. A number of state legislatures had been mulling over levying state sales taxes on Internet retailers.[6] Passage of the above suggested federal law would likely open up a floodgate of state taxation of the Net, possibly derailing the growth of Internet advertising.

This was the shock. Most important for this game, though, is not the idea of a tax itself but the effect the passage of such a law has on the key players in Internet advertising, an industry that is just beginning to find its legs.

Ironically, the scenario had the strongest psychological effect on fiscal giant Microsoft and on the ever-weakening AOL. Google and Yahoo!, the companies most alike in this game, were less bothered by the tax. The scenario and how each team reacted to it also taught the players a number of lessons about corporate relationships and deal making that no one had anticipated.

Stay Straight: The Google Huddle

Google team members retired to their breakout room and in only a matter of a few minutes came to the conclusion that the tax would not affect them. They believed this for a number of reasons: If Google was about searching for and finding the most valuable information, not necessarily buying anything, then it had little to fear from a tax. Even if all costs went up 5 percent to the consumer, it would still be cheaper to shop online than to walk into a store.

Is Help on the Way? The Time Warner–AOL Huddle

The AOL team did not feel terribly in control of its destiny. They felt vulnerable. Like a log in a river, they were still afloat and heading downstream with everyone else but with no real sense of direction or ability to maneuver very much. The basic conclusion was that the tax would hurt nearly everyone else more than it did AOL. AOL just sells advertising, the team members concluded; it doesn't sell actual product. Therefore, there is no sales to tax, just advertising to sell.

Although Time Warner's cable operations would feel the tax bite very directly, stay fast, the team concluded, and let's see what happens to us. But Time Warner did not talk like a company that knew where it was going. One company in the game was about to take advantage of Time Warner's vulnerability and change the game plan for AOL for some time to come.

Red Meat, Eat Meat! The Microsoft Huddle

If there was any question about the arrogance and sense of industry superiority in the persona of the Microsoft team, you merely had to eavesdrop on the conversation developing in the breakout room after the tax scenario was announced.

Microsoft was not chastened by the criticism heaped on it during the first encounter earlier that day. In one team member's words, "We could significantly increase the hurt of our competitors, or we can take advantage of them [when the tax takes effect]." Team members knew well that its cash hoard would allow it to place pricing pressure on the rest of the market as its rivals might feel the revenue squeeze resulting from the drop in sales. Microsoft would be able to ride out the storm as well as witness the failure of its rivals. Once they were weakened or on the brink of bankruptcy, Microsoft would be in a position to buy them.

This attitude within the Microsoft ranks led to a deal with AOL. Microsoft coveted the twenty-two million pair of eyeballs, otherwise known as AOL subscribers. The tax, Microsoft believed, would only weaken AOL further, allowing Microsoft to buy them at a fire-sale price.

Microsoft's proposal involved AOL's leaving Google and moving to the MSN service, as well as being given a sole spot on the Windows desktop. The implication: Anyone who bought a Microsoft platform would immediately be exposed to the AOL service.

Time Warner would not have to divest AOL at this time. Everyone involved on both sides understood that this proposed partnership could be a first step toward a Time Warner sale of AOL to Microsoft.

After a short deliberation, AOL accepted.

No Change: The Yahoo! Huddle

The Yahoo! team felt that for a variety of reasons AOL and Google would be somewhat equally affected—or unaffected—by the taxation scenario. The Yahoo! discussions mirrored Google's almost word for word. At the end of a very brief around-the-table meeting, most on the team believed that consumers would continue to buy online despite possibly being taxed.

The conclusion: No dramatic change in strategy. Stay on track. Do not become distracted by the tax issue.

DID ANYONE WIN THE WORLD SERIES?

All the teams returned to face one another one more time for a post–tax scenario presentation. They each were anxious to see how radically their rivals' strategies may have changed or not changed at all.

Google's Response: Search, Search, Search

Google drilled further into its strategy. Search. Search. Search. It was Google's search technology that would keep it out of the middle of the tax storm that was going to change how AOL or Yahoo! might conduct their business. The Internet tax was just a small blip on the long-term radar screen as far as Google was concerned.

Google's response to the scenario was a simple, elegant refinement of its earlier approach. When asked to deliver details, not just strategic platitudes, it did so—in three very specific parts.

Part One

> Continue to grow Google's geographic reach.
> Expand further into non-U.S. markets, such as China and India.
> Partner with Linux software developers to achieve a true Google inside strategy on whatever platforms they construct in global markets.
> Expand the Google experience on non-PC devices, such as cell phones or PDAs (personal digital assistants).

Part Two

> Increase the presence in the corporation.
> Use the Google search engine as a powerful data-mining tool that can index both structured (i.e., databases with formal records and data fields, such as a block of names and addresses for mailing lists) and unstructured data (i.e., critical information buried within mounds of text and possibly difficult to identify and extract).
> Expand services into the areas of financial services and the legal field since both deal in mounds of data that require analysis.

Part Three

> Deliver dynamic analysis of data with speed and agility.
> Work with large enterprise technology companies, such as SAP, to assist companies such as retailers to better sell their products. (Imagine if Neiman Marcus, a large U.S. department store chain, experiences different demand in one region over another for a particular type of sweater. Google's technology will learn from the different demand rates and change the pricing on the same product, based on region and level of demand.)

No one questioned Google's refinement of its strategy, not its rivals or the judges. Its response was specific and addressed the tax complication head-on.

Time Warner–AOL's Response: Find a Partner—Fast!

AOL, a bit dizzy during this final phase of the game, was also anxious about its falling market share. Its anxiety only worsened with the announcement of the Internet tax.

The Time Warner–AOL presentation contained, almost verbatim, the offer Microsoft presented to it: AOL would find a place on Microsoft's desktop in exchange for customer information and customer access. Be it in China or wherever the Microsoft desktop moves, AOL would go with it.

The Google team could not understand AOL's sudden departure from Google and this new deal it struck with Microsoft. Why, the Google folks wanted to know, would AOL move to a third- or fourth-rate search engine such as Microsoft? How would that solve AOL's dwindling market share? It wouldn't, was the implication.

Finally, Google wanted to know why AOL would agree to hand over all of Time Warner's content to Microsoft and its Windows platform. How would this arrangement ever compensate Time Warner for the full value of all its content, including magazines, newspapers, and TV?

The answer AOL gave Google was not convincing: It admitted it had not thought through all the details, partly because the deal discussions had proved extremely distracting. The AOL–Time Warner team simply ran out of time to plan anything other than the deal itself—and even that was half-baked.

The lack of planning was evident. By the time AOL left the stage, it had only discussed the Microsoft arrangement and nothing more. AOL appeared to have lost momentum—and some points from the judges.

Microsoft's Response: The Cash Machine at Work

In the short term, the Microsoft presenter made it clear that everyone would lose some revenue from the tax and the cost of business would definitely increase. For the long term, Microsoft was not worried and could stay the course, continuing to improve its position in search.

The AOL deal was far less of a distraction for Microsoft than it was for AOL, it appeared. Microsoft snatched AOL for two purposes: to gain the twenty-two million subscribers and to sting Google by depriving it of 13 percent of its revenue drawn directly from AOL.

As to plans going forward, Microsoft was not as specific or as clear as Google, but it did demonstrate a focus on continuing to differentiate itself in search. Similar to Google, it would drive to improve its local search capabilities, country by country. It would also develop the technology for GPS (global positioning satellite) advertising, advertising that finds you and changes depending on your location. For example, if you were in New England, an advertisement for a whale-watching tour would pop up on your mobile phone or computer screen; while in England, you might see an ad appear for a vacation spot in southern Spain.

In short, the Internet tax did not bother Microsoft. It had plenty of cash to ride out whatever revenue dip might occur. It would move forward in search technology and build its talent pool in this area. The Microsoft presenter looked right at the Google table and made it clear that building a talent pool will likely include stealing talent from Google. (No love lost among these players, all of whom by now had assumed their company's persona.)

Yahoo!'s Response: Don't Detour; Keep Building

Yahoo! viewed search as just one of a number of services it would sell and continue to sell. It declared the tax issue as a nonstarter, perhaps placing some pressure on both consumers and advertisers but not dampening the market all that much.

Team presenters spoke a great deal about the need for driving deeper into customer segmentation and offering complete customer solutions for advertisers. A complete solution in Yahoo!-speak meant providing the advertiser exposure to the customer through a variety of media and online communities that customers might have joined. Wherever the customer was, Yahoo! would offer the advertiser exposure to him.

The judges were not impressed. One judge thought Yahoo! left a number of opportunities on the table, such as technology partnerships or possibly partnering with other media companies or Internet search companies not necessarily present in the room that day.

THE REAL PRIZE: STRATEGIC INSIGHTS AND COMPETITIVE TRANSPARENCY

MIT's Google team took the prize. Google had pulled from behind by staying the course and building a strategy that played on its search engine strengths, but it won for other reasons. It used the war game as a means to explore and expose its rivals' weaknesses.

> > Microsoft generally saw its cash hoard as a strength,
> > whereas Google identified Microsoft's reliance on its

treasure chest as a deficit. Microsoft believed it could use its cash to ride out the tax storm or apply the brute force of its dollars to acquire its way to success, as it demonstrated by dealing with AOL.

> AOL's model was an early Internet age model of dedicated dial-up subscribers; Google knew AOL was mired in its own mud hole.

> Yahoo! was the company most like Google but became increasingly distracted as the game progressed. Google saw Yahoo! as playing with too many options, trying to pursue each one with equal force. As Porter warns, you cannot pursue all three strategies (low-cost consumer solutions, differentiated corporate services, and focused services to specific geographic or industry markets) at the same time. You'll fail.

War games are not crystal balls, but they do throw off lots of insight—and sometimes even foresight. This war game did presage both the quandary that the Yahoo! team had with its strategy and all the deal-making activity surrounding AOL toward the end of 2005.

Only four months after the game had ended, *The Economist,* in an article titled "Yahoo!'s Personality Crisis," noted how this very war game shone a spotlight on Yahoo!'s own strategic confusion:

Students from Harvard Business School and MIT's Sloan School of Management were recently invited to play a "war game" between the big four internet portals—Yahoo!, Google, Time Warner's AOL, and Microsoft's MSN. . . . Yahoo!, its team thought, is in essence a smorgasbord.

The article went on to criticize Yahoo! for losing focus even as it has improved its fortunes, concluding:

> *This fits a pattern. Terry Semel, Yahoo!'s chief executive since 2001, has "done a notable job turning Yahoo! around" since the losses of the dotcom bust, says Jerry Michalski, a technology visionary in Berkeley, "but in the process he has turned it into, well, a bit of a tart. . . . All things to all men."*[7]

Perhaps no surprise but reassuring nevertheless, Microsoft did pursue AOL throughout the final quarter of 2005, exactly as the game had predicted. This is where the similarity between the game and reality ended. At some point during the the Microsoft-AOL courtship, Google's management team took a stronger interest in AOL than the MIT-staffed war game team did during the game. Perhaps the regret that MIT's Google team felt in losing AOL after the game hit the real Google before it was too late.

In late December 2005, Google ultimately triumphed. It had won back the prize that it and Microsoft had fought over so fiercely in preceding weeks. The deal amounted to Google buying a 5 percent stake in AOL for $1 billion. AOL continues to use Google's search engine. In addition, AOL is now able to sell its advertisements directly to advertisers instead of sending those advertisers to Google. Google also wins because it still has access to Time Warner's content, something it apparently has begun to treasure. In the end, everyone was happy, except Microsoft.[8]

The game did test the tensile strength of everyone's strategy—that was its purpose. The fact that Google won the prize instead of Microsoft was more Google's brinkmanship than anything else. In all respects the game played itself out accurately and taught every-one involved valuable lessons.

I have witnessed and been involved in many war games inside corporations. No matter the industry, I have seen managers gain profound insights about how their market works, insights that teach lessons far beyond the development of a particular strategy. These are the reasons why war games are such an important strategic intelligence tool for anyone in any business.

Insight 1: Expect to Win at the Margins, Not Vanquish Your Rivals

Google's victory was not a case of destroying its rivals. It was all about who could reach the finish line first with the most inventive or most consistently thought-out strategy.

Most of the time revelations that surface during a game's vari-ous rounds teach management how to reposition—or jettison—a product and how to consider forming an alliance with a rival. War games serve as powerful tools to reshape company strategy for the best possible outcome. When I finish a game I see at least ten or fifteen to-dos for management to fine-tune its strategic position-ing. Consider the outcome of a war game as a new set of directions with which management can steer its very large battleship. Each instruction helps executives to adjust the direction and speed of the ship without tipping it over in the process. To carry the anal-ogy still further, a game can also identify where your rivals are likely to try to stop you or to cause you to misdirect your ship altogether.

There are times when companies need to pursue a zero-sum

goal, even if that goal is elusive. As you witnessed in the Battle for Clicks, Microsoft has successfully pursued a single standard based on its technology. For most companies, though, not only is this pursuit a waste of time, but it is also potentially dangerous to future fiscal health.

"I believe that if you frame companies with a zero-sum game, you will end up creating destructive competition in which nobody will ultimately win," says strategy professor Michael Porter. To win with a zero-sum mentality, you will bulk up your product line, cut costs, possibly restructure, and then downsize to reduce costs even further. All the while you become less profitable, if profitable at all. Management then writes down its investment as a loss, and suddenly the company's return on investment looks great. According to Porter, this is destructive competition that creates no economic value. That is often the result of zero-sum game playing.[9]

Winning at the margins is still winning. In Porter-speak, I would say the best outcome of a war game is to find your company's own unique strategy, one that sets it apart from the competition and gives consumers a reason to select your product or service. If you can discover how to be different you will have won more than a game; you will have found a way to win real revenues and profits.

Insight 2: Learn the Implication of Your Decisions— That's the Real Prize

What defines the winner in a war game? No war game can predict market conditions with 100 percent certainty. When a war game is successful, it provides a fertile environment for the players to create a variety of strategies or encounters with the enemy, customers, or even other entities, such as government agencies. The winner in a war game is usually the entire company that has played the game. Everyone learns lessons and gains insights, those "aha" moments they might otherwise not have had sitting alone in a quiet office.

The second difference is significant: At the end of every corporate war game, we bring all the players back together as one company. We have dissolved all the other teams but one, the hometown team. We instruct them all that they've been rehired by their old company, the one that has sponsored this strategic event. We ask all the newly rehired participants to express what they have learned and how they can use the newly won insight about themselves and their rivals to craft an improved strategy.

Sometimes the joint decision is to postpone a new product launch, or it may be to partner or merge—or acquire—another company. Whatever the decisions, management now sees the possibilities for each of its moves.

Seeing the implications of each decision you may make is the equivalent of a chess master looking at a chessboard. A chess master knows the opponent's strategy, understanding each countermove. The expert player can actually envision the chessboard two, three, or even four moves ahead.

Early in 2003, Larry Ellison, CEO of Oracle, the database software company, ran a series of war game scenarios to anticipate changes in his market. One of those scenarios described a number of triggering events leading to industry consolidation. The game armed him with strategies should consolidation occur. Therefore, when PeopleSoft made its bid for J. D. Edwards in June 2003,

Ellison identified this move as a triggering event and was prepared to act quickly.

The lesson he learned from his war game is that he wanted to be first among his rivals to select the best possible acquisition candidates. Ellison jumped into the fray, moving to acquire People-Soft itself. An eighteen-month contest in and out of court ensued. Oracle ultimately won. And, as of this writing, industry analysts believe Oracle made a shrewd and timely move, one that appears to be working.

Insight 3: Avoid the Merger Solution, the Easy Excuse

One of the first reactions many war game teams have when confronting an intensely competitive encounter or severe market shift (such as the e-commerce tax scenario) is to avoid the intelligence and follow the emotion. War games discipline you to play out your strategy in light of existing intelligence.

The Google team won because it chose to drill into its strategy and not get caught up in the take-no-prisoners, let's-take-our-rivals-off-the-table emotional approach. Google could have elected to buy out its rivals. After all, it has the money. Instead it truly analyzed its competition, examined its strategies, and made decisions based on the circumstances and available intelligence.

Besides, mergers often fail.[10] They should be the strategic choice of last resort. AOL found itself a bit lost and felt that the only way to salvage itself was to find a suitor. Microsoft, for all its available cash, saw AOL as a way to claw its way up in the Internet search ladder. AOL team members spent their time deal making and not digging into the intelligence to develop all their strategic options. Both AOL and Microsoft stunted each other's strategic opportunities. Instead, they fixated on a merger of sorts. No one benefited—at least not in the long term.

Mergers also tend to distract all involved parties. Despite Oracle's successful and even justifiable pursuit of PeopleSoft, both it and PeopleSoft became somewhat paralyzed during the eighteen-month acquisition battle. Customers also became unsure and confused over the merger, court gyrations, and delayed purchasing decisions.[11]

A member of the Time Warner–AOL team I spoke with after the game confirmed, "We were sucked into the discussions, rather than [thinking] through our strategy."

In the second round, AOL spent most of its forty-five minutes dealing and arguing over deals instead of refining or adjusting its strategy. The result: It walked into the second presentation unprepared. It had neglected its own strategy in favor of hammering out the Microsoft desktop offer.

While mergers are sometimes the only solution to a company's long-term strategy, they do tend to take on a life of their own. War games are not solely about mergers. Merging is only one of many options you need to explore. As an option that is frenzy filled, mergers can demand a disproportionate amount of time, energy, and emotion, which can cause a company's strategy to stall. All the while your rivals advance on the game board.

Insight 4: Let the Game Take You Back to the Future

If you let the game thrust you outside your competitive universe, you will find yourself mentally exploring other what-ifs. What if media mogul Rupert Murdoch decided to buy Yahoo! and enter our space? What if China or other Asia Pacific countries enforce state control and only allow certain companies to compete and not others?

Recent events are what form the foundation for any war game. Watching the players use these events to create strategy and find their own high ground will spark ideas and lots of other thoughts about the near future.

Google's marketplace today appears limited to the online world, the world of the Internet. It doesn't have to be that way and likely will push much farther out into other media opportunities in the near future. You only have to appreciate Google's true revenue potential to see where the real competitive game may take Google, Yahoo!, and the others in the next few years. The online advertising pie that everyone is fighting over today is worth approximately $10 billion, while the off-line market that includes traditional media is far larger, estimated at $265 billion.[12]

By the game's end, nearly everyone saw a much larger industry with lots of other shadow companies swirling around our little playing field, all looking to form relationships in order to win more customers through a better value proposition.

For example, Yahoo! and eBay are fighting for market share in China. There's a third player, an off-line company, that is currently bad-mouthing them but is likely to merge with one of them within the next twelve months. There are dozens of these second- and third-tier online players who are also changing the way Google and the rest of the rivals in the real Battle for Clicks do business.

Both Yahoo! and eBay will wake up one day and see the opportunity *is* China, not just online advertising in China. The Battle for Clicks reinforced this notion that if any of the online rivals are going to succeed, it will be because they join forces with the larger, off-line rivals who can then help them realize their true advertising revenue-generation potential.

War games can be remarkably emancipating experiences if you allow yourself to think about the players not yet invited into the room on that particular day.

Insight 5: In Times of Change, Pay Attention to Existing Relationships

Even winners can have regrets. Google had made a very big mistake in its march to ultimate victory. It had forgotten its friends.

The self-confidence a company can gain in the real marketplace is spread over time. In a war game, you can experience this feeling in a compressed two or three days. Such a self-confidence rush that helped Google build its rational, in-depth strategy also blinded it in other ways.

It turns out Microsoft also approached Google with a merger proposition before it landed the AOL deal. Google turned Microsoft down because it did not believe such a merger would succeed. At that point, Google just marched ahead with its own strategy, forgetting it needed to tend some of its past relationships, such as the one it had with AOL.

AOL's use of Google's search engine had provided a solid stream of revenue for Google. The relationship was now a couple of years old, very mature and stable by Internet standards. The Google team did indeed set AOL aside in its quest for the prize—and regretted its negligence.

In turbulent times—and those are the times most companies run war games—you need to reinforce relationships. Google forgot this in the game, just as many companies forget this fact in the marketplace.

CHAPTER 4

MAKE ME INTO
A PEPPERONI

Seeing the Trees to Understand the Forest

Seeing your competition clearly means seeing it rationally, if not necessarily perfectly. It is also about seeing, assessing, and understanding the details—and, perhaps, admitting to not knowing everything you wished you knew. The bottom-line questions that you face, of course, are which details are important and how much information is enough to see clearly?

The key to selecting just the right details often means knowing how your rival creates its product or service. It's not just that the devil is in the details; it's more like the profundity is in the process. If you (1) learn how your things are done, no matter whether it's meat processing or check processing, and (2) can find the major differences between yours and your rival's approaches, then (3) you can see through a competitor's smoke screen or even its penchant for secrecy. Process is your intelligence lens, the lens by which you can peer into the often obscure world of privately held companies or subsidiaries whose operations are buried inside large conglomerates.

WHAT HAPPENS WHEN *TOO LITTLE* INFORMATION BECOMES *TOO IMPORTANT*

Lucent in the mid- to late 1990s is a prime example of a company relying on too little competitive information, despite the raft of data that was floating around and available in the telecommunications industry. As a result, Lucent failed to see its competition clearly. It was a company caught up in a flood of rumors and denial rather than a company seeking insight by learning its rivals' process for competitive success.

Back then, Lucent saw its sales of analog telephone switches hit hard by new digital entrants such as Cisco. Cisco's proposition to prospective customers was that they would access more power and flexibility with Cisco's digital products than with the analog alternatives (or less-effective digital alternatives) offered by the lumbering, old-line phone equipment producers, such as Lucent.

Customers flocked to Cisco. While Lucent's 1998 annual report recorded a 14.1 percent growth in revenue over the prior year, Cisco reported a 31.3 percent increase, or more than double Lucent's. More important, Cisco was generating a very positive cash flow from operations, while Lucent's was negative. In short, Cisco appeared to be in both a great market and a great cash-flow position. Lucent had begun to stagnate.

Along with Lucent's stagnation came an inevitable boiling of frustration from within the ranks. And, along with frustration came lots of competitive rationalization—a very unclear vision.

During this same period, I ran a workshop for Lucent's engineers, marketing experts, and sales organization. It was a two-day session whose purpose was teaching them how to develop intelligence on their competition, competitors such as Cisco, Alcatel, and Nortel—all of whom were eating Lucent's lunch.

During one discussion on the threat of new entrants into Lucent's market, I mentioned Cisco. The mere mention set off verbal fireworks.

"Unethical sales," shouted out one irritated participant. "Cisco deliberately underbids us or tells the customer what they want to hear in order to close a sale," groused the Lucent manager who saw his group lose one bid after another to Cisco.

Heads nodded all around the room.

But when it came to offering details on Cisco's capabilities, some of the engineers begrudgingly admitted that customers told them Cisco's products were easier to use and more adaptable. Still, the Lucent folks in the room could not offer details as to how Cisco continuously made money.

Most still claimed Lucent's products were better, that Lucent understood its customers better than Cisco did, and that Lucent products would stand the test of time. Cisco, some thought, might be a passing fancy.

Others in the room claimed that Lucent's raft of Bell Labs–generated patents and new technology augured well for Lucent and its future. Unfortunately, the Lucent of ten years ago was not fleet-footed enough to take its products from the lab bench to the marketplace as quickly and successfully as it once could. Instead of trying to understand the details of what made Cisco so successful, all I heard that day was a lot of grousing—and fear—about the new rival, Cisco.

Lucent of the mid-1990s kept hammering away with its old technology, reassuring itself that success was within reach based on its enormous installed base of telephone switches located in nearly every phone company worldwide. Cisco, meanwhile, was an increasing irritation, but one that they could not explain away.

The late 1990s were not kind to Lucent (or perhaps Lucent was not kind to itself). In trying to achieve prominence in the then-exploding data and optical equipment markets, Lucent spent over $30 billion on acquisitions, with few market successes to show for all the cash it placed on the table. It promised sales and revenue projections but failed to deliver on them.

By January 2000, the markets began rendering harsh judgments. CEO Richard McGinn announced that Lucent would substantially miss its revenue targets for that quarter. Before long, the markets had lopped $23 billion off the company's market capitalization.

Then came the worldwide recession, combined with the telecom collapse. Lucent continued to implode, selling off assets and terminating large numbers of employees. By late 2003, Cisco was outselling Lucent and showing a far healthier market cap and profitability. Cisco was now the leader and Lucent the laggard.

One thing that appears not to have changed substantively was Lucent's assessment of the competitive landscape. Denial locks out good intelligence, which in turn results in poor strategy and irrational decision making. The formula is a common one:

Denial − Facts = Irrational Strategy

Unless you are willing to look under the hood at your competition, you may find yourself chasing the wrong problem. It's not so much a can't-see-the-forest-for-the-trees problem as an inability to even find the forest because you've never located the trees.

WHERE'S THE BEEF?
LOTS OF MEAT WITH NO SUBSTANCE

A number of years ago, the president of a large producer of precooked meat topping for pizza gave Mike Sandman, a consultant, a tour of his facilities. The president wanted to meet with Mike because he needed help understanding how one of his competitors could consistently beat them out on price, client after client. This company's clients included Pizza Hut, Domino's, and numerous smaller regional chains of pizza parlors and restaurants.

The president did not want to enter into a price war with this rival. Although his firm had continuously lost market share, it still had plenty of cash. Yet if a price war started between the two of them, how long could either last? Even worse, the president mused to Mike, what if such a price war would result in a permanent lowering of all prices across the board? Then where would their profit margins be? He needed to know more and he knew he was flying blind.

"Make me into a pepperoni," Mike said as he turned to this senior executive.

Mike used this phrase not for its silly-sounding nature but

rather to create a platform for helping management to understand its own operations. To truly know how his client's rival operates, he needed to start with the production details, the process itself. And to understand the numbers, Sandman believes, you have to know the process intimately—in this case, the process for producing precooked meat for pizza toppings.

PROCESS IS THE MOTHER OF COST

Process is the mother of cost. If you understand a rival's process, you can derive its cost structure—plus a great deal more. By piecing together a company's process you can learn how to better produce your own product or improve your service. Knowing a competitor's process can teach you much about its management's thinking and strategic direction, as you will see in this case.

There's more to cost analysis than simply piecing together a floor plan of how your company produces its product or service. Whether it's a bank, a software firm, or a pepperoni producer, knowing how, where, and—most important—why a rival spends money in a particular area or function can teach you volumes about how it thinks strategically, what markets it hopes to conquer, and how it intends to get there. Process is the mother pearl of competitive knowledge. Understand process and you will likely understand how your competitor behaves today and into the future. Your costs dictate how much cash you have on hand to invest in R&D, conduct marketing and advertising campaigns, and offer incentives to your sales organization and others.

Costs for the pizza-topping industry are difficult to manage.

Mass production is difficult. Typically, a pizza-topping company produces dozens of meat and spice blends—some very much unique to one particular store chain. Unlike Henry Ford's one-size-fits-all approach to mass production of Model Ts, pizza-topping producers can react only to the highly different needs of various restaurants and pizza parlors.

The reality of this customized approach to pizza-topping production meant that each time the company would change topping blends, workers would have to hover around the machines, much like race car mechanics in the race pit, changing parts, cleaning equipment, and so on. The more product-line changeovers, the more downtime, and the more inefficient the use of labor, the higher the cost to produce the topping.

Yet this particular company, the one under assault, was one of the leaders in the industry and one of the pioneers in the development and creation of the pizza-topping market. Its management made sure to invest in the highest-quality equipment, including stainless-steel ovens and computer-controlled heating and processing devices. Given all this technology it invested in a relatively low-tech business, senior management could not believe one of its upstart rivals constantly underbid it and won the bids despite having once had lower-quality toppings.

The salespeople did not make management's losses any easier. One after another, regional sales managers knocked on the executives' doors. "We need to lower our prices," they complained. "Unless we lower our prices, we will continue to lose business."

Management knew that if it simply reacted to sales pressure and indeed did lower prices without making any significant production changes, it would suffer from lower margins, soon followed by a cash squeeze. To do so would likely throw the company into a cash-starved death spiral. Management needed to know more about this rival.

BECOME THE PEPPERONI, BUT FIRST
CLEAN OUT THE DENIAL

During this first meeting, Mike Sandman toured the entire plant—its receiving bays, manufacturing floor, and packaging and shipping area. He saw a relatively large facility, containing long belts and tunnel ovens that would slowly cook the small pieces of sliced meat as they moved through the heated chamber. The meats, Mike observed, rested on a mesh belt that would allow the fat dripping from the cooking meats to fall into a water-filled trough below. Equipment removed the excess fat, which was then sold to a secondary market as renderings (which then could be used in the manufacture of soap, cosmetics, lubricants, and even plastics). The wastewater was also recycled.

It didn't take long for Mike to see that costs quickly added up. The changeovers for each of the roughly two dozen meat-topping combinations, the waste-disposal costs, and the relatively inefficient use of labor could all take its toll on profit margins. None of this was a problem when this company owned the market, or when it had manufactured just a few blends, but it can make a difference when you have low-priced competition and when customers demanded an increasing number of product varieties.

Make me into a pepperoni. There are other ways to make pizza toppings, other similar processes, but this was how this plant had produced it for many years now—and management was not planning to make any changes.

By the time he finished his plant tour, Mike understood the types of machinery needed to produce the pizza toppings, the labor costs, and the overall configuration of the facility.

Next came the hard part. He had to talk to management. After all, ossification is a human condition, not a mechanical one. The machinery wasn't stuck; the people were. Senior people knew something was wrong, but they believed they had the best, highest-quality process in the business. Other company managers saw market share loss year after year and started taking sides. Operations blamed marketing; marketing blamed operations; sales blamed everyone except sales.

The VP of sales and marketing said, "The operations people here don't know how to make this product at a reasonable price." The VP of operations responded, "You people don't know how to sell."

Mike scheduled discussions with all of the interested parties: senior management, marketing, R&D, and operations. The half-truths and rationalizing revealed an almost paranoiac atmosphere.

"A few years ago," the president told Mike, "we were interested in buying this rival and actually toured their facility. We saw their thermal screw process for grinding and cooking the meat toppings and weren't very impressed. The quality was low. It had a high fat content, far inferior to our overall product. Sure, the thermal screws were cheaper and more flexible to operate, and even their waste disposal cost less, but we still believe we have the better process. I don't expect much has changed at all with them."

Uh-oh! Denial is creeping into the conversation, Mike observed. Why, Mike thought, would the president of the firm think nothing has changed at the rival's facility? After all, it's been a few years and the rival continues to successfully sell against them.

The marketing people, too, caught the denial bug. At their meeting with Mike, they indicated their belief that the rival was able to produce the meat toppings at a low cost. They also acknowledged that the rival had a smaller sales organization, mostly because it focused exclusively on the large pizza chains, not the mom-and-pop stores.

Then came the zinger. Everyone except the VP of marketing was saying in effect, "On the other hand, it's possible the rival operates with little profit."

"Why," the marketers questioned, "would the rival keep its price so low, even if it built up a 36 percent market share?"

Why, indeed? thought Mike.

The R&D folks could only report on what they knew. It appeared that the rival used roughly the same meat, spice, and filler blend as they did.

Mike jotted down these comments and thought they might prove useful later on.

He conducted the final interview with the manufacturing staff, which wildly imagined the rival was illegally dumping the fat renderings and other processing chemicals into a local river instead of disposing of them legally—and at a substantial cost. They also wondered whether or not the competitor managed to figure out the futures market for meat and buy their meat at the lowest possible contract prices, since spot market prices fluctuated as much as 10 percent in a week.

These managers were grasping at straws by assuming that the rival may have hired someone who figured out the futures market for meat. You are more likely to find that genius making millions in a Wall Street investment house or, alternatively, lying under a shady palm tree in Bora Bora with a satellite phone than in a Midwestern meatpacking plant.

So many irrational thoughts, so little evidence. Yet everyone Mike interviewed admitted they were losing business.

To build a true, unbiased competitive picture on the rival, Mike sliced his pepperoni production picture into discrete pieces. Essentially, he developed a profit-and-loss statement spreadsheet that compared his client's operations with that of the competitor's. He knew he needed lots of operating details, most of which were still missing.

The categories were deliberately chosen. He needed to understand, with reasonable certainty, specifics on raw materials costs, labor costs, number of employees, incentive structure, the type of equipment used, and overall administrative costs. If he could piece together the answers to these questions, he would know where and how the rival was saving on costs—and where its marketing intentions led it in the near future.

Over the next couple of months, Mike and his analysts gathered the raw data. Some of the initial findings were amusing and even anxiety provoking. One Department of Agriculture report of the rival's facility, released through the Freedom of Information Act, reported: "Live roaches spotted in the women's locker room. . . . Dead roaches found in the men's locker room, break room, cabinets."

To corroborate and build on some of the insights gained from government filings, Mike's team conducted dozens of interviews with ex-employees; equipment suppliers; meat suppliers; and government inspectors who worked for the Department of Agriculture, the Occupational Safety and Health Administration, and the local town hall and assessor's office.

The local newspaper had run several profiles on this hometown employer. The articles, perhaps not news by big-city standards, provided insight on the town's largest employer. Included in the articles were such tidbits on salary and incentives, number of shifts, and overall management direction. For example:

PRODUCTION: "Slices and ships 210,000 pounds of its cured pepperoni weekly in the form of almost 43.6 million 0.05-inch-thick slices . . . to ten pizza retail and wholesale clients."

PLANT SIZE: "Were almost doubling the plant size to 70,000 square feet by investing another $2.6 million."

EFFICIENCY: "In another room, cooked bite-sized chunks of beef sausage . . . frozen at 8-minute intervals at the rate of 3,500 pounds an hour for Pizza Hut."

PRODUCTIVITY: "One work shift turns out 75,000 pounds of pizza topping." (Altogether, the paper reported, the plant operates on two shifts.)

BONUSES AND INCENTIVES: "Hourly workers are considered earning bonuses averaging 25 percent to 35 percent of their take-home pay and sometimes more from their average $12-an-hour wage." (The article spent nearly half its allotted space reviewing the incentive and benefits package in great detail—no doubt a topic of great interest to relatives of those who work in the plant as well as to prospective employees who read the paper.)

Follow-up interviews with the reporter and some former employees confirmed the labor picture. The rival produced nearly the same volume of pizza toppings with only two shifts and at a far lower labor cost than Mike's client.

The reporter also confirmed the rival's aggressive expansion plans. This was not good news for Mike's client. "Someone told me, oh four to six weeks ago, that they're expanding even more for Pizza Hut. They took all or some of Pizza Hut's business from one or two of the biggest guys in the industry."

Uniform Commercial Code[1] filings indicated the rival leased five batch ovens and three thermal screw cookers, along with other production equipment tied into the ovens and the cookers, further confirming expansion plans. Again, this supported some of the information the president had already reported to Mike during his initial interview. But it also added new information that showed an unexpected sophistication and improvements made by the rival.

In this case, Mike felt it important to request a routine review of the rival's floor plans, filed with the town's commercial building inspector, which confirmed the layout and placement of the equipment. The floor plan made it clear that the rival had a far more flexible production process, one that was subject to less downtime. Mike's client had only two large tunnel ovens. If one tunnel was down for cleaning and maintenance, 50 percent of production was down; since the rival had five smaller, more efficient production lines (each requiring far less manpower to operate to begin with), one production line out of commission would mean that only 20 percent of production was halted.

The rival, Mike discovered, also had no advantage in its raw materials costs. Interviews with meat suppliers made it clear that the rival bought its product on the spot market, with little or no advance purchase. In other words, the rival did not employ some commodities expert, sitting in the back room of the meat plant with a sophisticated computer model to anticipate price fluctuations in the meat market. The rival purchased its raw material and meat the same way every company did—when it needed it. No price advantage here.

At the end of the assignment, a very different picture of the rival emerged. This is a resilient business whose operation was inherently lower cost and one that promised to continue its growth. No longer could management argue away the rival's capabilities.

Mike's final report rattled management. They saw the forest among the trees clearly for the first time. If Mike could have delivered his final assessment to the president in the form of an old-fashioned telegram, it might have read as follows:

> STOP. NEW RIVAL ABOUT TO SURGE AHEAD IN MARKET SHARE. STOP. RIVAL WILL OUTLAST YOU IN PRICE WAR. STOP. RIVAL HAS COST ADVANTAGE THROUGH LOWER LABOR COSTS, LOWER WASTE-DISPOSAL COSTS, AND A FLEXIBLE MANUFACTURING PROCESS, NOT STATE-OF-THE-ART TECHNOLOGY. STOP. YOU NEED TO MAKE IMMEDIATE ADJUSTMENT TO SURVIVE. STOP.

The president understood the message. The finance people, nearly in unison, said, "Aha!" They accepted the findings. The manufacturing group, under a great deal of pressure to become more efficient and, at the same time, trying to grapple with union demands for higher wages, stormed out of the meeting frustrated and upset. They felt too many fingers all pointed at them.

A few months later, as the reality of Mike Sandman's message sank in, the company found ways to become more efficient in their production methods. Managers knew they had to drive for less downtime to lower overall production costs, which they did. They also used some of the findings to gain a few concessions from their restive unions.

Could this company have taken even more drastic measures to become competitive? Yes! Did they? No.

Coincidentally, this exercise revealed the rival's trade secret for production of meat toppings (although that was not the initial goal). The client could have used this knowledge to redesign its own facility and install similar thermal screw equipment and ovens. All this would have cost many millions of dollars and even some more downtime in perfecting a similar process. Considering that this was a company needing to find a way to regain the market share it lost, it would have been unlikely to expect management to dramatically risk the integrity of its current process for the potential of another. Old-line companies do not typically leave inertia behind so readily.

As for the details, this company now knew them. Management was finally able to see the trees that made up the forest or, rather, the pepperoni that made up the pie.

———

PEPPERONI was about the here and now, about the necessity of truly seeing your rival clearly in the context of the existing marketplace. What about tomorrow's marketplace? If you are in R&D or in long-term planning in your company, or if you are the owner, you need to project yourself and your market some years into the future. That is where seeing clearly does not stop at the door labeled "this month" or "this earnings period." If you are to succeed in the future competitive market, you need to clear your vision of that future. The next chapter on early warning provides an approach to project yourself around that unknown corner just a few years from now.

CHAPTER 5

EARLY WARNING

Getting Intelligence on Competitors That May
Not Exist in a World That Has Not Arrived

Seeing the competitive reality of today is one type of intelligence, but what about the possibilities of tomorrow? Walking through a pepperoni factory to compare your costs and process to that of an actual rival's, a here-and-now threat, can be challenging enough. Yet how do you prepare for competitors that may not exist in a world that has not arrived?

Believe me when I state that building a clear view of distant competitive scenarios has a discipline and a structure. You will see.

However, before looking ahead, let's take a lesson from the lowly chessboard.

Today my eldest son, Elan, beats me handily in chess. Five or ten moves, if I'm lucky, and it's typically all over. That wasn't always the case. When he was five years old and just learning the game, I hesitantly won a match by moving my bishop opposite his king. Elan could not find a piece to protect his king, nor was he able to move his king out of the line of attack.

"Checkmate!" I declared.

He responded by saying something to the effect that he didn't expect me to move there, anticipating that I would move my piece back to its starting position and remove the threat to his king. He did not expect my move; therefore it could not happen in his mind.

When I retold the story to my wife, a preschool teacher, she said this was very much an appropriate reaction for a five-year-old, since a child of that age views the world in black and white. That's it, no questions asked.

Many businesspeople similarly see the world around them as would a five-year-old, with a fixed set of rules and expected behaviors. Our habits tend to limit how we consider current and future competition. In our minds we often fight the last war, replaying events of past years over and over again as if they will always occur the same way. I have seen managers at numerous companies view a competitor as unchanging, even when this competitor has truly altered its approach to a market.

The credit card business is one example. Credit cards and charge cards blossomed in the United States and in western Europe shortly after World War II and reached a mature stage by the late 1980s with three-quarters of all U.S. households owning at least one. The dominant players were MasterCard, Visa, Diners Club, and American Express. Each planned its strategy in this oligopolistic world by watching the moves of the other. Market share, signing up merchants, and collecting transaction fees made up most of the strategic ingredients for running a successful credit card business.

It was also a wonderfully profitable business. Card issuers

could count on a minimum of card hopping and customer loyalty, in part ensured by the annual fee common throughout the industry. This "sticky" environment, where customers remained loyal to a particular card, was all the more amazing considering the fact that credit card issuers charged substantially higher rates for outstanding balances than most other bank credit products—even during times when interest rates fell. Credit card issuers were a moneymaking machine.[1]

In March 1990, the credit card chess game changed dramatically. AT&T introduced its own named card, the Universal Card, and promised no fee for life. An added advantage was that it doubled as a calling card. AT&T rewrote the credit card rulebook forever. No one had ever offered a "no annual fee for life" deal in addition to the 10 percent discount on calls consumers made when using the card. Just over one year after introduction, AT&T had signed up over ten million cardholders.

The credit card business had experienced the equivalent of an earthquake registering 9 on the Richter scale. The name of the game suddenly became cobranding and heaping on new card features and benefits. What features could other card issuers fold into their cards? Myriad market segments rapidly emerged—airlines, hotels, universities each demanding attention—each further adding marketing cost and complexity. Airline credit cards, for example, promised frequent-flyer miles or point systems that led to gifts or vacation packages. Mass marketing and direct mail campaigns mounted, dropping dozens of solicitations in a consumer's mailbox every month. Card hopping soon became commonplace. Loyalty to one or another bank-issued credit card nearly disappeared.

The turmoil AT&T generated took place in 1990. More than

one credit card issuer was caught flat-footed that first year with no new options to explore. Citicorp's dominance of the credit card market with thirty-seven million Visa and MasterCards outstanding was threatened by AT&T's potential to convert its then forty-six million calling-card holders into owners of its new credit card/calling-card combination.

Check, but not quite checkmate. The other credit card issuers still held the bulk of the market. Still, AT&T had just moved them into an uncomfortable corner of the competitive chessboard. The no-fee feature plus its use as a calling card were powerful incentives that no other card on the market at the time could match.

The incumbent credit card companies should not have been surprised. The warning signs were all there. AT&T very much wanted to hold on to its eroding long-distance telephone customer and saw the credit card as one product that could help with this problem. AT&T had made noise about entering the credit card market some three years earlier. It even hired credit card experts away from First Chicago and MasterCard over a year before its card launch. All this was in public view. Why then was everyone apparently surprised?

Besides, the credit card industry's barrier to entry was fairly low. AT&T had all the earmarks of a new entrant. It had enough capital from its long-distance telephone cash-cow business to fund a credit card start-up such as Universal Card Services. Delivering cards into consumers' hands was easy. They were just sent by mail. AT&T also had the best mailing list in the business (the crown jewel asset of any card company)—its own telephone subscribers, or over 75 percent of the country at the time. There were few government regulations, other than the usual accounting reports required by any other credit card company to keep companies such as AT&T out of the picture. Add it all up and the question for AT&T was not "Should we enter the card business?" but "Why not enter the credit card business?"

SIGHT, NOT FORESIGHT

I have found that people confuse monitoring with early warning. They are not the same. Early warning is about seeing into the future, into a market that may not yet exist or is just beginning to emerge. Monitoring is the task of keeping watch on existing competition and competitive threats or opportunities. Monitoring is about the here and now; early warning is about the future.

I recently met with the senior management at two very different companies to talk about early warning. I wanted to know what kept these executives up at night with concerns that might not materialize for many years.

One group ran one of the largest energy companies in the United States whose century-old roots were as an electric power producer; the other company was a biotech less than ten years old. The energy company, pumped up by the Enronesque hubris of the 1990s, made numerous acquisitions that saddled it with a lot of debt. It had suffered terribly in the last few years and was now retrenching to its core power generation business and dropping its energy trading and international interests. The biotech had had a very successful run with a number of its treatments to reduce or practically eliminate chronic diseases but was coming into contact with true competition for the first time—and it was not prepared for some of the recent shocks it received. Suddenly, it was dealing with problems such as me-too products on the market, alternative treatments, generics, and pricing pressure from managed care insurers.

Imagine that you are able to view these two meetings side by side, like a split-screen television picture.

I asked both the energy company strategists and the biotech product managers and marketers, "How do you know when you need to learn about a long-term threat (or opportunity) or what those threats might be?"

No one had an answer.

Okay, I suggested next, let's say we looked at only two factors: (1) the level of impact a particular set of events might have on your company and its bottom line and (2) how certain you are that the event will happen in the first place. This made sense to both groups.

I first listed three potential events that might occur over the next few years in the energy industry and asked the managers at the energy company to apply my two criteria. Here is how they responded:

> A single market will emerge within the next three years in which power generators will have to compete on price throughout the United States. Uncertain, they said, but high impact.

> Regional and national mergers of energy companies will continue to heat up. Well, they said, this is already taking place, so it's very certain. Of course, this also can have a high impact on us and on our business.

> Massive power failures, like the August 2003 power outage in the northeastern part of the United States, become commonplace. Highly uncertain, they responded, but extremely high impact.

I then turned to the biotech executives and asked that they use the same criteria on the following issues:

> Generic forms of their leading drug will enter the market within one year after their patent expires. They responded, It is a very certain event whose impact will be extremely high.
> Genomics, the art and science of manipulating genes, will replace the need for biotech solutions within ten years. While a very uncertain outcome, they agreed, should it occur, the impact will be extremely high because such technology will replace virtually every traditional pharmaceutical and biotechnology company that works to treat the disease rather than fixing a particular gene that causes the disease in the first place.
> It is highly certain that Medicare reimbursements for one of their key products will drop precipitously over the next few years. Everyone agreed that this was a likely scenario with a high impact.

Wherever you experience high-impact events that are almost certain to occur, that means the problem or the opportunity is already here at your doorstep. Energy company mergers and generic entries into the market when the biotech's patent expires are both examples of high-certainty and high-impact events. You need to track them now, with all of your resources—databases, heard-on-the-street information from your sales organization, and so on. These are tactical intelligence problems. There are no mysteries on this side of the list.

What happens when you believe that a certain event would have both a high impact on your business and a great deal of uncertainty surrounding it, mostly because it is just a bit too far into the future for you to be sure? For the energy company, the prospect of massive power failures exemplifies such a low-certainty, high-impact event; for the biotech company, the genomics scenario hit that mark. The competitive environment for them does not yet exist, nor do most of the future rivals that would serve these markets. Yet should the right market forces emerge, such a future will be certain to eliminate a whole raft of companies currently in this market, including the very two companies in this example. These are futures to watch. These are both prime candidates for early warning.

Seeing a few steps ahead does not mean you need a crystal ball, just that you need to prepare for the uncertain possibilities. What makes an early warning process valuable is its ability to help a company avoid driving itself toward one specific outcome, which increases its chances of being wrong. That's risk. Taking the time to sketch three or four outcomes—and to plan strategies that account for each outcome—gives you a safety net. You know you will be prepared no matter how the future unfolds.

THE FUTURE IN FOUR STEPS

All this seems so logical. Although no one has a crystal ball, most will admit that change will occur and that the future will not be the same as today. Why, then, are companies so unprepared for the inevitable change? Maybe because the people who make these companies run, the people for whom I wrote this book—the marketers, product managers, scientists, strategists, financial managers—simply don't know how to anticipate these futures.[2]

The early warning concept—the ability to see into the future—is easy to understand. Early warning consists of four very simple steps: (1) drawing the road map of possible futures, (2) identifying the signals you need to watch for each of these futures, (3) finding the people who will watch those signals in the course of their everyday work, and (4) making sure you create an approach to act quickly once one of the futures you have identified begins to emerge.

Formulas, such as the four steps I listed above, are not enough. You need to know your colleagues and the amount of risk they can tolerate. The best way to learn about early warning and how to make it work for you and your company is to learn how others have made it work for them.

WIRED FOR WARNING

We all know people who can see around corners. There are some individuals who bet on the right stocks, pick the winning sports team at the beginning of the season, and forecast future events. They see just a few steps ahead.

Two people I know, Melanie Wing, formerly a marketing strategist for the credit card Bank One, and Clare Hart, CEO of Factiva, a Dow Jones–Reuters company, both pointed me to a news report revealing that knowledge of the Ford Explorer rollover problems surfaced far earlier than originally thought—nearly two years before this issue filled the U.S. business press in mid-2000. "Look at this. The signals were all out there," both Hart and Wing told me. Each handed me a similar article, published in late 2000, months after the Ford-Firestone debacle had appeared on the U.S. news scene.

A *Wall Street Journal* article stated that as early as October 1998, reports leaked out of Venezuela regarding tread separation on Firestone tires mounted on Ford Explorers. This was nearly a year and a half before the Ford-Firestone investigation began in the United States in May 2000. In August 1999, Ford launched a tire replacement program for its Explorer customers in Saudi Arabia, after tread separation problems cropped up there as well. People at Ford's U.S. operations realized the mounting problems that Ford and Firestone were facing, but only a few accurately predicted the seriousness of the threat.[3]

The central nagging concern I have with all these news stories is one of hindsight. A good reporter can find and review the evidence once the event has arrived. It takes some digging, but investigative reporters do this all the time. The signals are out there. Like a radio telescope that observes the explosion of a supernova, the event we now see (the Ford Explorer rollovers) is something that began years before. The radio waves detected by our instruments see evidence from the past, not the present and certainly not into the future. The skill or talent in early warning is the ability to tag these bits and pieces of intelligence ahead of time and then divine their true meaning—like a prophet—before the expected event unfolds, not after the fact.

In another conversation with Melanie Wing, she recalled an incident with her former employer, PECO Energy, where she accurately forecasted the troubles Enron would have nearly two years later. At that time, though, no one would believe her, when *Fortune* magazine, the *New York Times,* and other media crowned Enron as a corporate superstar who could only do right.

"When I was at PECO in early 1999, we were competing against Enron in power-trading contracts and everyone kept saying, 'How can Enron compete at the price they were competing at?'

"We looked at their financials in depth to figure out their cost structure. . . . I kept coming back to management saying that it doesn't add up. We paired up the press releases about all their partnerships and joint ventures and their expected income from those and paired them with the expenses. Our team had figured out that Enron had an awful lot of off-balance sheet debt and predicted that they would fail in one year. No one at PECO would believe me."[4]

They wouldn't believe her because it was Melanie. Her conclusions came from the same published data everyone else saw—and dismissed. As perceptive as she was, it was not enough to move her management. This was not her fault. She knocked on many doors but was dismissed, as far as her Enron theory was concerned.

Why was her forecast dismissed?

Melanie was indeed the nay-saying prophet of corporate doom

at a time when Enron, Tyco, WorldCom, and others could do no wrong. Another strike against her: She was a voice of one (or of very few within PECO at the time). She was an outsider, not a member of the executive committee or of the board of directors.

Samuel, Job, and Isaiah delivered messages foretelling the fall of a kingship or of a kingdom. Melanie Wing delivered bad news about the energy empire of which PECO was a part. Altogether, Samuel, Job, Isaiah, and Melanie were delivering the news as prophets without a process. Few accepted the prophet's message, and the intended audience failed to see the message as clearly as did the messenger. The audience felt threatened or divorced from the prophet's message and found it easier to reject the message than to wrestle with the implications and accept it.

PROPHET WITH A PROCESS

Approximately a decade after the shock of AT&T's credit card entry hit the industry, along came another. This time it was not a company but a technology—the Internet—that threatened to change the credit card business forever.

Corporate prophets must involve their executives in their stories. Tell the story; sell the story. The prophet must help them recognize and agree to the signals they must watch. Dale Fehringer, vice president of market intelligence at Visa International, is just such a prophet. The process was critical to his prophecy. He enlisted the support and constantly kept his executives involved. At the same time as he opened management's eyes to the possibilities, this prophet also brought comfort. Comfort intelligence, he called the news he delivered.

Unlike the prophets in the Bible who also tried to tell their stories but who mostly alienated their audiences with doom-and-gloom scenarios, Fehringer succeeded in convincing his audience of the changes ahead. He was a prophet with a process.

Starting in 2000, Visa International felt threatened.

Visa International does not actually issue credit cards. It is the organization that owns the brand and works with its member institutions, such as banks and credit unions, to market and distribute the cards. At the same time, it must work with and satisfy those accepting the cards from consumers. Visa also needs to satisfy the customers (known as "acceptors," in Visa parlance). These are the merchants, government agencies, utilities, and other service providers.

Through the years, it had achieved amazing success. Visa is a powerful brand that was processing $2 trillion of transactions by 2000, its thirty-seventh year of operation. Despite its size and reach, Visa felt threatened by a new category of entrant, known as emerging payment solutions companies.

Emerging payment solutions are Internet-based companies, such as PayPal, that allow consumers to pay for merchandise or services with electronic chit. "No more need for plastic cards" is the pitch the PayPals of the world offer the consumer. Open an online account and use it to do all your trading on eBay, for example. Generally, emerging payment solutions companies charge merchants less than the traditional plastic-based credit card companies. They have also struck lots of deals with other online merchants, such as Amazon, making it easy to use their alternative to the traditional credit card.

Visa International's fear then and now: If the plastic disappears from consumers' wallets, then so could Visa's market power.

Dale Fehringer, back then spearheading competitive intelligence efforts at Visa International, began to take a serious look at the emerging payment solutions market in early 2000. Unlike the biblical prophets whose language and disposition was one of doom and gloom, Dale sports a clearly vibrant and optimistic appearance. He is an insatiably curious individual. He loves to read, clipping and collecting scattered bits and pieces of information from newspapers, competitors' advertisements, and brochures. On certain projects, he takes news clippings and ads home with him, spreads them out over his kitchen table, and tries to discern less-than-obvious patterns not immediately clear from the headlines.

During the years 1999 and 2000, magic—black magic—was in the air at Visa International. Fehringer and his team were operating in a frenetic, almost chaotic industry environment at the time. Burn rates (the rates in which companies used up the invested capital) were more widely reported than revenues. Somehow the emerging payment start-ups defied the financial laws of gravity. The start-ups continued to threaten the Visas of the world while eating up capital at a rapid rate. The credit card universe Visa International and its brethren had known and inhabited for so many years appeared upended. Profit was no longer important. The press and the public believed that the Net would become the new business universe, and those who could not compete on the Net would lose. Nothing else—not sane business practice, true profit goals, cash flow, and actually making money—mattered anymore.

The dynamics of doing business in the Internet world consumed boardroom discussions throughout the world. The credit card industry was no exception.

"When VISA USA [Visa International's separately incorporated sister corporation] board members discussed competitive threats at a special meeting in December, they didn't dwell on American Express Co., or MasterCard International. Instead the directors fretted about the likes of PayPal Inc., eCharge Corp., Flooz.com and eCount," reported one article in the *Wall Street Journal*.

These start-ups—payments companies developing new Web-based ways to send money—had seemingly unlimited access to cash. Not long before that, Visa's chief Internet developer, Bond Isaacson, summed up the menace in an interview: "I have 200 people standing in front of me, shooting with unlimited ammo called venture capital."[5]

Fehringer, who faced a list of over a hundred of these venture capital–backed PayPal-like start-ups, knew he had to narrow the list of rivals and bring some sanity to the ever-growing list of Net-based rivals.

The feeling inside Visa at the time was confusion. Which of these threatening paperless, plastic-free rivals would succeed?

"The message about the downfall of plastic cards was strong and loud at that time," recalls Fehringer. "We were paranoid but we didn't know whom to be paranoid about. Our CEO at the time was once asked about what Visa had to watch and his answer was, 'We really don't know!' "[6]

He still shakes his head about the level of confusion caused by the constant stream of news announcements and rumors that sent management into a dizzying spin. As if to highlight this point, he recalls that the only company everyone had on their list as a universal threat was Microsoft (although little uncontested proof existed at the time that Microsoft was a serious contender for the credit card throne).

Dale and his staff of two then proceeded to track the remaining list of start-up companies, examining news feeds, press releases, and Web sites. His team did manage to identify the likely offenders but initially found it difficult to write the future storyboard for these upstarts. The upstart rivals Dale did identify as real threats appeared to have enough cash to last through the 2001 shopping season (another eighteen months from then), long enough to become a viable threat. Visa's management needed to predict what these new rivals would do next and their likelihood of success, as well as help management prepare a response to one of those futures.

TELLING AND SELLING THE FUTURE

Dale and his team had reached an impasse. He knew he had to do more than prophesize or preach in the form of a report that would merely land on the CEO's desk with a thud—and go nowhere. For a forecast to succeed, he had to create a three-part platform. First he had to involve his management in creating the prophecy (not just present what would be perceived as an outsider's viewpoint). Second, he had to find signals that would tell him and his team which of the potential futurecasts was becoming reality. Finally, he had to get management to agree to a means to act on the future that was about to land on Visa's doorstep.[7]

Yet the noise outside his office made it difficult to begin. Even narrowing down the targets, Dale and his team foresaw too many ways in which the story could unfold. Just as one news announcement faded, another took its place, each screaming another Internet possibility for the credit market of the twenty-first century. He could not rank the various possibilities, and he could not foretell how the selected rivals would play in those different competitive settings, at least not with any degree of certainty.

One upstart in particular, NetYouPay (not its real name), became the symbolic target for the Visa team. If this Internet-based company succeeded, it could grab market share as well as validate the market for other emerging payment rivals.

NetYouPay had more than just the necessary investment capital, according to Fehringer. It knew how to recruit merchants to endorse and use its credit services, and it had already begun to talk to banks about helping it sign up merchants and customers. To make matters worse, NetYouPay's CFO had been recruited from Visa.

NetYouPay's promotional message took direct aim at Visa, MasterCard, American Express, and all the other traditional charge card companies. "Using credit cards on the Net is not safe!" was its message during fall 2000, supported by news reports, such as the December 1999 theft of three hundred thousand credit card numbers from CD Universe, an online music dealer. This propaganda buzz sent shivers through the ranks of credit card issuers.

The problem was even more complex than a potential steep

drop in market share. Visa feared that its rivals, who also worried about the same upstarts, would react faster than could Visa in shoring up their online security. If that were to happen, Fehringer and Visa management fretted, consumers would have many switching choices, from going to new-age Net credit systems to moving back to its traditional, but supposedly more secure, rivals.

Visa's competitive picture moved away from a straight, linear zero-sum formula to a complex market that looked more like balls flying around a billiard table. One ball bumps into another, which causes another ball to move in a direction not anticipated. Visa's billiard ball had been moving in a straight path in years past but was now deflected. Was Visa heading along a vector that would mean loss of market share (Visa International could lose as much as 10 percent of its business, some within Visa speculated), loss of merchants, defection of customers, and poor performance with respect to other rivals' security initiatives (a response to the new Net rivals entering the market)? Or would these new rivals, the PayPals of the world, just disappear altogether, leaving the market essentially the way it was before 2000?

Wearing the prophet's hat, Dale had to make sense of all the apparent confusion. While most at Visa suspected that the "disappearance" scenario was unlikely, that left too many other alternative futures for Visa to consider and flesh out in detail. Dale needed to create a road map with a limited set of reasoned, rational directions in which the market could take over the next two years.

Whenever Dale's team found they hovered over a particular scenario, saying "It depends," they knew they had hit upon an uncertainty. It felt real but at the same time did not. If the it-depends scenario would eventually materialize, everyone knew the impact could be enormous. For Dale's team this type of uncertainty immediately called for them to flesh out one of these alternative futures.

The process for Dale began by drafting his road maps of future events. This part was probably the most agonizing. He followed five steps that allowed him to (1) determine critical questions; (2) identify drivers and cluster similar drivers; (3) develop the scenario or story from the drivers; (4) research and fill in gaps, the result of questions arising from building a scenario; and (5) revise the scenario based on the new information.

The process became very important to Dale. He realized that unless the organization had bought into the message, his prophecy— no matter how cogent and rational—would be meaningless. In particular, he needed to involve senior management without talking to them each and every day.

For this the prophet used his messengers.

The two Visa organizations, both Visa International, Dale's employer, and the sister organization, Visa USA, agreed to form a review committee consisting of managers from strategic planning, marketing, legal, and product development. These were his messengers to management. In the nearly five months of scenario-building work, this committee met six times.

In theory the group, from Visa's major U.S. and international regions, would sit down and help Fehringer refine and build the scenarios and construct a means to track competitive threats. The reality was far different. Visa International and Visa USA were sometimes politically at odds with each other. According to Fehringer, the regional offices were very autonomous and very independent. They served on this team as volunteers, reporting what they saw fit to management. What brought them together was the common—but yet unidentified—enemy.

Aside from internal political squabbles with the Visa affiliates represented on the committee, Fehringer had to deal with individual agendas of the committee members themselves. While some of the committee members became very invested in the early warning efforts, others did not.

"I recall a skeptical attorney, one of the company's legal counsels, continuously questioning the process. He kept repeating, 'What is the end product going to be? What are you going to have at the end of this thing?' "

Dale, a very patient, soft-spoken individual, had to calmly explain to this attorney that he was not necessarily going to receive a three-dimensional concept, gift-wrapped with a bow on the top. The result of the committee's deliberations might be a series of possible directions or options for Visa, he explained, but not something you could place on a bookshelf.

The hypercritical attorney might have been in the minority among committee members. Nevertheless, his incessant how-real-will-it-be questions did prod Dale to ask himself how he could make the future real. How could he make committee members see the future as clearly as they saw today's reality? Reality was the proverbial elephant in the room that no one quite discussed but about which everyone had to understand.

SHOCK AND SHAPE

Sometimes there is no better way to sense reality than to see a news report. At one of the first meetings with the committee of messengers, Dale crafted a fictional newspaper headline and flashed it before the group.

VISA GOES UNDER

The headline's purpose was to shock the committee into realizing the responsibility each member had. The mind game worked. The future somehow felt real, perhaps for the first time since Dale began his initiative.

Fehringer kept pushing them forward, meeting after meeting, with the goal of developing a road map of Visa's possible futures. One of those futures could be bleak, he warned, if management either ignored the warning signals or failed to prepare a strategy to reduce potential damage.

During the committee's first meeting, Julie Boland, an analyst on Dale's staff, reviewed the scores of potential new entrants into the emerging payment solutions market and concluded that Net-YouPay was the entity that the group must focus on first.

At least they now had a target, and it wasn't Microsoft.

NetYouPay was a true threat, Boland concluded. It was well financed, was beginning to negotiate with banks to help it sign up merchants, and offered merchants lower transaction fees than did Visa, MasterCard, or American Express.

That is today. Now what about the future for NetYouPay? Once the target was decided, Fehringer's next goal was to have the com-

mittee begin to examine the major events that were expected to
change the credit card industry. These major industry-shaping
events are called drivers.

Drivers are common parlance in the world of scenario building. Drivers are the rules by which you design your road map that
contains the various scenarios. They are the key ingredients for all
future scenarios. Drivers can emanate from technology, government regulation, shifts in the economy, or shifts in competitive
power, as would occur through mergers or increased buying
power of a particular customer, such as a Wal-Mart.

In thinking about the drivers, the committee of messengers
were always thinking about the three groups that made up Visa's
universe: the merchants (or acceptors, as they are called in Visa-
speak); the financial institutions, such as the banks, that distribute
the Visa-branded cards; and the consumers, both individual and
corporate. This was Visa's world and any drivers it considered
would emanate from this world.

Thus, the drivers that Dale and his team drafted included the
following imperatives:

> SUCCESSFULLY SIGN UP MARQUEE ONLINE MERCHANTS.
  Any would-be contender in the online credit card industry
  would need at least one to three premier merchants, such
  as Amazon or eBay, in order to succeed.

> FOSTER BROAD CONSUMER ACCEPTANCE AND TRUST OF THIS
  NEW EMERGING PAYMENTS APPROACH. This acceptance and
  trust would be driven in part by fear that the old-economy
  plastic credit cards are not secure online.

> **BUILD A BRAND.** The new entrants would successfully build a brand through marketing and advertising.
> **DEVELOP TECHNOLOGICAL SECURITY BREAKTHROUGHS.** The Internet start-ups would be successful in both allowing the consumer to easily establish an account and creating reliable security features to digitally identify both the consumer and the merchant.
> **GARNER INVESTMENT CAPITAL.** Because these new entrants would have to spend a great deal to establish their brands, they needed investors and investment capital to sustain themselves for at least the next eighteen months to two years it would take to survive the 2001 holiday shopping season. Were they to choose to start their attack on Visa and the other incumbents outside the United States, the new contenders would need similar investment partners in western Europe or the Asian Pacific.

Over the next few sessions, Dale, the prophet, and his committee of messengers refined and shaped the road map of scenarios, all the while minding the drivers. Following each meeting, the messengers would return and report the results as the process evolved. Each scenario they shaped was unique and distinct and would take Visa in different directions.

Scenario A: U.S. Success Comes First

The U.S. success narrative told how NetYouPay would fire on all its cylinders. It would do everything right, including signing on a number of marquee merchants, such as Amazon. It would have enough cash from its own investors, successfully develop digital methods to certify both the merchant and customer (thereby strengthening both the merchant's and the customer's reliance on such a service), and establish its brand.

Scenario B: International Business Comes First

Essentially, the picture would be the same for this scenario as for the first. The major difference is that the launch would take place overseas. Available evidence supported this argument. NetYouPay already had investors in Germany, Korea, and Japan, all of which are large, developed markets that Visa considers important. Barriers to entry were lower in these overseas markets, allowing online purchases to be charged on customers' telephone bills. European and Asian telecoms were looking for more value-added services they could offer their customers.

Scenario C: Acquisition or Alliance

Should NetYouPay run out of capital or fail to secure new financing, it might place itself up for sale by mid-2001. Before this could happen, Company X would have to demonstrate long-term viability and continued value, including a suitably large consumer base (which it had already built).

At the time, the acquisition scenario seemed likely, given NetYouPay's dwindling cash and its rapid burn rate. This scenario also differed from the first two because it painted a bleak picture. Chief among the failures in this story would be NetYouPay's inability to sign marquee merchants—key to winning a broad customer base. In the 2000–2001 period, dot-com acquisitions were plentiful, especially of companies with these two key ingredients: good ideas and lack of operating capital to finish their mission. NetYouPay was a perfect fit for this scenario.

Dale probably feared this outcome the most. In this scenario, NetYouPay's concept and technology not only would survive but would become reinvigorated. No longer would it be burdened by a dwindling cash hoard. It would have a new parent with deep pockets, which could leverage the brand. Wherever Visa would turn in this scenario, it would be confronted with serious threats, Dale thought. It was not a pretty picture, this part of the road map:

> If a non-Visa customer bank issued NetYouPay products, Visa's banks would likely lose volume.

> If a member bank became the new owner, Visa's relations with that new owner would become strained to the point where Visa might lose its business altogether.

> If a nonbank rival, such as American Express, became the new owner, it could place pricing pressure on Visa to develop a low-cost emerging payment solutions alternative far faster than Visa might want (possibly introducing a product that would be inferior and damage the Visa brand or one that would cannibalize Visa's existing credit card business).

> Finally, a technology company or telecommunications player might pose a new class of competitor, which would compete against Visa with different core competencies,

different regulatory restrictions, and a different business model.

Scenario D: Failure

This scenario involved NetYouPay's failing outright because of a single or a combination of failures: failure to convince and convert merchants and consumers, failure to deliver a less than user-friendly Internet technology, failure to secure additional funding, and, finally, failure to convince consumers of the site's security.

Even if NetYouPay failed, Visa needed a response. The team believed that this outcome would only further reinforce consumer fears of online card shopping. Because NetYouPay and others tried—and in some cases succeeded in—converting merchants, the merchants already had a taste of lower-cost alternatives, alternatives that Visa would have to face at some other point in time if not now. Finally, even in failure, NetYouPay's attempt would almost certainly encourage other emerging payment solution companies.

The last step in sorting through the scenarios was to place them on a probability-impact chart. That is, the Visa team had to identify and place the scenarios in a relative position, one to the other. An outcome that had a high impact but also had a low probability of success might be ranked less important than an outcome with a high impact but high probability of success. This simple but important ranking would dictate what Visa could do with limited marketing resources. Like any business, Visa's management would have to make choices as the outcomes emerged. The probability-impact relationship would help move them toward one set of decisions or the other.

Dale made sure that his committee constantly fed senior management the various scenarios as they unfolded. He wanted no surprises.

HOIST THE SIGNAL FLAGS

Before he could act, the prophet needed a sign, a signal. That was the trick, the prophet's early warning secret.

While Dale saw each scenario as equally believable, at some point, everyone around the committee table agreed, the various scenarios would eventually part ways. Some would drop out and some would emerge as real. The key to success in early warning is to identify the early warning indicators or milestones that would send an alert signal to Visa in enough time for it to deploy one of its chosen strategic responses.

Starting with the 2001 Christmas shopping period and working backward, Dale identified what goals NetYouPay had to accomplish each quarter to be ready for the next event. At least two to three online merchants would have to sign up to its service by the end of the first quarter. The digital certification technology would have to be ready for prime time by the second quarter. NetYouPay would have to have lured more bank partners into deals by the third quarter to extend its consumer reach. The early warning team knew if NetYouPay wasn't ready by that Christmas, it likely wouldn't have enough funding to survive another year.

Depending on which signals appeared and which did not, Dale and his crew determined the scenario that would likely evolve. He then devised a strategy for each potential outcome—whenever it would occur. If the alliance scenario emerged, Dale had a strategy ready for that one. If the international markets scenario appeared to mature, Visa would have a strategy for that as well.

CHECKMATE NEVER ARRIVED

Julie Boland kept track of the signals throughout the eighteen-month period. As the year 2000 ended and 2001 began, she and Dale watched NetYouPay's cash position through press accounts in *Barron's* and other media that periodically reported on funding of start-ups. They also monitored advertising expenditures and the rival's attempts to sign online merchants to their services.

Visa's prophets read the signals and began to see a picture take form. They saw, as the year progressed, that NetYouPay found itself unable to sign more merchants. In addition, it could not sign up banks to help deliver its services, either because banking prospects melted away over time or bank deals had failed. This left it with little cash with which to successfully market during the critical holiday season. By the second half of the year, Visa began to see the failure scenario emerge as the likely candidate.

Dale fed the signals back to his committee and prepared them for the likely scenario of failure. "Our group suggested that Visa develop a series of countermessages to merchants and consumers," Dale stated, "to demonstrate our value proposition to merchants and to assure consumers it is safe to use their cards to shop on the Internet. We suggested that NetYouPay be closely monitored—along with other similar emerging payment solutions. We also recommended that Visa sponsor market research to track consumer concerns about shopping online with a card."

By the time Dale presented the official findings at a formal meeting of Visa's senior management, his audience was already prepared. They were prepared because they were part of the process all along.

"Our management was comforted that someone in the company was watching," Dale recalled, "and that a plan existed for dealing with them—no matter what happened."

The news that NetYouPay would be out of business before very long also brought with it implications for Visa. Dale recommended that Visa continue to promote the message that online shopping with Visa is safe. Visa also beefed up its antifraud protection activity, consumer education on the use of the Net for transactions, and development of secure technologies on the Net. It kept hammering home "Your number is safe"—and backed that up by stating that cardholders were not liable beyond $50.

At Visa International Dale Fehringer became a prophet whose mission was to deliver future possibilities to management. He realized that the history of prophets is littered with failure and frustration. His approach was different. He became a prophet who felt it as important to sell the process, and to involve management in shaping the vision, as it was to sell the vision itself. Even in unsettling times, he gave management comfort, despite rattling the corporate cage with a range of predictions from the dire to the desirable. His process was methodical, not miraculous.

First, he worked with managers, involving them from the very beginning in painting the future landscapes. They became part of the prophecy, not apart from the prophecy. They understood the rationale and reasonableness behind each potential outcome and were reassured. Second, he derived the signals, the indicators they would watch. Finally, when the signals "lit up," Dale and the managers met yet again to discuss the most and least likely scenarios about to emerge.

From scenarios to signals to a call for action, Dale allowed for few surprises. When the moment finally came, when Visa's management saw the holiday season approaching, it knew what it had to do. That is why for Visa, checkmate never arrived.

———

N o w let's rewind this book a bit. I have shown you a number of effective frameworks that can strip away the mystery and myth surrounding an impending competitive threat. Frameworks are indeed an intelligence reality you must come to respect and to use.

Where I have taken things out of order is the fourth intelligence reality, the Internet. I have done so because the Net is just a means to an end. It is a path to finding critical intelligence. War games, cost analysis, and, yes, even early warning need the informational power the Internet's World Wide Web brings with it. It's generally an unbridled power, appearing to the untrained user as a chaotic, knotted ball of yarn. Absent the Internet, your intelligence efforts become more time consuming or potentially impossible. You need to find a way to untangle this important resource to truly develop your X-ray vision, and you will learn how to do that in the next chapter.

CHAPTER 6

THE INTERNET
HOUSE OF MIRRORS

Seeing Through the Confusion
to Gather Intelligence Gems

Like a house of mirrors, the Internet tends to refract, bend, and altogether confuse your sense of reality. At the same time, it remains one of the most valuable intelligence sources. You need X-ray vision to see past these distractions, these Net-created distortions. If competitive intelligence is the product of clear thinking, then I'd like to help you build this Internet X-ray capability one concept at a time.

<<<<<<<<< INTERNET X-RAY CONCEPT 1 >>>>>>>>>

**The Internet has dramatically altered what
libraries once stood for: information standards
and unfailing trust in that information.**

The Internet has transformed how business must use and must distrust information, all at the same time. Politics, emotion, and corporate and professional interests are all factors that help shape

165

the world the Internet sees—and how you see the business world through the Net.

For me the concept of the Internet was not created in the 1990s with the launch of the World Wide Web and the browsers that made the Net accessible. It was born on June 4, 1927, in Boston, Massachusetts, with the dedication of the Baker Library on the new Harvard Business School campus, located just across the river from Cambridge.

George Fisher Baker, the then eighty-seven-year-old New York banker, donated $5 million toward its construction. He believed that this business library, which was one of the first of its kind, was destined to become the world's preeminent business library, a central information resource.

At the time of the dedication, he explained why he had decided to give the $5 million, when Harvard representatives had asked for only $1 million. "My life has been given over to business, and I should like to give a new start to better business standards."[1] Standards. That is how Baker viewed the library built in his name.

When the four thousand people standing on the expansive lawn in front of the Baker Library on that June day looked at the building's face, they saw a majestic structure, a building epitomizing Baker's image of an eternal repository of business knowledge. Six three-story-high white columns topped with Ionic capitals greeted those walking up its dozens of steps that led to the giant wooden doors. The brick building was topped off with a Harvard signature bell tower and golden cupola. Inside, the hallways were marble lined. Portraits of Harvard's other donors, professors, and giants of industry hung on the walls leading up to the library reading room on the third floor.

The reading room became my second home in the late 1970s and early 1980s, when I first began my competitive intelligence practice. The Baker Library was my Internet. It held a nearly unimaginable volume of business knowledge—at least all the information that could possibly be in print—including more than a half-million volumes and more than seven thousand periodicals from nearly every corner of the business universe.

The two-level reading room hall (it contained a second-tier balcony of bookshelves) felt totally accessible. Section upon section of dark wooden shelves lined the room's perimeter. Business information of every kind surrounded you wherever you sat. Investment surveys, *Moody's* manuals, the *Encyclopedia of Associations*, *Standard & Poor's Registers* all were out on the tables for anyone to review.

Back in the early 1980s, I often entered the library when it opened in the morning and was nearly the last person to leave at midnight, when the remaining few business students would shuffle off to their dorms to finish reviewing their cases for the next day's class.

I knew that all the information contained in that library was legitimate and true. One of the many highly skilled librarians would review the collection and weed out unnecessary material. What they kept was cataloged and filed. A librarian was always walking the floor replacing returned books or reference books lying on the study table. I knew that with a combination of the card catalog and a knowledgeable librarian, I would find what I wanted when I needed it.

I recall one assignment that required I chart P/E ratios (price/earnings ratios, or the market price per share/earnings per share ratios) for a client who was considering a number of acquisition candidates. I would head to the far left corner of the reading room (this was before the age of the Bloomberg terminal that would aggregate large gobs of electronically available data) where I would find scores of softbound books containing the daily stock prices recorded from the national and local stock exchanges for the last few years—even for the difficult-to-locate penny stock companies. These obscure books helped me uncover target companies with lower-than-average P/E ratios, indicating a potential and earlier unseen bargain.

If I needed to go back further, I could always visit the back-stack archives. The back stacks contained the true treasures. If I had to research historical activity of a particular publicly traded company, I would visit the stacks where I would find Securities and Exchange Commission filings going back to the commission's founding in 1934.

Moving from the microeconomic to the macroeconomic world, the Baker Library did not disappoint. Industry statistics found in trade association publications, United Nations population and productivity statistics, and U.S. Department of Commerce industry analyses were all here—and easy to find.

Toward the end of a long day of research, I would drag my pile of books and magazines to the bank of nickel-fed copying machines and run off the photocopies of all the earmarked pages. By the time I walked out of the reading room at midnight, my bag filled with informational booty and the odor of burned Xerox toner suffused in my nostrils, I felt I had captured most of the published business data the world offered at the time to answer my questions.

I had a sense of focus, a feeling (true or not) that if I could just burrow myself into the mounds of publications that someone else had meticulously spent time reviewing in advance at the Baker Library, I would have the foundation for an analysis. What the Baker contained was most of the published information I could ever hope to find and need. I saw the Baker as a jumping-off point, a key to a doorway through which I could collect all the other information I needed on a company, the unpublished information—the gossip, the customer–sales force conversations, discussions on trade show floors, and so on.

The Baker Library was the Net for me back then. It supplied the expert names found in news articles, the financial footnotes in hard-to-find annual reports, obscure stock prices, critical industry analyses, and names of organizations I needed to contact.

Then, some fifteen years later, the Internet arrived on the business stage. What took me two days in the Baker Library would take me only a couple of hours to assemble by trolling through Google or some other search engine.

What would George Fisher Baker think about his $5 million investment today? Would he believe that his pantheon to business information was wasted? All this brick and mortar, facing the Charles River, is just a hollow monument to an idea whose time has passed?

"Standards," the octogenarian Baker preached.

Standards is exactly what the Internet lacks. Focus is something that is very elusive on the Net as well. The Baker Library with its four walls gave the researcher a feeling of completeness, of integrity. It was vast but finite. Enter the Baker Library, follow the typical path of "ask the reference librarian," or search through the intricately cross-indexed card catalog and you will find it—if it truly exists. Within the Baker you could see everything there was to see that was published on business in the twentieth century.

The Internet, by contrast, is unstructured, with lots of false or untrustworthy information in this virtual library. It's more like an endless labyrinth, a house of mirrors. Some paths are real and lead you to a partial answer; other paths waste your time or mislead you altogether. No longer do you have a single path. Gone is the library catalog, the all-knowing I've-touched-every-book-on-every-shelf-in-this-place reference librarian. No one knows it all on the Net. That's impossible.

TRANSACTIONS EXPOSE THE INFORMATION

<<<<<<<<< INTERNET X-RAY CONCEPT 2 >>>>>>>>>

**Follow the transaction trail to uncover the
Internet's intelligence gems.**

Ah, but the Net does have a standard, a catalog of sorts. It's the catalog of business transactions. By knowing where the money is exchanged, you can find the intelligence.

It is the Net's vastness that makes it such a powerful—yet frustrating—intelligence tool. For the first time, competitors large and small feel compelled to reveal gobs of information—from self-promotional press releases to a historical archive of their annual reports. Suppliers create links with their customers; a senior executive's presentation on his firm's strategy finds its way (Power-Point and all) onto some obscure investment Web site or onto a university business school professor's class page. Discussion threads include experts inserting their opinions on everything from a clinical trial of a drug to a conspiracy theory or corporate malfeasance.

The Net has it all. It is a strange blend of Baker Library–like archives with the informational dynamics and hurly-burly of a Middle Eastern open-air bazaar. It is all there—knowledge, insight, and even malicious gossip and destructive rumor. You need to find a way to see through the distractions and distortions and select the powerful information gems that may be hidden on corporate home pages, in discussion groups. You need to understand the reasons and motivations behind why various Web-based authors couch information in a certain way. By doing so, you can begin to harness its power.

There will always be places for Baker-type libraries. Historical archives are not likely to find their way into electronic form anytime soon. Yet libraries place artificial barriers on information. They cannot reflect the dynamic nature of how information flows.

One of my cardinal intelligence principles is "Wherever money is exchanged, so is information." This means that whenever a business transaction takes place, someone or some group passes along information. That "passing along" may take the form of a conversation, a government filing, a reporter writing a news article about a major corporate acquisition. Traditional libraries can only capture what the publishers place in their documents. Most of this information is limited by whatever the publisher deems it will include (or exclude). Besides, most of this information is also out of date by the time it reaches the library shelf. Library information, therefore, does not generally give you a competitive advantage. It's just information (old information at that), but it is not intelligence.

The Internet more accurately reflects the way information flows in the real world than does any library archive. More of the transactions and the information they convey appear on the Net. Instead of a bank of editors deciding what should appear in print and what should not, the parties involved in the business deal control what details they want the world to see and read.

Even small or low-profile companies expose themselves whenever a major transaction takes place. For example, when Ontus Telecommunications Corporation, a Portland, Oregon, builder of international telecommunications routes, signed a joint venture with SingTel, a Singapore-based telecommunications firm, it sent out a detailed press release.

Ontus Announces Joint Venture with the SingTel Group

PORTLAND, ORE.—(Business Wire)—December 13, 2004—Ontus Telecommunications Corp. (OTC: ONTC) an FCC licensed international and long distance telecommunications carrier, today announced that it has closed on a Joint Venture agreement with Sunrise Internet & Communications Services (PTE), Ltd. Of Singapore.

. . . The Sunrise joint venture will be managed and operated from Singapore. The joint venture will target both Sunshine's vast broadband ISP audience and the ISP audiences of regional competitors, with a combination of traditional and grass-roots advertising campaigns in Singapore, Indonesia, Australia and Philippines. The launch is scheduled for 2005.

Under the terms of the agreement, the joint venture will deploy the Ontus soft switch to deliver IP [Internet Protocol]-based telephony services to enterprise customers using a range of communications devices including PC-based soft-phones, personal digital assistants (PDA), and standards compliant IP phones.

How can a rival use such a release and what questions does it prompt? A rival would now know which technology has cemented this deal: Ontus's soft switch. It would also see in which Asian Pacific markets Ontus will market its product (through Sunrise). It also might suspect that this is the first of many opportunities Ontus will find to work with Sunrise. The details of this deal certainly will cause the rival to find out which customers the joint venture will approach and how well this joint venture is progressing. Among the rival's likely questions: At which price points is Sunrise selling the bundled offering? When are they winning accounts and with whom? This press release prompts the sorts of questions that can lead to highly specific answers, answers that lead to vital intelligence.

Why did Ontus or SingTel (Sunrise) release this information? The superficial answer is that as a publicly traded company in the United States, Ontus was required to do so. But another answer is that the two companies just completed a substantial deal that should—if it works well—generate a lot of revenue on both sides. Success presumes that customers know about the new opportunities this deal represents. Thus, you need to tell the world about the deal in any way possible. Salespeople are expensive, and knocking on doors takes time. Sending a press release out is easy. Once again, the wherever-money-is-exchanged-so-is-information rule holds sway in this case.

The Ontus-Sunrise press release is an example of these real-world nuggets you need to find. You need to cut through the turgid, incoherent cloud represented by the million-plus hits you encounter when trolling through Google. While the Net itself still does not represent all the world's knowledge, it's a far more comprehensive—albeit seemingly incomprehensible—information storehouse than any single library.

Cutting through the Net's distractions and false information and knowing how to unearth the intelligence nugget is an art, a way of thinking. I have discovered that the experts in this find-the-insight-on-the-Web game come from different ends of the company, but not necessarily from the traditional library world. Because these Net-savvy individuals are involved in the transactions themselves, they know what critical informational bits and pieces to look for and what to discard. Mostly, they know how to focus their view and cut through the Internet haze and confusion.

NOVARTIS AND THE NET'S LAW OF INVERSE NUMBERS

<<<<<<<<< INTERNET X-RAY CONCEPT 3 >>>>>>>>>
Look for what is not said or for what is missing.

Novartis's management appears to have discriminatory taste when it comes to using information streaming off the Internet. Novartis is one of the pharmaceutical world's true powerhouse companies. (At the time of this writing, it was the sixth-largest pharmaceutical company in the world.) It has managed to do a lot of things very well, from traditional pharmaceuticals to generics and animal health. Formed out of a merger of Sandoz and Ciba-Geigy in 1996, it has gained the reputation as a market-savvy Big Pharma concern. It has a healthy pipeline of new products, and among its creations is Glivec, a very successful cancer therapy.

CEO Daniel Vasella and Mark Higgins, an early commercial development manager, are both Net-savvy individuals within

Novartis. Both understand the Net, both for its foibles and for its advantages.

Neither has an information science degree. Curiously, both are trained physicians. What they exhibit is an instinct for how the Web can help them see the big picture. Each uses the Web to see the many facets of reality, as if the Internet were a many-sided prism with every side reflecting a different part of the world around it. In addition, they each bring a deep knowledge of their business that helps them interpret any one of the Web's reflections of reality.

When I spoke to Vasella a few years ago, he had been CEO for little more than one year. He has a reputation as a demanding, direct CEO who overhauled the once-staid culture of its Swiss Sandoz/ Ciba-Geigy heritage. He spoke very calmly but deliberately. Vasella is constantly finding ways to look outside the company as well as seeking to bring new information into Novartis. As an example of his outward-reaching personality, Vasella recently made the decision to move Novartis's R&D headquarters from relatively quiet Basel to Cambridge, Massachusetts, a hotbed for biotechnology research. Novartis is sinking $4 billion into this facility and betting that it will become a sponge for absorbing and instituting new ideas, which in turn will create new drugs. This Cambridge facility is in many ways a reflection of Vasella and his goals—always outward looking, always critically reviewing new information.

Vasella never sees the Net as a sole source of information but rather as a mirror reflecting evidence of the many industry forces swirling around Novartis.

At one point in our conversation, I had asked him about how successful he is in his ability to forecast five or ten years out. He responded by talking about major overseas investment decisions, including that of China, that he expects to make in the next few years and how complex a picture he expects to confront.

"What formulates my mental picture of China?" he asked. "I have visited many times and have had discussions with politicians, physicians, and my colleagues. My picture is composed of data and experience, failures and successes." The data he refers to come from scientific journals and papers as well as information he may find on the Net. He almost never accepts the raw data alone before making a decision. He tends to blend any data he finds in medical journals or Internet news groups and combines them with his experience.[2]

"Every day I read material on the Internet using key words to find a selection of articles and publications," he explained. "I then extract the essence, or the facts, from a variety of formats. Additionally, organizations generate information, such as market research data or reports on research symposia, which help to complete a certain picture. In any case, it is important to separate the facts from the interpretation as the latter varies greatly depending on the perspective."

Vasella always wants to know the source. For instance, he recalled reading an article on the Net about the monarch butterfly and genetically modified crops, an area in which Novartis once held a stake. The article's author apparently stated that the butterfly was dying because of its eating genetically modified crops. Vasella didn't readily buy into the conclusion. "Upon further investigation, or study of the data, you learn that this conclusion was derived from laboratory data and that the study was not conducted in nature."

Vasella understands the politics coursing through the Net. "One has to be careful when reading such 'information,' " he said, referring to the author's assertion that the butterfly's threatened extinction was the result of its feeding on genetically modified plants. "But one always learns something from it, even if it was only the political agenda of certain activists."

Mark Higgins contends with similar issues. He, too, must evaluate what he finds on the Internet and help the scientists with whom he works distinguish between fiction and reality, between panic and an actual competitive intent.

Part of Higgins's job is to develop intelligence on Novartis's rivals at the very earliest, preclinical stages of pharmaceutical development. He is a physician and a marketer by training and education. A soft-spoken man, he sees the value of the Net, but, like his company's CEO Daniel Vasella, appreciates it for what it is and for what it's not.

Like a mirage in the desert, the Net can play tricks on the mind. For many who search for information nuggets on the Net, volume is a virtue—but it's also a trap. Don't fall into it. For the astute, Net-savvy manager, red flags should pop up every time you join the million-hits club by using the Google search engine. Knowing where the lies lie can help you define a rival's true competitive position.

Higgins knows about the Internet's house of mirrors. Reality is sometimes just the opposite of what appears on the Net. Lots of noise, he would contend, does not mean lots of substance. For example, Higgins is wary every time he sees articles pouring out of the laboratories of one of his company's rivals and into the journals or on one of many non-peer-reviewed Internet sites. "If you see a lot written about a molecule," states Higgins in his typically quiet way, "it usually means that the rival is not pursuing it."[3]

According to Higgins, you cannot assume that once a patent appears or lots of articles suddenly spill out into the market that this firm is about to pounce, about to aggressively move a drug to the next stage of development. In fact, he concludes, you should consider that the rival is planning to do just the opposite—canceling this compound altogether. "This appearance may be equally wrong," he says. "The question you should have is: 'Why are they publishing this just now?' "

Higgins has used this Internet volume-publishing principle to strategic advantage. He recalled a chemical compound found naturally in the body, known as neurokinin. Drugs or molecules targeted to this compound or its molecular pathway were being examined for use in treating anxiety and depression.

A number of scientists working in this therapy area approached Higgins with a doomsday scenario. They searched the Net and discovered, to their dismay, that a competitor had just released a large number of technical articles in this drug category.

"We saw someone publish an awful lot [on their version of neurokinin-directed compounds]," he recalled, "which meant that their molecule did not work. They indeed did already have patents on the molecules. Yet the inference was that they were canning the molecule, which means that we still had a lead in the field."

Higgins saw through the mirage. He saw past the mirrors.

This sudden release of information on neurokinin was not likely a corporate sleight of hand or some underhanded manipulation on the part of Novartis's rival. Pharmaceutical companies and other R&D-driven businesses generally try to control how, when, and where one of its professionals can publish. Management at Novartis and at the other pharmas treat their scientists as quasi-academics whose standing and professional advancement somewhat rely upon their ability to publish. It is this push-pull between a scientist's need to publish and a corporation's need for secrecy and avoidance of competitive surprise that Higgins has recognized in his assessment of the science he reads on the Net.

This inverse signal—where the rival indicated it was no longer interested in the drug by publishing volumes of information on its experiments—told Higgins that Novartis had one less rival in the marketplace for this particular pharmaceutical.

VALUE IN ANGER . . . THE F-COMPANY WAY

> *Rumor is a pipe*
> *Blown by surmises, jealousies, conjectures*
> *And of so easy and so plain a stop*
> *The blunted monster with uncounted heads,*
> *The still-discordant wav'ring multitude*
> *Can play upon it.*
>
> —HENRY IV, Part 2

<<<<<<<< INTERNET X-RAY CONCEPT 4 >>>>>>>>>
Seek the language of anger.

If the Internet were a library, you would undoubtedly find a large portion of that library's collection cataloged under "Insult, Anger, and Rumor." Consider once again the cardinal intelligence rule: Wherever money is exchanged, so is information. When someone is laid off from a job or feels mistreated by an employer or a company in some way, you can take that same rule and rewrite it ever so slightly to read: "Whenever I lost money in a transaction, or whenever my company may have stolen from me (translate that as mishandled or misappropriated my retirement fund), I would be more than happy to tell my tale, my truth, to whoever will listen."

Daniel Vasella filters out the political bias, and Mark Higgins reads inverse signals. What about anger? How can you use anger to uncover a rival's soft underbelly? More to the point, how can you find the right listings in the Internet's vast "Insult, Anger, and Rumor" section of its library catalog?

Unfortunately, some of the best intelligence reveals itself when people's emotions are stripped raw and naked. That's when a lot of four-letter words appear in print. These words are your link to some valuable competitive insights.

Let's look at some Internet history once again—albeit a brief history.

The dot-com era reached a boiling point in the late 1990s. New companies rose and collapsed overnight. One start-up I ran into received millions of dollars in funding by showing investors no more than sixteen PowerPoint slides. A landlord I spoke with would only rent my firm additional space in a nearby office building if we would give him equity in our firm in lieu of rent. This was a crazy, unbalanced gold rush period in American business history.

The Internet taught me, during the crumbling of the dot-com era, that unchecked exhilaration is one side of a coin whose flip side is unbridled anger and retribution. Not only did numerous Internet start-up companies collapse, but large, established icons of business success, such as Enron, WorldCom, Tyco, and others, unraveled as well. All these implosions were the result of irrational and illegal behavior coupled with outright greed. Unfortunately, at the bottom of the collapsed pile lay tens of thousands of employees who could do little about their company's failure, their demolished pension plans, and sudden job loss.

The one recourse those individuals buried under the fiscal rubble had left, aside from applying for unemployment and joining in a class action lawsuit, was to scream. And scream they did, ironically using the platform upon which many of their companies once thrived: the Net.

Scores of Web sites sprang up and chat rooms buzzed with anger, bitterness, and accusations. These people felt victimized and they were not going to wait for the courts to settle their complaints.

A number of sites became magnets for the high-tech corporate failures during that period. One of the most popular sites for corporate rumors in the Internet and technology arena is FuckedCompany.com. It encourages rumors on just about any company by anyone. The site's founder sees FuckedCompany.com as a virtual bettor parlor. Its very direct purpose is to encourage users to bet when a company will fail.

Philip "Pud" Kaplan is the site's founder and operator, a man in his mid-twenties who reports that his site received as many as four million visits each month during the peak of the dot-com bust.[4] According to Kaplan, his site plays a game of "deadpool." "Your classic deadpool is a game of picking celebrity deaths," Kaplan states on his home page. "Points are generally earned based on odds . . . but instead of betting for (or against) people, you're betting on companies. The lines are a little blurred when dealing with companies because there is rarely a clean-cut death. To make up for this, FuckedCompany.com rates different levels of a company's demise and awards points based on the level of severity."

The entries are frank, often raw expressions of someone just laid off.

> I was laid off on Tuesday, along with 40%+ of the staff. You won't see the reports on any news site, since Conxion wants to keep it quiet . . . I have heard IBM who hosts their Global Services managed hosting customers with Conxion is pissed. The company blew through $84 million in one year, and still nothing to show for it . . . I don't think the rest of us will have jobs here soon. (2/10/2002; points 150)[5]

> Rumor has it SwitchHouse.com's planned AOL partnership fell through (no sh#t) and the company is going down . . . word is sometime next week. (2/10/2002; points 190)[6]

> "NextCard is no longer accepting credit card applications," said the e-mail sent to NextCard advertisers, asking them to remove all NextCard ads. Apparently the gub'ment shut down the bank they were running due to "operating in an unsafe and unsound manner." (2/8/2002; points 299)[7]

What should the marketing manager, a Dale Fehringer at Visa, do when spotting the above remark? Perhaps nothing. Then again, maybe he needs to verify or confirm the fact that NextCard may be shutting down.

An astute manager would take the names of the participants on this bulletin board and start a conversation with the sender. He or she may send a private message, not using the established bulletin board (realize, though, that any message you send on the Net is never private).

Anger usually leaves behind a long information trail, similar in some respects to the contrail of puffy white vapor left by a jet plane flying in the stratosphere. A contrail is aerospace shorthand for "condensation trail." Contrails are clouds of water vapor blended with small particles shot out of jet engines. World War II fighter pilots first used contrails to track and locate enemy aircraft. Similarly, following an intelligence contrail may let you uncover a competitor's strategic direction.

Anger leaves a contrail on the Web as it incites one person after another to respond to his or her own personal indignation, which in turn will likely lead to another rumor, which will likely lead to someone else relating the first rumor or anger statement to another unrelated experience. Your challenge is to follow the trail to its end. The intelligence jackpot is often worth the effort.

Pud Kaplan understands a piece of this intelligence physics. He knows how to provide a platform from which to create an anger contrail, then expose it to others for comment and further advancement. Kaplan, who launched his site in 2000, was not the first.

There is an entire Internet subculture that sees the Web as a social (or antisocial) soapbox upon which to express all types of anger. For example, hundreds of sites contain the word "sucks" in their Internet address. PayPalsucks.com, WalMartsucks.com, HomeDepotsucks.com, and so on. These sites typically assemble news items and public bulletin boards where outraged customers can vent their views or sad experiences with the company under discussion. For example, if you wanted to confirm some details on

Wal-Mart's personnel policies (let's say you were doing an analysis, benchmarking your firm's hiring and retention practices), and you discovered a site where current and former Wal-Mart employees complained about their vacation or personal leave requests, wouldn't you want to contact that person to try to verify or at least place a range on the policy's limitations, taking into account such factors as how many days of vacation, the amount of notice, pay ranges, human resources training, consistency across the Wal-Mart organization, and so on? Such sites can be gold mines for confirming or disproving human resources practice fact from published press release fiction. Wal-Mart may indeed be a model employer, but finding some of these information cracks in this vast empire could provide you with invaluable, formerly unpublished insights on the company.

Anger has its place on the Net, as long as you, the seeker of the truth, realize the sender's perspective. Just as Daniel Vasella of Novartis cautiously accepted scientific information on the Net, you should also verify employer-shredding remarks on public bulletin boards. Once you have spotted a useful site, searching for statements about your target company is not an endless quest. Because the messages you do uncover are written in anger or frustration, assume you are dealing with a false statement until you have had time to verify it.

Take heed. When someone says a company is "going down," there is likely some truth to the statement. In any number of assignments, I have found that such statements often are true, or at least a portion of the statement is true.

If you can think of the invective, then someone has probably appended a company's name to it and formed a Web site containing controversial, angry information. Juicy and filled with inaccuracies, no doubt, but one that leaves a long, visible line pointing directly to your target. The contrail begins here.

BLOG YOUR WAY INTO A DIFFERENT REALITY

<<<<<<<<< INTERNET X-RAY CONCEPT 5 >>>>>>>>>

Use blogs and discussion groups to refine your competitive hypothesis.

Have you ever attended a party and had to listen to someone opposite you ramble on about a topic you didn't want to hear? We have all had this experience to one degree or another. But have you ever thought about seeking out such a ramble and actually enjoying the prospect of listening to endless preaching and speculation? I do and so do the analysts who work in my firm.

Blogs are Web sites dedicated to one person's musings or opinions. Most blog sites invite others to comment and respond. If the topic is exciting enough, you will see an entire discussion thread emerge over hours, days, or weeks.

To possibly gain competitive insight, you need to think of a blog or a discussion board as a psychologist would a patient's conversation. Take a turn in language, a change of topic, or a new sense of emphasis as a cue to ask or refine a question. Just as patient-doctor discussions provide psychologists with opportunities to ask a question in order to pry open the next answer, so too must you use a blog or discussion board in the same way.

Because individuals participating in a blog or a discussion

group often are very much involved in their industry or with the issue under discussion, they know the hot buttons all too well—even if they themselves don't always realize it. Sometimes you need to just watch the stream of words they write in order to identify the central issue. You can then use this central issue to formulate a hypothesis about a rival. Spin a few questions around your hunch about this rival, and then ask your list of experts these very specific, very targeted questions.

The pharmaceutical and biotechnology industries are filled with discussion or chat groups. Among the two most popular bulletin boards we often go to are Cafepharma.com and Biofind.com. Both contain thousands of discussion threads, many of them about the sales and marketing side of the business. For example, the following discussion began on Cafepharma.com on August 4, 2004, at 8:00 A.M.[8] The anonymous posting was intended to evoke discussion. It did.

The question concerns selling the oncology drugs Tarceva and Iressa. Tarceva is produced by the biotech firm Genentech; Iressa is produced by the pharmaceutical company AstraZeneca (AZ). Iressa had been approved for sale by the Food and Drug Administration in May 2003, while Tarceva received approval on November 18, 2004, shortly after the discussion below. Both are relatively expensive, life-prolonging medicines costing from $1,800 (Iressa) to $2,000 (Tarceva) per month of treatment. Treatments don't sell themselves in this highly competitive market. Competition among salespeople is intense. Knowing the high cost of these drugs and the competitive nature of selling into this market will help you appreciate the conversation that follows. Look at how the bulletin board conversation flows and where it takes you.

Question and posting:

> I've been told that this drug is a me-too drug as compared to Iressa, with more side effects. It is not filling an unmet medical need, so how is it going to be fast tracked?

The first response appears at 8:23 A.M. that same day.

> Simple . . . dosing. Due to dosing differences (based on clinical data) Tarceva will be boatloads less expensive. The only way AZ can change their dosing to compete price-wise is to EAT millions now, go back to the drawing board and crank up the Clinical Trials. They will surely do this, but look for Iressa to get killed for at least 2 years from the word GO. KILLED. And 2 years in this industry is almost forever.

The next response occurs at 9:28 A.M., only an hour later.

> Can you say . . . "survival advantage" with Tarceva!?

Another party interrupts and comments on the first writer's naiveté.

> Quote:

> > I've been told that this drug is a me-too drug as compared to Iressa, with more side effects. It is not filling an unmet medical need, so how is it going to be fast tracked?

> U been lied to.

On August 6, 2004, at 8:55 A.M., yet another individual adds a comment.

> I've also heard that Tarceva is a me too that is more expensive and has more side-effects than Iressa?

A little later that day comes this cynical critique.

> Come on. Either you are flat out lying or you don't really know what you are talking about. I think you mean Iressa is safer and less expensive?? Go back to the Pfizer or Merck [message] board.

Shortly after 9:00 P.M. that same day:

> The drug is not approved yet, so the price hasn't been announced. You don't know if it's going to be more or less expensive than Iressa, idiot.

Two days later on August 8, this insight:

> No, one of my local research site docs was telling me about pricing, while that may change on approval he said it was supposed to be a little more than Iressa.

On August 9 a very down-to-earth observation on the product's salability:

> Tarceva and Irresa [sic]. . . . Two big yawns. Response rates in, at best, 10% of patients on an oral medication. Does Medicare pay for it? No. Sounds like a couple of barkers to me. Good luck.

A new door in the conversation opens the next day, August 10:

This could be a very tough sell!!!

Someone else seconds the comment with an off-colored embellishment:

Could be. Could also be a job making $95k in base salary and a nice bucket of options and a free car where if you are a good sales rep, you can make another 35k in bonus. WOW. That sucks.

By August 20, the conversation starts turning to other opportunities:

Going to be a dog to sell, already said that going to be more expensive than Iressa with more side effects. I am not looking forward to wasting my time with this one.

This continues around another opportunity corner:

Is Avastin [another cancer drug produced by Genentech] as easy to sell as they say it is? My friend told me he hardly has to do any work and will make nearly 60k in bonus this year. This on top of his starting base of almost 100k. If this is the case, I'm sending my resume.

A discouraging note follows only a few minutes later:

Sorry, I think the Avastin train has already left the station, unless you happen to be located where there is an opening, very, very few of those.

This bothers one of the participants, an Avastin supporter, enough to truly delve into details:

> Your friend is exaggerating. I came on late last year with nearly five years of biotech experience at a base of 75k, and I'll probably make about 40 this year in bonus, and I'm currently the number two rep in our region. One of the things I've learned here is that while the culture isn't bad, many people are out just to further their own careers and like to exaggerate their salary and bonus numbers just to tick off outsiders. Honestly speaking, DNA is no better place to work than a lot of the places I'm reading on this board, whether it be Amgen or Centecor or Merck. The big difference is whether you get a good manager or not. And forget about those promises of big bucks. The management here knew Avastin was going to be big so they structured the bonus plan to benefit the company. Still, even if I was one of those people who came on board at 70k with a chance of making 25 in bonus, it still wouldn't be a bad place to be, although things are going big pharma as we speak.

A day later, August 21, this discussion begins to resemble a poker game, with each participant showing his or her hand. Here are the salary cards this discussion member is willing to expose to the group:

> Let me get this straight, are you saying you're selling Avastin, are number 2 in your region, and will be lucky to make $40K in bonus?
> If so, there are only three possible conclusions:
> 1. Your region sucks, or

> 2. You don't know how your bonus is calculated, or
> 3. You're a liar.
> Your choice.
> In terms of base, if you've got 5 years in biotech and you're only making $70 K base, you suck, don't blame DNA. What were you making in base at your last company—$60K? I came over last year, according to my 8/13 pay stub, I've earned $15K in bonus and Avastin has not even kicked in yet. I got a base of $72k in 1998 with my second [oncology] company and only 2 years experience. DNA is my fourth and last oncology company.

The above discussion thread is rich with intelligence possibilities, marketing messages and sales incentives among them.

Imagine you are trying to understand the key messages an organization has developed for a newly launched product. Examining the postings from a discussion thread, such as the one above, can help you to develop hypotheses concerning these messages. You can take your theory about the messages and market positioning statements and test them by directly interviewing sales and marketing professionals.

The conversation that you just finished reading will help you shape your messaging hypothesis because (1) now you have a sense of what a rival's marketing message could be *("Simple . . . dosing. Due to dosing differences [based on clinical data] Tarceva will be boatloads less expensive.")*, and (2) you can see possible roadblocks to product success *("Tarceva and Irresa. . . . Two big yawns. Response rates in, at best, 10% of patients on an oral medication. Does Medicare pay for it? No. Sounds like a couple of barkers to me. Good luck.")*.

It was just such a discussion that could lead my health care analysts to highly productive conversations with industry insiders about their products, asking questions such as "Do you believe it's the simple dosing regimen that is Tarceva's strong suit? If so, why (or why not) do you believe this is so?" The drug's formal literature may not say a lot about the low-dosage issue, but the salespeople were apparently making some noise about this treatment approach. Only a discussion thread would reveal such subtleties.

Satisfied with this approach? You shouldn't be. Attempting to pinpoint marketing messages a rival telegraphs to a market is just one way to milk this discussion. Look at the conversation yet again. You certainly can see many self-serving and somewhat smug comments about salary and bonus structure. Assuming you need to fully appreciate the sales prowess of a rival, you will find no better place to begin than right here. Call this second exercise building-a-salary-and-incentive hypothesis.

This time you wish to understand the nature of a sales organization in a pharmaceutical organization. Let's say your company is about to ramp up sales because of a newly approved drug, and you need to build a highly motivated sales force. Part of your job would be to benchmark your plan against that of your rivals or of companies similar to yours. Where do you start? How do you know that your sales incentive and compensation scheme reflects market reality, or even what these salespeople want?

A review of the thread will reveal that (1) you have a sense of a rival's salary-plus-bonus structure, as well as salary ranges you would be competing against *("I came on late last year with nearly five years of biotech experience at a base of 75k, and I'll probably make about 40 this year in bonus, and I'm currently the number two rep in our region"),* and (2) you can see how salespeople perceive company management and how management can motivate them (*"The management here knew Avastin was going to be big so they structured the bonus plan to benefit the company"*).

A few years ago we were attempting to understand the compensation structure for sales reps among competing pharmaceutical companies. By reviewing a particular set of statements on the Cafepharma.com site, similar to the ones you just read, we noted that a number of participants cited salaries and compensation schemes for similar sales rep positions. From these discussions we were able to then determine reasonable salary ranges. We used these informational tidbits as anchors to ask better questions of sales reps whose names were mentioned or who signed their postings in open discussion groups. By speaking to a number of the reps and comparing their answers, we pieced together details on a rival's salary and compensation plan for its sales reps.

CORPORATE DNA CAN MAKE THE INVISIBLE VISIBLE

<<<<<<<<< INTERNET X-RAY CONCEPT 6 >>>>>>>>>
Track down corporate DNA to unmask a competitor.

A company uses a language that is all its own. This language may be the language of promotion or the language that describes how it markets or assembles its products or services. Nonetheless it is unique. I call this corporate DNA—unique patterns of words and phrases that form the substance of a company's Web site, its press releases, and its advertisements.

Siemens, the German industrial conglomerate, uses the phrase "accelerates business processes through to real-time enterprise" in a way that is unique to its business. Awkward a string of words as this is, it is a DNA marker pointing a search engine directly to Siemens. For IBM, "We strive to lead in the invention, development and manufacture of the industry's most advanced information technologies" is a DNA marker, and "It's why you fly" is a promotional tagline that belongs to American Airlines.

Search engines, such as Google, are your best tools for tracking down any other locations on the Web that employ the same phrases, containing a rival's corporate DNA language.

If you catch yourself looking at a Web site or trolling through an anonymous discussion group and you stop to ask yourself, "Where have I heard this before?" or "This sounds like promotional language emanating from a corporate PR shop," you have probably identified a unique phrase, a piece of a company's corporate DNA.

An intellectual property attorney knows the power of corporate DNA to track down those that plagiarize concepts or violate trademarks. But for those seeking competitive intelligence, it can help you pierce the cloak of anonymity the rival has attempted to hide behind.

A case in point: Some years ago, we needed to assess the hiring and marketing strategy of companies in the data mining software business. This included companies such as Verity, Autonomy, and others. Their products are designed for large companies or law firms to intelligently sort through and identify unstructured data, mostly in the form of text, not numbers.

The search began simply enough. Targeting Verity first, we typed "verity problem" into the Google Groups (the discussion groups section of Google) search box. We were hoping to find people complaining about Verity. Instead we found job postings for companies wanting to hire technology troubleshooters in the data-mining area.

We pursued one job posting, labeled innocuously "Project Manager (74605)." It was a job posted through a recruiter. The company wished to remain anonymous. This ad contained a lot of information on the company's overall strategy, including who it considered its chief rivals and its target customer groups. If we could only uncover the company itself and connect this ad with other public information on the company itself. . . .

Scrolling down to the bottom of the ad, near the Submit Your Résumé button, was the phrase "Europe's leading search engine software company providing intelligent indexing and search technology for users of the Intranet and Internet." Helene Kassler, the librarian conducting the search, thought this phrase sounded too PRish, too canned, as if the recruiter simply lifted it from a piece of corporate literature.

This was her key to tearing away the recruitment ad's cloak of anonymity. By typing in the exact phrase "Europe's leading search engine software company," bracketed between two sets of quotation marks (this tells the search engine that you want the exact phrase) and commanding the engine to find references to this same phrase, she found the very same phrase embedded within the Web site of a rival European data-mining competitor. The company was Muscat. Muscat, she subsequently learned, merged into another similar company, Smartlogik. The corporate Web site contained extremely valuable information on the company's strategic plans, adding nicely to the insights gained from the original job ad she uncovered through Google.

Consider any odd or unique-sounding phrase as the equivalent of corporate DNA. If you spot such a phrase, even if the reference omits the company's identity associated with it, you have likely identified a special pattern not used by anyone else. Apply the tracking power of an Internet search to see where this pattern has appeared elsewhere. Match DNA strand to DNA strand, phrase to phrase, to tear away the cloak.

RECOGNIZE THE NET'S GREAT CULTURAL AND LANGUAGE DIVIDE

<<<<<<<<< INTERNET X-RAY CONCEPT 7 >>>>>>>>>

Find the right words to mine the Internet's hidden worlds.

Finding a home page is easy, as is jumping around the Net through search engines such as Google. Why then does so much of the Web remain hidden from those seeking the information? There are forces at work on the Net, in the form of language and culture, that help shape the way the information appears as well as your ability to find it. Web sites and news may be perfectly invisible if you, the searcher, examine the Web using the wrong phrase, idiom, or cultural concept.

The Web has no passport control, no green cards or visas. For the most part, anyone who can design a Web page can participate in this greatest of all intellectual democracies in any way he so chooses.

It's this last phrase, "any way he so chooses," that can make the information invisible. While the information's creator does not intentionally want to hide the information—otherwise why bother publishing a Web page at all—he may inadvertently do so because of his background and culture.

I have been trolling through the online world since the mid-1970s. My staff has completed thousands of assignments all around the world. This global perspective certainly helps.

In a series of conversations with my staff librarians, I asked them for some of their recent experiences, particularly asking them to comment on the subtleties in their use of language and culture when searching on the Web. That is when we first started talking about the French language or, shall I say, the many French languages.

A project manager needed some basic information on a multinational company in order to begin a competitive analysis. First, searching in English, we found little. But because this company had strong roots in France and in the French-speaking world, we switched over to searching in French. Not only did we find a large number of articles on the company's activity in France, but also references to France's Spanish and Dutch neighbors and the company's activities there as well.

Even the seemingly simplest task on the Web can become muddled unless you know the correct expression. For example, if you are looking for job postings in France, you type in "offers d'emploi"; in Belgium the word for the same concept is "vacatures."

One word shines a light on information hidden on France while the other works equally well on Belgium, but they are not interchangeable. Use the wrong phrase in each case and both sets of information remain shrouded in darkness. They are there, but you cannot see them.

Surprisingly, English itself can present a similar barrier to the intelligence seeker. When George Bernard Shaw stated that America and England are two countries separated by a common language, his prescient remark foretold the vagaries of the Net. For example, if we were to look for information on the labor force in a company and wanted to troll the Net for details on a company's use of part-time help, in the States we might type the words "temporary" or "part time." In the United Kingdom, however, you instead would use the word "supply" plus the type of position. Each term defines the point of origin. Type in one and the Net sends you to the United States; type in the other and the Net beams you to the United Kingdom.

American Business English Versus
British Business English:
Know the Different Terms to Get the Right Answers

1. An American manager examining Kimberly Clark, producer of Huggies, or Procter & Gamble, producer of Pampers, would say they were both in the diaper business. A Brit doing the same research might search Google under the word "nappies."
2. To a Brit, "in the City" would mean someone who works in the financial district; an American, on the other hand, would refer to "Wall Street."

3. "Redundant" means laid off from a job to someone in the United Kingdom, but to an American it may only mean something superfluous and not connected to jobs at all.

4. "Enjoin"—now there's a word that divides. In the United States it means to legally forbid, but in Britain it means to legally force or to compel.

5. The official tax collector in Britain goes by either Inland or Inland Revenue, while in the United States it is the IRS or the Internal Revenue Service.

6. In Britain, "to table" means to place a topic on the agenda. In the United States it means exactly the opposite—to put aside a topic indefinitely.

7. To end this list on a somewhat humorous note, the phrase "on the job" in the United States conveys learning while working, as in "on-the-job training." In the United Kingdom, however, it means having sexual intercourse—still considered work by at least one profession.

Even so-called simple language concepts, such as "car," can involve very different terms. Again, use the wrong one and you find nothing; use the right word and you unlock a treasure chest. For example, in France you would say *voiture* (or *vaihre* or *vaiture*) for the word "car"; in French-speaking Canada, they say *char* (which means "chariot" in France).

Switch to Chinese and the word for "car" demands context. Without context, the meaning may differ dramatically. If you simply use the Chinese *che* (the transliterated word for "car"), depending on where you are, it can mean a bicycle or an automobile. In parts of China it would mean "bicycle" simply because bicycles are more prevalent than cars. The same phrase in other Chinese-speaking regions, where there are more cars, would mean "car."

<<<<<<<<< INTERNET X-RAY CONCEPT 8 >>>>>>>>>
Recognize cultural bias and the Web site's originating country or political leanings.

If you could don a pair of high-tech reading glasses that would allow you to see parallel information universes, that is what you would see when looking at the Net. We should really call the Net "the Nets." Each Net represents a different culture or sub-culture with different ways to depict the same issues or even the same corporation.

A country reflects the national mood, political structure, and social mores of that region. Just as you can walk into a stranger's personal library and assess that person's interests by reading the titles on the shelf, you can do the same with the Net. A country's or a region's virtual bookshelf contains more information on issues and concepts central to that culture than in yours.

For instance, you may need to search for details on the demand for employment in different sectors. My firm has done so for various clients who are considering entering a market and need to understand the competitive forces at work there. It is quite amazing to see how that which is on the surface, while appearing to be a straightforward topic, can mushroom into a complex, multi-faceted issue. Labor is one of those complex topics, especially in Europe where many governments have socialist influences. Such countries have a strong interest in employment issues and workers' rights.

In Belgium or France, for example, you will have a better chance of finding information on labor conditions than you will in Hong Kong. Hong Kong simply does not have as many unions or as many parties who are historically interested in the welfare of the workers as does France or Belgium. The result: In France you can often locate vast amounts of information on different classes of workers—male, female, full time, part time. Not so in Hong Kong.

A comparison of two Net-based services starkly contrasts the cultural differences on the Net. Hoover's is a U.S.-based site that supplies concise details on companies around the world. Transnationale.org is a popular French-based site. While Transnationale reports its mission as providing information on ninety-five hundred companies worldwide, its aim is to "report social and environmental behaviour, financial data, list brands, communication policies." In contrast, Hoover's states its mission as delivering "comprehensive company, industry, and market intelligence," with no direct aspirations to report on social, labor, or environmental issues. Let's look at how Hoover's portrays Walt Disney, for example:

The monarch of this magic kingdom is no man but a mouse— Mickey Mouse. The Walt Disney Company is the #2 media conglomerate in the world (behind AOL Time Warner), with operations in television, film, theme parks, and the Internet. Disney owns the ABC television network, 10 broadcast TV stations, and about 55 radio stations. It also has stakes in several cable channels such as ESPN (80%)."[9]

While Hoover's offers straight corporate news and information on corporate structure, the news from Transnationale.org takes an entirely different view, a view that examines corporate injustice wherever it's found.

An investigation on labor conditions in 12 Chinese contract factories producing for Disney reveals that employees work 13 to 17 hours a day, 7 days a week, without a union, health coverage and retirement money, for a base salary of 1.2 US$ a day."[10]

This is the same company on the same planet, but the viewpoints are very different. How you paint your competitive picture will depend on which Internet lens you wear at that moment as well as in which framework you will analyze the data.

INTELLIGENCE FILTERS THROUGH "DUST MAGNETS"

<<<<<<<<< INTERNET X-RAY CONCEPT 9 >>>>>>>>>
**Think about "dust magnets" and eliminate
the distracting mirrors.**

Once you appreciate and leverage the Net-based forces of language and culture, you still have to contend with the elements and how to combine and manipulate them in order to retrieve the critical information.

The Web, as I have already stated, is a mulligan stew of information—a blend of truth, exaggerations, politically skewed viewpoints, and outright lies. It's too valuable and vast to ignore; at the same time, however, you cannot assume it will turn up *the* answer. Search engines, for all their amazing capabilities, retrieve a less-than-perfect search (the best will likely miss over 80 percent of the material on the Web, much of it not even searchable by the major search engines).[11]

The Web's statistics are beyond belief. Using Google as a barometer, it had indexed over eight billion pages by late 2004. By 2004, according to an article published by the Reston, Virginia–based Internet Society, the number of Web sites worldwide approached one hundred million. In numerous cases, Web sites can contain their own databases, each housing tens of thousands of pieces of data not necessarily cited in the global Web site count.[12] How can you expect any service, even one as effective as Google, to index the tens of billions of Web pages now in existence? The answer: You can't.

Although fee-based online information services have been marginalized in this age of free information, some have existed since the late 1960s and are still superior to information on the free and free-ranging Web, particularly for traditional news and scientific databases they do index. Systems such as the Dow Jones–Reuters Factiva information service, Dialog, or the LexisNexis service have editorial oversight and allow the searcher more control and reassurance that he or she will find the right piece of information. In Factiva's case, the system is fully indexed. That means editors literally assign index terms to each and every article or record.

Factiva, LexisNexis, Dialog, and their other online competitors have continuously improved the search and analytical capability of their archives. Factiva includes Reuter's newswires, content from the *Wall Street Journal*, as well as a wide variety of news, articles, and other content from nearly nine thousand sources with hundreds of millions of articles. LexisNexis, too, claims a large archive. In its case, the claim is for 4.1 billion documents stored online.[13]

Clare Hart, CEO of Factiva, emphasizes how applying taxonomy (editorially selected terms that are attached to each and every news item on the Factiva system) provides an edge to her system— an edge worth paying for. She maintains that services such as Factiva can deliver faster and more accurate information, explicitly because of the cataloging system built into the system. She lists the indexing built into the Dow Jones–Reuters data pool: "Factiva supplies technology that helps you crawl a large mass of data using Factiva's intelligent indexing, as well as its 300,000 company codes and its 372 geographic codes, 426 subject codes, 735 industry codes . . . We can work with companies to add codes to the taxonomy. Getting access to the most relevant articles," Hart concludes, "means that you must pay attention to the taxonomy."[14]

The online databases, such as Factiva, have become my Baker Library. I need them for their accuracy and fast fact-finding capability, but I also recognize their limits. Online services are timely archives, containing only reviewed or edited documents. For that they are invaluable. At the same time, true competitive advantage comes from peering into a world way beyond the online domain, and even beyond the Net.

The Net, though, is a convenient bridge into the real world and all its transactions. Sure it's free and filled with inaccuracies, but it also courses with unbridled chatter, virtual water-cooler conversations. The most savvy information gatherers I've met all gravitate to this virtual world in order to learn where to begin their intelligence hunt in the real world. Besides, what if you cannot afford to pay thousands of dollars yearly to regularly tap into a proprietary, well-indexed information machine? Most large companies can and should subscribe to such services. It's part of their competitive due diligence.

Where does this leave you—the product manager, marketing manager, and salesperson—seeking answers on a competitor and you just can't pry those funds loose? Just over ten years ago, before the advent of the World Wide Web, your only recourse would have been to take a trip to the local library or to tap into the fee-based world of online information. Today you have the Net.

Its very free-ranging nature makes it invaluable. Yet what about its accuracy? Factiva's, Dialog's, or LexisNexis's accuracy is far higher than that of the Net overall. But the breadth of the Net's reach is unmatched. How then can you harness the less-than-perfect search engines to catch just the information you need?

You may understand the language and cultural overtones of the Net's content, but so far you are not equipped to rationally sort through the critical information. It's akin to standing on Speakers Corner in London and shouting out with a megaphone the question "How do I find the cost of operations of a pepperoni pizza topping company?" Assuming a passerby doesn't knock you off the box or the authorities lock you away, you will likely have thousands of suggestions to your broadly worded question.

The Web offers a very similar experience, unless you can find a way to target your questions or somehow radically limit your field of view. For example, you will uncover the word "pizza" connected to Internet ads and as part of home pages belonging to pizza equipment manufacturers, novels and popular magazines, recipes, and on and on. Of the more than nine million citations of the word "pizza" I found through Google, there are a mere handful of useful articles, press releases, and industry information that would truly help you complete a cost analysis on a pepperoni pizza-topping producer. Digging through them all is mind-numbing.

The trick is to distill just the right information from the Web and see clearly through the thousands of distractions, through and around the many mirrors, reflecting the many bits and pieces of information—some true, some not, some relevant, some just pure distraction. To do this, you need to create intelligence filters. These are not special software algorithms. You can build these filters by combining the right words, concepts, and the Web's own somewhat hidden indexing language.

These intelligence filters start with a concept I call "dust magnets." A dust magnet is a series of words or phrases you string together in a search, each representing an intelligence objective.

Librarians call the connecting words Boolean "operators," and they include words such as "and," "or," and "not." Both the traditional online world and the open Web search engines, such as Google, employ these or similar terms or phrases to exclude or include concepts in your search. Dust magnets place a strategic spin on this idea. A dust magnet is a phrase that combines the elements of the idea you are trying to capture. Like a filter, if they are well constructed, they tend to send a Google in the general direction of the sources you need to identify.

If you are a product manager working for a soap and detergent company, such as Dial soap, Henkel, or Procter & Gamble, you certainly would like to know about one of your global rivals,

Unilever. For example, let's say you wanted to interview an ex-employee of Unilever's or scientists working with Unilever in its detergent business. My solution is to create a dust magnet from the words "résumé" and "Unilever," and "surfactant," a key chemical component in detergents. I turned up twenty-nine hits on Google with at least four or five of them leading me to former employees of the company and to scientists who collaborated with Unilever in its research at some point. "Résumé-Unilever-surfactant" is the dust magnet of choice here.

Knowing that trade shows and scientific conferences (or congresses, as they are known throughout Europe) are extremely fertile ground for locating experts in the relatively obscure global industry of surfactants, you may want to shape a dust magnet that filters the information in this direction. In this case, the dust magnet might consist of a combination of the words "Unilever," "surfactant," and "conference." The results on Google yielded 186 hits, including a link to an upcoming World Conference of Detergents in which Unilever scientists and managers play a leading role during many sessions.

SHHH! DON'T TELL ANYONE ABOUT THE SECRET SEARCH LANGUAGE!

<<<<<<<<< INTERNET X-RAY CONCEPT 10 >>>>>>>>>

Harness a search engine's secret language to give you a type of intelligence night vision, an ability to see into a competitor when others cannot.

You can pull away a few more distracting mirrors by focusing your search even further. Even the best of dust magnet filters are crude and may allow in hundreds if not thousands of potential references in Google, but by using the little-known "filetype" search phrase, you can further target your findings and eliminate many of the distracting mirrors.

By combining the Unilever-surfactant-conference dust magnet with the phrase "filetype: doc," I will reduce the hundreds of results to fewer than a dozen. That is because by requesting only files whose suffix is .doc, I am asking only for Microsoft Word documents. This particular search yielded lots of résumés of current and former Unilever employees, reports from industry experts on conferences they attended, and even one chart describing a very specific research project conducted by a number of university and private laboratories, including that of Unilever.

When I switched the filetype to .ppt, in effect I was asking Google for any PowerPoint presentation files linked to the concept of Unilever + surfactant. I received only seven search results, but one of them came from the Center for Chemical Processing Technology, at Texas-based Rice University. The center's research is supported in part by Unilever. The presentation offered a broad list of research projects, some funded by Unilever.

When I switched the search to "filetype: pdf," I now asked for all Adobe Acrobat–formatted documents, which included a number of long reports, including one identifying Unilever's work in China and another batch of expert résumés. You will find lots of white papers issued in Adobe's PDF format, such as the one above.

Oh, yes, back to the pepperoni search. By adding the word

"manufacturing" to "pepperoni" (which yielded over 250,000 citations on Google) and linking it to the phrase "filetype: ppt," I reduced the number of citations to only eleven. Nearly all contained information on some aspect of pepperoni manufacturing. I downloaded a table of U.S. government–approved importers of pepperoni products and the volume imported. Other presentations concerned the manufacturing process itself. This information is a gold mine for someone trying to understand who potential suppliers might be as well as the different methods for producing pepperoni.

WHAT OF THE NET'S INTELLIGENCE FUTURE?

The Net will get smarter. The Googles of the world will build better search engines and smarter filters. Publishers will do a better job of indexing their material, making it easier for us to find.

Robert Crandall, the IT-savvy former CEO of American Airlines, had similar thoughts when I walked into his Dallas office a few years ago. At the time, he spent two to three hours each day trolling through the Net, both out of curiosity and for potential business opportunities. He sees a more sophisticated Web evolving at a very rapid pace.

"Purveyors of information have got to have much, much smarter search engines, and people are out there doing that," he muses. "The guy who has the best search engine is going to have an enormous advantage. People don't really want to go and have to look through the entire *Encyclopaedia Britannica* or through the entire list of magazines that have been published in the last twenty-five years. They don't even want to read the articles; they want the answer. We're not very far away from that."[15]

How far have we come from George Fisher Baker's 1927 vision for his pantheon of business knowledge, Harvard Business School's Baker Library? While the Baker Library is not going to disappear anytime soon, it is working on reducing the size of its formal collection, just as most libraries worldwide are doing. Business libraries today are becoming archives and less a central repository of current knowledge.

Business information standards, as Mr. Baker so desired, are fast becoming fanciful imaginings. The world moves too quickly for any single group or governing body to dictate what information we should read and absorb. There are too many information-generating sources holding up too many mirrors. The best we can hope for is to improve our ability to capture slices of this moving target, this intelligence.

CHAPTER 7

COMPETITIVE FOG

How Rothschild, Buffett, Walton, Dell, and Branson Saw Clearly and Others Did Not

Anyone in the twenty-first century who thinks himself or herself the first to discover the intelligence concept is more than a bit naive. Whether or not past entrepreneurs ever labeled their ability to clearly see through or ahead of their competition as intelligence is irrelevant. The fact is that they did and they do. Equally important, we can learn from yesteryear's profiteers and magnates.

One of the first things we learn by examining intelligence concepts invented in the eighteenth century is that speed, security, global tracking of events, and other such critical intelligence components have always existed in these entrepreneurs' kit bags.

Often empire builders who launched new ways of doing business or entirely new industries at the same time invented new approaches to develop and deliver intelligence. Mostly, it was necessity that drove them to seek out critical intelligence. Many were the new kids on the block, the new entrants, not the entrenched stalwarts. They had everything to gain and little to lose. Rothschild,

211

Buffett, Walton, Dell, and Branson are among just a few of those who have discovered new and inventive ways to make intelligence a profit-generating force to grow their businesses. They were able to see through the competitive fog, where others failed.

They also have many intelligence lessons to teach us.

SPEED WITHOUT BANDWIDTH

The Rothschild family invented the bond market at the end of the eighteenth century. They were a banking powerhouse, financiers of the first order, serving governments, kingdoms, and industry. But first and foremost, they were believers in intelligence. In an age before trains and telegraph, they pioneered speedy, accurate communication of business and political news, any news that would affect their investment strategy.

One of the most famous Rothschild intelligence stories is also mired in myth. It is the story of how Nathan Rothschild capitalized on Napoleon's loss at Waterloo in 1815. As told and retold over the generations, Nathan Rothschild made a bold bet during the Battle of Waterloo in 1815 and profited on Napoleon's defeat. True or not, the story was typical of Nathan Rothschild's ability to assess the broad competitive panorama, both in the near term and into the future.

I have imagined what it would be like to interview Nathan Rothschild on the subject of intelligence, to explore the thinking behind his family's communications innovations. Here is how it might go:[1]

Mr. Rothschild, it's been a couple of centuries since your coup at the Battle of Waterloo. Can you tell me how people describe it to you?

ROTHSCHILD: As the story goes, my brothers and I had a network of correspondents located throughout Europe. Of course, we did not have cell phones at the time. Why, we did not even have telegraph.

Most versions of the story I've heard and read in newspaper accounts report that a number of these correspondents sent the message of Napoleon's defeat to me in London via carrier pigeon. In truth, we employed a speedy courier system via horse and boat. (We did not start using carrier pigeons with any regularity for another nine or ten years after the Waterloo battle.)[2]

What is true is the fact that I did hear the news of Napoleon's defeat some hours before my competition, the other bankers. While I cannot divulge all the details—even at this late date—I can tell you that we did dump our British securities on the market, making it appear as if I had heard of a Wellington defeat. My competitors saw my action, hastily gathered all their securities, and sold them as fast as they could. [Rothschild emits a muffled chuckle and reveals a slight grin of satisfaction.]

As soon as I saw the market bottom out, I bought back every piece of paper at fire-sale prices. I made a tidy profit.

Thank you, sir. May I ask you another question, regarding those messengers or couriers?

ROTHSCHILD: Certainly.

The speed. The speed in which you—and all your brothers, Amschel, Salomon, Carl, and James—received these messages is truly remarkable. Can you comment on how you built such a network? These carrier pigeons and couriers were like the e-mail of your day. Everyone had the same so-called technology. What exactly did your family do to give you such competitive advantage?

ROTHSCHILD: Your point is well taken. Let me see if I can elaborate.

You have to understand that secrecy, as well as speed, was at the heart of our success in using intelligence to our advantage.

Communications, as you call it today, was very unreliable. Postal services were slow and could be infiltrated by our rivals. That is why we were the first group to build our own private courier service throughout Europe.

It became the forerunner of a Reuters or a Bloomberg news service of today with scores of correspondents and messengers located on the ground. To ensure receiving the news of any governmental or economic upheavals where even a half day's advance knowledge could net our family a tidy fortune, we made sure to send out more than one messenger along similar routes. It was very easy, you see, for a courier along one route to become waylaid.

Proudly, I have to say, we became the de facto news service for Europe's royal houses and highly placed government officials. We were more reliable than any single country's consular network.

This is fascinating, but what if your message was intercepted?

ROTHSCHILD: This did occur. That is why we used codes wherever possible. This was part of the game.

Anything we could do to delay a message or speed the receipt of our message offered competitive advantage. For instance, a blue envelope received at the post office indicated that the exchange rate rose; a red envelope disclosed that it fell. If we used a carrier pigeon instead, a note received with "AB" meant "buy the stock," and "CD" meant "sell the stock."

Of course, none of these systems remained unique for long. Our rivals soon started imitating us. That is why we constantly had to find faster and more efficient ways of sending messages.

It's all about speed and accuracy. Isn't that what I read in your modern-day business press whenever you create new communications technology? Bandwith, encryption, and so on. That's what it's all about, isn't it?

Yes, Mr. Rothschild, that is what it's all about. I'm still confused over something else you just said. It's about the encryption and speed. Was that your insurance policy, so to speak? In other words, if you had all the speedy communications you could want, would that ensure your success?

ROTHSCHILD: Good question. The answer is basically no. Nothing can ensure success. Not speed, not accuracy. There is always risk.

I recall the time I remitted a note of payment for £100,000 to my brothers in Frankfurt, which unexpectedly flooded the market with more pound sterling than it could absorb, in turn dramatically dropping its value in the Frankfurt markets, as well as in Amsterdam. Speedy communications did not help us in this case.[3]

What I am trying to say is that even the best information, the best intelligence, cannot eliminate risk altogether.

By the same token, I have seen companies that have superb communication networks in your world today, the best technology. The problem is their low tolerance for risk. They choose not to act even when the intelligence is telling them to make a decision.

The lesson in speed is critical. Remember it. Also remember that you must get used to applying less-than-perfect intelligence. Most of the time that's all you will have. Risk and intelligence are part of the same coin. One comes with the other.

I have to ask your patience. Please clarify something for me. It appears that all this effort concerned what I would call a bet. That is, the speed, the rapid communication, even your tolerance for risk, all centered about placing your money on a single outcome. This does seem rather short-sighted. What about the larger global picture? Do you use your intelligence for looking into the future or for assessing longer-term problems or opportunities?

ROTHSCHILD: I am sorry if I misled you. My brothers and I always looked at the larger picture, at the complex machinations of governments, potential outbreaks of war elsewhere, the strength of stocks or bonds in various countries' markets. The Waterloo bet, as you call it, was actually part of a long string of events we connected together. Until Napoleon's escape from his island prison on Elba, my brothers and I were buying up stock in the Vienna and London markets. Napoleon's escape changed that move. We then became involved in helping to finance Wellington's armies.

While in the end we did not make the great fortune everyone originally thought we had, my four brothers and I created a powerful network that allowed us to see competitive activity in multiple markets at once.

We believed that peace was always better for business than war. We often used our political knowledge to advise European governments to avoid war. This was our long-term goal. Waterloo was unavoidable. It was a single incident, one that involved a series of short-term decisions. Yet all along my brothers and I were always looking beyond Waterloo. In fact, by the 1830s we essentially saw our long-term efforts help—perhaps in a small way—to bring peace throughout most of Europe.

You must understand that peace brought with it other challenges. We shifted our couriers and our network toward underwriting industry instead of armies. For example, my family supplied much of the financing for the growing pan-European railway industry.

Our thinking at the time went far beyond just financing the railways. Certainly everyone saw the railways as a more comfortable and efficient transportation system. We believed the railway system represented something far more important to the European and global economy. The railways—and all the political and market intelligence we needed to collect about them—were important because they would serve to unify and integrate regional commodity markets in coal, iron, and other products. The railroads would consolidate enormous markets.

As history recorded our story, we would certainly win by investing in the railroads themselves. Perhaps what historians did not see so clearly was that our truly great profits came from the larger investment opportunity the railroads themselves would bring to our banking houses. In effect, intelligence on the railroads was just a means to an end. That was the ultimate use of the intelligence.[4]

I hope this somewhat long-winded explanation has helped you see the bigger picture, the reason we were so intelligence hungry in the first place.

Just one more question, if I can.
ROTHSCHILD: Go ahead.

You must have been elated at the advent of the telegraph and how it could speed the dispatch of vital intelligence on a railroad investment opportunity or some other competitive opportunity. Is this true?
ROTHSCHILD: Yours is a sadly amusing observation. In reality, we were nearly despondent over the rise of the telegraph. Before the instant nature of the telegraph, our courier network reigned supreme throughout Europe. No one would receive vital information faster than the banking houses of the Rothschilds. But by the late nineteenth century, such was no longer the case. The telegraph became the great equalizer. As more information became available faster to everyone, our competitive advantage began to disappear.

If there is a lesson in all this, it is that one must always find a means of thinking ahead of one's competition, not just relying upon the speed of the messages themselves.

That was the strategic success the Rothschilds were able to accomplish. It was in our ability to piece together a complicated picture very quickly, such as with Waterloo or with the railroad, as well as tolerate the risk that came with the less-than-perfect picture we formed. Speed, risk, and analysis—these were our secret intelligence ingredients.

I am sorry if I seemed to have been preaching for a moment. I hope you found my answers helpful.

Thank you. Your answers do help a great deal. I am glad we spoke.

CLARITY THROUGH EXPERIENCE

One day, a few years ago, Warren Buffett walked into my life. This chance encounter taught me a number of essential lessons about investing and the use of intelligence. One of those lessons is that information has a tendency to repeat itself. Industries tend to follow certain immutable rules. Learn how one company within an industry operates and take those lessons with you when assessing another in the same industry.

If you can build up a sufficient "mental database" on an industry by constantly focusing and collecting information on companies in that industry, you can make spot decisions quickly. What appears to be a snap decision is really a decision based on one new piece of information added to years of prior knowledge. That is the lesson I learned when I encountered Mr. Buffett.

I met Warren Buffett indirectly through one of his investments, Jordan's Furniture, a family-run chain of Boston-area stores that are the most unusual furniture stores you will ever visit. When my wife, a friend, and I walked into the Jordan's in Natick, Massachusetts, late on a Saturday evening, we did not enter a store but rather an experience. First, a greeter welcomed us by handing each a colorful beaded necklace. Next we encountered the store's New Orleans Mardi Gras theme, including an hourly, automated show featuring animated mannequins of such jazz legends as Louis Armstrong. The store was packed at a time when most retailers were quiet or had already ended business for the day.

The entire concept of the Jordan's chain is to give the shopper an exhilarating experience. Even the company's yellow pages ad screams this message:

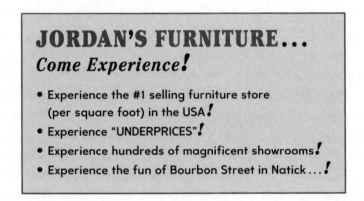

JORDAN'S FURNITURE...
Come Experience!

- Experience the #1 selling furniture store (per square foot) in the USA!
- Experience "UNDERPRICES"!
- Experience hundreds of magnificent showrooms!
- Experience the fun of Bourbon Street in Natick...!

While we bought the beds we needed, I came away wanting to know much more about this company and the people who run it. I quickly learned that some months before, Warren Buffett, through his company Berkshire Hathaway, had bought out Barry and Eliot Tatelman, the brothers who owned Jordan's Furniture.

"Jordan's Furniture is truly one of the most phenomenal and unique companies that I have ever seen," said Buffett after encountering and presenting an offer for this regional furniture company.[5] What Buffett envisioned when he entered Jordan's was a business that met all of his criteria for success. For instance, an average furniture store sold approximately $150 of mattresses per square foot. Jordan's sold $2,000 worth of mattresses per square foot. The Tatelmans' stores sold out their inventory thirteen times a year, five times the industry average. Almost without hesitation—and without reportedly looking at the company's books—Buffett made a purchase offer to the Tatelman brothers in late 1999.

At the time, Barry and Eliot Tatelman had not put their company up for sale. Yet they agreed because Berkshire Hathaway's offer gave them the money they needed for expansion and left them in control—without the Tatelmans having to consider selling stock to the public. It was a proposition that worked for both parties.

This was not the first instance of Buffett swooping down on a good deal, acting on observations, insights, and intelligence. In 1983, he had heard that the Nebraska Furniture Mart's eighty-nine-year-old owner, Rose Blumkin, was interested in selling. He had known of the store for years and was originally rebuffed by Ms. Blumkin when he approached her to buy the mart many years earlier. It was the largest furniture store of its kind in Omaha and had driven many rivals out of business, selling so low that no one could successfully compete against it.

When he approached Rose Blumkin for the second time in 1983, the exchange between the two of them was short. Buffett asked if she wanted to sell the store to him.

Mrs. B (as Blumkin was known around Omaha) said, "Yes."

"How much?" Buffett responded.

"Sixty million," she stated.

They shook hands. That was the deal. Buffett fashioned a

one-page agreement and a few days later paid her 90 percent of the agreed-upon amount—with the Blumkin family retaining a minority stake.[6]

Buffett's buying Jordan's Furniture was not an impulsive purchase. Buffett does not make impulsive purchases. Even as a nine-year-old child growing up in Omaha, he would very deliberately go to a nearby gas station to count the soda machine bottle caps tossed aside to determine the market share for different soda brands in his neighborhood. In later years, Buffett would examine and build a mental database of investment data in the same way. Investment was a discipline built upon rational sets of data. That is how Buffett looks at the numbers. Everything has a history. And generally history does repeat itself in how companies operate within the same industry.

Whether it is Rose Blumkin's or the Tatelmans' furniture store, Buffett always asks himself what would it feel like to compete against this particular company. If the answer is "tough," then he knows he has solid opportunity. This is always how he examines a potential investment.

Much of Buffett's approach to investments began with his teacher at Columbia University, Ben Graham, who taught Buffett to insist on a large gap between the price he was willing to pay for an investment and his assessment of what the stock was worth. Toward that end, Buffett constantly searched for cheap stocks, or "cigar butts," as Graham labeled them. With each cigar butt, with each undervalued investment he picked up, he learned more about the specific business. The furniture business was no exception to this disciplined information-gathering-cum-assessment approach to investing. In the retail furniture businesses he acquired, Buffett watched for evidence of a fun shopping experience as well as high inventory turnover.

At the same time, Buffett remains focused on the factors underlying success in the first place. He builds on the same data and looks for businesses that work on those same principles.

Following the Nebraska Furniture Mart purchase, he bought Utah's leading home furnishing retailer, R. C. Wiley. This is a business that had grown from $250,000 in 1954 to over $342 million in 1999.

In the Berkshire Hathaway (Buffett's publicly traded holding company) 1999 annual report, Buffett acknowledges Rose Blumkin and her family as the ones who educated him and who provided him with the foundation for his company's highly profitable furniture business:

> There's no operation in the furniture business remotely like the one assembled by Berkshire. It's fun for me and profitable for you. W. C. Fields once said, "It was a woman who drove me to drink, but unfortunately I never had the chance to thank her." I don't want to make that mistake. My thanks go to Louie, Ron and Irv Blumkin for getting me started in the furniture business and for unerringly guiding me as we have assembled the group we now have.

The Jordan's Furniture deal seemed to have happened fast, but it was the result of over twenty years of Buffett's absorbing Rose Blumkin–generated data on what makes for a successful furniture store. He is, as a rule, willing to wait until the right moment, but once he believes the timing is right he jumps in with both feet.

Berkshire Hathaway had already signaled the market about its strong interest in home furnishings. Its 1998 annual report (the year prior to the offer made to the Tatelmans) showed that $793 million of the $9.9 billion in sales came from home furnishings. Therefore, if Buffett saw a good buy, he had to act quickly. Intelligence, he knew, is only as valuable as the speed at which one acts upon it. To wait was to give others a chance to realize the same opportunity (something he apparently does not let happen too often).

SEEING THE COMPETITION
THROUGH THE EYES OF THE CUSTOMER

Recent business history suggests additional lessons about intelligence. As I explained in the previous chapter on the Internet, business intelligence is invariably the outgrowth of a business transaction; all transactions begin or end with selling to a customer or buying from a supplier; therefore, control the customer or supplier and you control the resulting intelligence.

It's exactly this type of logic, methodically executed by retail iconoclast Sam Walton and computer industry wunderkind Michael Dell, that has provided each with an enormous competitive advantage over his rivals. Piece by piece, each found a way to lock in both suppliers and customers to their business machine.

Worry more about the supply chain than about the competition, Sam and Michael suggest. Concern yourself with intelligence from suppliers and customers. They are more important than your competitors, plain and simple. Fulfill their needs and you will control the market and your rivals.

Most people think of so-called intelligence gathering (I believe you develop, not gather, intelligence) as an exercise in combing the outside world for vital information and then analyzing that information. What if you were able to turn this approach on its head? What if you could develop all the intelligence you could need by trying to control the very information environment in which you do business?

Instead of worrying exclusively about the competition, Walton and Dell decided to take control of their competitive environment by learning as much about their suppliers and their customers as possible. Arguably, Walton and Dell might claim that customer and supplier intelligence is a far more valuable commodity than competitor intelligence. This is the intelligence legacy they leave behind. This is their intelligence history lesson.

Nearly a decade ago, I recall a friend of mine, owner of a company that manufactured desk lamps, traveling back and forth to Bentonville, Arkansas, the home of Wal-Mart, as often as three times each month. Serving Wal-Mart was vital to his business. Sure, they squeezed him on price, but they bought in large volume. Wal-Mart's buyers kept him very busy, and he learned a lot about market conditions in return.

Sam Walton had been involved in retailing since the end of World War II. He had experimented with various retail styles and customer service approaches throughout his career. Most of his early stores were modeled after the traditional variety store, such as Woolworth. In 1962, he saw a new concept that changed his approach to retailing forever. The S. S. Kresge dime store chain launched a new discount store, known as Kmart. The well-organized, self-service style impressed him. He opened his own version, also in 1962, and called it by a similar-sounding name, Wal-Mart.

As I have seen with many successful entrepreneurs, Walton was an incessant collector and assessor of competitive information. He flew from store to store in his private plane and, while in the air, sized up new possible store locations. When he visited one of his stores, he always asked employees their impressions of the store and its level of customer service, and he would personally respond to any employee—among the tens of thousands—who offered a comment or idea or wrote to him about a store problem.

But Walton's real intelligence genius began with his buyers. He charged them with the responsibility of cutting out excess cost, thereby lowering the prices charged to Wal-Mart. From nearly the very beginning, Walton determinedly refused to see manufacturers' reps, cutting their commission slice out of the system.

The secret to his competitive knowledge stemmed from his need to squeeze costs and his desire to keep his customers highly satisfied. Like the Rothschilds, Walton and his Wal-Mart successors have always employed technology to both speed and control information on the market and on Wal-Mart's supply chain.

As early as 1987, Wal-Mart deployed its own Hughes satellite network. The network controlled everything from thermostat settings in each individual store to watching customer shopping patterns. By 2005, Wal-Mart had required that its top one hundred suppliers embed RFID (radio frequency identification) tags into all their products, forcing the suppliers to better track, more efficiently ship, and ultimately squeeze further costs out of the shipping and distribution of their products to Wal-Mart.[7]

All this technological control has given Wal-Mart a transparent view inside the suppliers; it has also allowed Wal-Mart to see a few steps ahead of the market. SupplierLink, Wal-Mart's hundred-terabyte-plus supply-chain database and its related extranet, is used by all Wal-Mart's *buyers,* as well as its ten thousand suppliers, to monitor sales and inventory levels in every store (outside of the Pentagon, Wal-Mart reputedly has the largest data-processing operation in the world). No longer can suppliers overstock or undersell. They have the same information and contribute to the same information pool as everyone else.

Forecasting, including predicting consumer buying habits at Wal-Mart, is a much more deliberate, accurate undertaking than it is with nearly any other company in corporate history, specifically because Wal-Mart's suppliers contribute to the intelligence mix.

One example of Wal-Mart's joined-at-the-hip knowledge of its suppliers begins with Levi Strauss & Company. Levi Strauss, the famous manufacturer of blue jeans, had fallen on hard times in the mid-1990s, with sales peaking in 1996 at $7.1 billion. Sales through fiscal year 2002 were just over $4.1 billion. Since turning to Wal-Mart in the fall of 2002, Levi Strauss has had to revamp its information technology and distribution system in order to conform to Wal-Mart's requirements. It had to rethink its entire supply chain in order to efficiently serve Wal-Mart's thirty-four-hundred-plus stores and its over one hundred million customers.

The power of control has given Wal-Mart an ability to do collaborative—and likely far more accurate—forecasting. To become as efficient as Wal-Mart required, Levi Strauss created a scanning device that would allow its own manufacturers to more accurately determine when cartons were ready to ship. It shares all this information with Wal-Mart's buyers who work with Levi Strauss executives to forecast both supply and demand into the near future. This kind of forecast gives Wal-Mart executives the ability to see more than just Levi's sales; they can also predict the market for blue jeans overall.

While Nielsen and IRI, the traditional database reporting services of store inventory and sales, work well for historical, or retrospective, market views, only Wal-Mart's information-sharing activity with its suppliers can yield truly explosive, future-cast competitive trends.

This nearly religious adherence to sharing information, which in turn reduces costs, certainly gives Wal-Mart the competitive edge but may not do the same for its suppliers. "If I look overconfident, I'm not," says David Bergen, Levi's chief information officer and the individual responsible for executing Levi Strauss's successful jumping through of Wal-Mart's informational hoops. "I'm very nervous about this change."[8]

He ought to be. After all, the knowledge that makes Wal-Mart more competitive may not do the same for its suppliers.

By controlling its suppliers, Sam Walton's intelligence legacy offers lessons to us about approaches to staying ahead of the competition by watching and collecting information on market forces other than the competitors themselves.

COMPETITOR INSIGHTS, BYTE BY BYTE

Shortly after IBM announced the sale of its personal computer division to the Chinese computer company Lenovo in late 2004, a reporter asked Michael Dell if he was concerned about mergers in the PC business. He said no, he was not worried. He could not recall a large merger in the computer business that had actually worked as promised. "We like to acquire our competitors one customer at a time," he said. It was this final statement from Dell that spoke volumes on his view of the competition and how he will attempt to outmaneuver them in the future.[9]

Michael Dell is in many ways Walton's spiritual heir, inheriting Walton's penchant for controlling market conditions, as well as absorbing vital intelligence from both suppliers and customers.

Dell Computer's rise is nothing if not meteoric. Started in Michael Dell's college dormitory in 1984, Dell has become predominant in almost every category it has entered. It has become the largest seller of personal computers and in 2000 even surpassed Sun Microsystems as the largest seller of workstations.

Like Wal-Mart, it has harnessed technology to both collect market data and reduce cost of operations. It has done so in a gargantuan fashion.

According to a fact book located on Dell's site, "Today, Dell operates one of the highest volume, most frequently visited e-Commerce Web sites in the world, with approximately half of the company's $32.1 billion in annual revenue being generated online. Dell.com ... receives an average of 9 million page views per day at 80 country sites written in 27 languages/dialects. It manages 400,000 customer transactions a month in 40 different currencies."[10]

Unlike Wal-Mart, Dell's target market is not the individual consumer; it is the corporate customer. Dell aims to sell nearly three-quarters of its computer and computer products to corporations. This makes its extranet an even more powerful tool, a force to control supplier costs as well as to harness its knowledge of market demand.

The Dell extranet has succeeded in reducing the number of suppliers by 75 percent and its inventory to no more than five days' worth—an industry low. At the same time, Dell has used its extranet with its largest corporate customers to learn in detail who their customers are, their buying patterns, and the kinds of problems they have had in corporate computing (which in turn gives Dell an intelligence jump on the solution needed).

Dell's customer reach is deep, very deep. At least ten thousand customers communicate with Dell each and every day. With such active customer participation and communication, buying patterns and trends become evident quickly. For instance, if Dell begins to see it is running short on a fifteen-inch monitor, it may begin to lower the price of the seventeen-inch monitor. This real-time customer data (perhaps only matched by the airline industry's ability to balance its load factors to fill airplanes) allows Dell to forecast accurate market demand and customer trends as far as three months into the future.

Michael Dell's drive for ultimate customer intelligence—that is, knowing what the customer needs perhaps even before the customer does—came through during a talk he gave at the giant Consumer Electronics Show in Las Vegas. "I started off like pretty much all of you as a customer and I was frustrated by the computer dealers at the time who weren't offering much in the way of service and support and at the same time has high markups . . . if you have a problem and you tell the dealer, does the dealer tell the manufacturer, does that get all the way to the guys that are designing the products?"[11]

"No" was the answer to his question. Dell's need to eliminate the "no" is what drives him to close the intelligence gap between his suppliers and his customers.

Sam Walton would have been proud.

POLITICAL AWARENESS: SCANNING INTELLIGENCE FROM MANY DIMENSIONS

The flight was about to take off. I shimmied my American frame into the European-cut economy seats on the Virgin Atlantic flight and off I went to London. The flight was packed and I was barely able to move my arms (I felt more like RoboCop than some suave international traveler). At the same time, I very much enjoyed my nearly seven-hour trip, much more so than the British Airways experience I had some months before.

It was not the seat. Seating in the economy section was pretty much the same in every airline: tight.

Nor was it necessarily the service, although I do recall the Virgin staff being friendlier and more attentive than those from British Airways. (Unfortunately, I did not have a masseuse offer to work me over as Virgin's first-class passengers get to experience.)

It was something else. It was the video screens planted in the back of each and every headrest throughout the economy cabin. While my seat was less than comfortable, the video served as a distraction between the meals, any reading I could do, and the short naps.

Imagine that: video for the price of an economy trip. Today we can all smile. Video screens are fairly common on all but the short-haul airplanes. Back then, though, they were not. This was an innovation, a Richard Branson special. To my knowledge, the only carrier at the time that used video was Singapore Airlines. In western Europe and in North America this was a first.

This story is evidence of the drive and the far-sightedness that Branson has exhibited throughout his stormy, tumultuous career. My experience also demonstrates the very broad view Branson brings to assessing any industry. It's an outsider's view.

He is an outsider and appears to like the role. In general, he prefers to enter industries where customers have very few choices. He enters as the upstart and often changes the rules by which others play (very similar to Rothschild, Walton, and Dell).

He has a long string of both business successes and failures. Virgin Records upended the recording business. He then moved into air travel, where he was successful in gaining market share against entrenched and seen-as-stuffy British Airways. His Virgin Cola never quite succeeded at winning share from the giants Pepsi and Coke. Other businesses include cell phones, Virgin-branded music and movie stores, and even a British-based rail line, Virgin Rail.

Branson also likes flying balloons in an attempt to break various world records. Whether or not he succeeds in his flights, balloon flying is perhaps a metaphor for how he views market entry into a new business. He first looks out from on high, surveys the landscape, and finds opportune spots for a landing—despite the intense competitive brush surrounding him.

Francis Aguilar, a retired Harvard Business School professor and father of the concept known as environmental scanning, would describe how Branson perceives the market as exactly that—scanning. Professor Aguilar, a quiet man, dressed in a cardigan sweater when I met him many years ago in his office, believes in the need for gathering information from a wide range of sources, including government and regulatory groups, competitors, suppliers, and academia. Aguilar sees intelligence in many dimensions. So does Branson. As Branson perceives it, both threat and opportunities can emerge from out of a dark, unexpected corner. You need to watch the ever-changing landscape in order to be ready for it. Both Aguilar and Branson agree on this intelligence philosophy.

The difference is that one teaches the idea and the other lives it. Francis Aguilar impressed me as an introspective, thoughtful individual, with a Mr. Rogers–like quiet but perceptive personality. Richard Branson, on the other hand, has been described as a showman, a P. T. Barnum, who attempts to fly hot-air balloons around the world.

His showmanship allows him to both establish a presence in a market as well as open information conduits that might be closed to others. Branson invites controversy, even revels in it. While the mayhem over one outrageous act or statement ensues, he is always watching and listening. He is scanning.

A good example of this played itself out in the early 1990s. Branson had already run Virgin Atlantic Airlines for approximately a half-dozen years when he wanted to move out of Gatwick (London's secondary and less-trafficked airport) and win gate slots at Heathrow. He also wanted to expand into Tokyo. He knew that British Airways would try to resist any expansion attempts by this relatively new, upstart airline with only four Boeing 747s to its name.

While he clearly saw his nemesis as British Airways, Branson realized that his competitive position could improve or languish if he ignored intelligence from a number of other arenas—all surrounding his expansion strategy.

According to Branson's own account, Lord King, the then chairman of British Airways, met a representative from the Rothschilds' bank (yes, from that same family who brought you the winning bet at Waterloo) for lunch in early 1991 and was reportedly "badmouthing Virgin" to the Rothschild bank. Branson was immediately concerned that news of Virgin's supposed financial troubles could cascade down to a number of influential groups, any one of whom could begin to sink Branson's airline.

Branson was watching.

His own words described the environment he must scan: "An accusation of financial weakness coming from highly placed Lord King can rapidly become a self-fulfilling prophecy, particularly when it comes from such a lofty and authoritative source as Lord King . . . Lord King's accusation of Virgin Atlantic's financial weakness had a number of key audiences."

Branson constantly watched the press. He wanted Virgin's story—not British Airways's—to reach the press first. Next, he knew he must keep his feelers out with London's bankers and financiers. Virgin had indeed run into cash problems in recent months. Branson very much needed additional financing. He also monitored the airplane manufacturers and leasing companies who might fail to extend credit to a financially distressed airline. Finally, he would have to take the pulse of the Civil Aviation Authority (CAA), the government body that would permit or refuse Virgin the additional gates it would need for the expansion.[12]

Virgin placed key people in negotiating positions with the CAA. He also used the press to his competitive advantage. The battle between British Airways and Virgin entered the public arena at the end of January 1991. Virgin was painted as the underdog being assaulted by the far larger rival, British Airways.

Branson won this particular battle, in what was (and is) a long, protracted war. By the end of January, the CAA granted Virgin access to Heathrow and ordered British Airways to turn over four landing slots to Virgin at Tokyo's Narita Airport.

This was a multidimensional battle, requiring Branson to look at a threat from a number of angles.

I have seen too many businesspeople discuss the subject of intelligence and interpret it as just "competitor intelligence," that is, intelligence only about and from your rivals. Wrong, wrong, wrong. Intelligence, when it provides true competitive advantage, emanates from many sources, from many perspectives.

If there is any history lesson here from Rothschild, Buffett, Walton, Dell, and Branson, it is this: It does not matter whether you use carrier pigeons or airplanes, or you walk on the ground and look around. Competitive threats and opportunities are always present and may reveal themselves through the many actors in your business drama. Competitors, suppliers, new entrants, and government regulators are all participants in your marketplace.

Act quickly, learn from past performance, and look at all the other forces in your market, not just at your rivals. Most important, know who your targets are and watch them.

The past masters of competitive intelligence would offer you four pieces of advice:

> *Act on critical intelligence with speed.*—Nathan Rothschild
>
> *You will need less information if you build on past experience.*—Warren Buffett
>
> *See your competitors through the eyes of your customers— probably the clearest view of all.*—Sam Walton and Michael Dell
>
> *Scan the market from all dimensions, including the political one.*—Richard Branson

Wonderful advice if you're a business genius, some of you might say. What about the rest of us, though, the mere mortals in the business realm? There are very few Bransons or Buffetts among us. How do we adopt global lessons from these sometimes swashbuckling mega entrepreneurs to our own lives? How do product managers, small business owners, marketing managers, company scientists, purchasing managers, and everyone else find ways to live a life of competitive clarity? By working the essentials of competitive intelligence into your everyday life—the subject of the next chapter.

CHAPTER 8

DAY TO DAY

Integrating Intelligence with Your Work

Some people are just hard-wired for intelligence. Intelligence—seeing through and ahead of your competition—is part of their makeup. The word "intelligence" may not be in their daily lexicon, but they know its meaning nevertheless. They apply intelligence to achieve competitive advantage. Curiously, though, they achieve their results without necessarily moving bureaucratic mountains, without reengineering an entire corporation, without sucking away large budget dollars. Intelligence is part of their daily lives. It makes them successful. It makes their companies more competitive. When intelligence is part of your life, it's a win-win for everyone, for you and for your company.

A CEO such as Herb Baum has strengthened company after company that he's headed by breaking down internal intelligence barriers. Mavericks like T. Boone Pickens, former corporate raider and oil and gas millionaire, understand the value of gathering information at street level. Gary Roush, once Corning's corporate marketing manager and internal Mr. Fix-It, has helped his organization realize that valuable pieces of intelligence are very close by and shows them how to find it. Tom Berkel, formerly a financial expert at Best Foods, has learned how to manage the information gathering of others without stepping over ethical or legal bounds. Dale Fehringer, onetime Visa International vice president of market intelligence, knows how to let data simmer and develop to achieve that competitive insight, that "aha!"

Not all their stories are dramatic; not all are cliff-hangers. These individuals use intelligence as a bricklayer does a brick. They build competitive advantage, one piece of intelligence at a time. As in life, success is often gradual. Yet success—no matter if it takes a month, a year, or more—is still success. For Baum, Pickens, Roush, Ferhinger, and Berkel, that is the magic of intelligence. Each of them has a lesson to teach us.

SEEKING TRANSPARENCY

"A t'ing of beauty," the contractor declared as he asked us to turn around and look at his handiwork, at the newly remodeled kitchen he had just finished for us. It was remarkable. He squeezed in every cabinet, every appliance into a very small space. We could see it all. Nothing was hidden. All was transparent, every pot, every dish. We could find it all, and everything was within easy reach. Yes, it was a thing of beauty. Not so with many companies.

Transparency (or the lack of) is the most significant problem I encounter in assessing the competitive preparedness of companies. Instead of pots and pans, it's the information that managers can't find. Someone has it, but no one seems to know who.

A couple of years ago, I had nearly completed a project to tune up a company's intelligence process when I happened to drop by unannounced into the CEO's office. The five-minute conversation I had with the CEO revealed a shocking problem, a potential intelligence nightmare that overshadowed some of the advice we were about to dispense to management.

The company, a producer of enterprise software, was a fast-moving operation, constantly having to adjust how it executed on its strategy in a very rapidly changing market. I asked the CEO to tell me his top four or five strategic priorities for the company. He did without delay. I scribbled these down.

Then I decided to do something with this list. I removed the CEO's name from any association with this list and jumbled the order. Over the following week, I asked approximately two dozen senior managers to rank this list in order of importance. No problem. Everyone responded very quickly.

The shock lay with the type of response I received. Fewer than 40 percent of those who answered got it right. More than 60 percent ranked the strategic priorities in an order different from the CEO. Outrageous. In some cases, individuals completely reversed priorities. And most of these people see and speak to the CEO each and every day.

Sure, the office interior itself was modern and sleek. Most offices had glass walls so everyone could see everyone else. This was open-office architecture. Ironically, management's understanding of its own strategic priorities, knowing what information was most critical to the competitiveness of this business, was anything but transparent.

Lack of transparency can mean that management doesn't see or doesn't want to see important, vital competitive information. At times this can lead to crisis.

For one company I worked with, the flow of vital intelligence actually ground to a halt, the CEO confided. It was a story with a nearly fatal outcome. Approximately one year earlier, a purchasing manager was approached by a salesman from a key supplier—in fact, a sole-source supplier. The salesman was very willing to cut his prices considerably to win a sale. When the purchasing manager asked the supplier's rep why he was suddenly so generous, he disclosed that his company was having cash-flow problems, persistent cash-flow problems. The salesman said no more and left the buyer with the offer on the table.

As soon as the buyer heard this, he tried to get managers to listen. No one did. They did not consider this a serious news item and essentially ignored it. After all, they thought, this was just purchasing giving us the information.

Nine months later, the *Wall Street Journal* broke the news that this supplier's holding company reported severe losses and would have to divest itself of a number of subsidiaries to raise cash. Now the management team listened and became alarmed. They pulled out all stops to find out the fate of this precious supplier with technology that could not be easily reproduced.

The answer came quickly. It was true that the holding company would have to divest, but it assured the client that this particular supplier was not on the block. Pure luck saved management from losing out because of valid intelligence, intelligence it had in its possession nearly a year earlier.

This story is a lesson in intelligence transparency, or lack thereof. The intelligence was there, inside the company, but it was not believed and therefore not "seen."

Transparency is Herb Baum's secret strategic weapon. There's no doubt that Baum has marketing moxie. But lots of marketing experts and managers have that. What he also has is a personality and a drive to open up information channels in a company to allow critical intelligence to flow from outside in as well as from inside and within a company. He cannot stand bureaucratic barriers, particularly when they blind him. When he first joined Dial Corporation, a leading soap and detergent company, as CEO in 2000, he described the climate within the corporation as oppressive. Since then, he has opened up the organization to sharing information of all kinds. His three-times-a-month "Hot Dogs with Herb," where he meets with a cross-section of the organization, and his think-tank strategy sessions, encourage employees from across the organization to share data—without fear. Baum has been successful, perhaps too successful. He jokingly notes that this open-door policy has succeeded to the point where he once received an e-mail request to fix bathroom problems in the accounting department and even a complaint about a dead bird found outside Dial's headquarters that needed to be removed.

Perhaps Baum's greatest achievement in his marketing career—and the one that best demonstrates the power of intelligence transparency—took place over two decades ago in 1981 when, as president of Campbell Soup USA, he launched what is now one of Campbell's megaproducts, Prego spaghetti sauce.

The U.S. pasta sauce market is valued at $1.5 billion.[1] It's a staple found in nearly every household. Back in the late 1970s, that was not the case. Pasta sauce was a home-grown market mostly manufactured by local or regional producers. By the late 1970s, Ragú, first introduced in 1946 (now owned by Unilever), became popular and began to catch the interest of large national food companies, such as Campbell. Today Campbell's Prego Traditional sauce alone sells over $250 million each year, and there exists over twenty-five other varieties of Prego, from Mini Meatball to Three Cheese.

Back in the 1970s and early 1980s, Campbell Soup USA was a sleepy, old-line, mostly family-controlled company. Joseph Campbell founded it in Camden, New Jersey, in 1869. The company invented condensed soup in 1897 and parlayed its soup products into an American industry icon.

Yet the company did not launch many new product classes until Baum introduced Prego in 1981, nearly a century later. Camden itself was an economically depressed town in those years. Following World War II, traditional manufacturing businesses began to close their doors with much of the middle class leaving town as well. Three days of rioting and looting in August 1971 acted as a catalyst, speeding the urban decay in Camden. Shuttered buildings and a rising crime rate became this city's symbols. Although located just across the river from cosmopolitan Philadelphia, Camden, New Jersey, was in its own economically depressed cocoon. This was Campbell Soup's backyard, front yard, its panorama. Look outside Campbell's headquarters and it was difficult to see what was really happening in the market.

Imagine Baum's challenge. He had to boost this company's

ability to see outside itself and to inject critical intelligence into Campbell at this time if he was going to overtake Ragú early in the race.

It turned out that around 1980 Campbell Soup had just bought a tomato paste plant in Davis, California, and was now confronted with excess capacity it needed to fill. This gave Campbell capacity, but capacity for what?

According to Tony Adams, Baum's marketing research chief, tomato paste was considered a commodity item. Campbell had to move up the value chain. Its management did not want to fight for pennies in the marketplace. What could Campbell do with its tomato products, other than produce more soup?

Both Adams and Baum knew they had to consider a higher-margin product, certainly one with a higher price point than tomato paste. Adams thought through the problem and constructed a value chain for Baum, illustrating which type of product would generate the greatest return for Campbell. "We started with tomato paste (a commodity), then added value," Adams says, in describing how he and Baum built the value chain proposition. "That took us to [higher value] tomato juice, to ketchup (more profit there), and become a Hunt's and Del Monte. Finally, at the end of the pipeline, you come up with [highest value] spaghetti sauce. At the time, this category was dominated by Ragú. When we talked with consumers, they were pretty happy with Ragú."[2]

The fact that consumers already found a satisfactory product in Ragú did not deter Baum or Adams. It challenged them. It fired up their desire to trump the entrenched rival.

Yet Baum knew that there is a large gap between recognizing a market opportunity and defeating an ever-growing competitor.

Baum and Adams also knew that no one knew more about mass production and distribution of tomato-based products than did Campbell.

One thing could have stood in his way to success: inertia. Once a company has achieved market dominance in soup, what is left to do, after all? At least that was the thinking, in part. Herb Baum needed to supercharge the information flow within Campbell; he needed to gather data quickly and develop the necessary intelligence. Ragú was moving quickly. Besides, who knew who else might be entering the fray, perhaps usurping Campbell's chance at catching up to or surpassing Ragú.

That is when the duo of Adams and Baum created what they called the Prego war room, a place where the product management team could meet, surrounding themselves with market data and competitive knowledge. No longer would the product team have to worry about lost information or rabbit warrens of hard-to-find data. It was all there. The competitive world outside of Camden was suddenly there and very transparent.

Nothing was held back, nothing.

The team met once a week. Baum instructed that all the rivals' ads be placed on the walls. They reviewed everyone's sales by region. All that was posted in the room as well.

Marketing, strategy, tactics, advertising messages. This was no exercise. In Baum's view, this was central command, the core of Campbell's brain trust that would launch a Campbell-branded sauce that would out-Ragú Ragú.

This group developed eighty-five promises, promises of how much better Prego was than the competitors' products. The focus groups, market research, and competitors' sales tactics resulted in

Campbell's promising consumers "the most authentic Italian . . . imported spices from Italy . . . Tastes like homemade," and "Rich with little herbs and spices that you can see." These slogans then translated into advertisements, which showed Prego as resting on top of a plate of spaghetti, while the rival's product just dripped right through to the bottom of the plate.

"We took a panzer division view of the market," says Baum. "We grew the category to about 25 percent of the market . . . If we had followed our instincts we would have only had 10 percent of the market. You felt the war room. It gave you a dynamic, an excitement. You could see the ads on the wall, the competitive packaging. We talked about the competition market by market."

Baum's voice even now rings with excitement when he recalls the intellectual birth of this product. "It became contagious and an obsession to succeed. They were not chummy meetings. There were a lot of battles, verbal battles on which markets and which market, level of advertising, deal structure. All the factions were represented, advertising, market research, manufacturing, R&D."

At Campbell Soup, immersion combined with transparency truly did drive revelation. Transparency—not serendipity—gave the team the insight that led to a 25 percent market share.

A double irony here. I remember walking around the Campbell buildings, a combination of gray-walled, deck paint–filled hallways with little glass. It all seemed like a maze. Contrast this to the software company above with its glass-walled offices. Campbell had achieved transparency in a facility that was nearly opaque. The software company with all its open office architecture was an intelligence black box.

Baum's lesson to all of us: Transparency does not just happen and it's not the product of architecture alone. You need to direct intelligence, to give people a place to send it and to provide a purpose. You need to direct it. You need to find places, portals—such as a war room—where all becomes visible.

For Tony Adams and Herb Baum of Campbell Soup, the pressure cooker atmosphere worked best. Hence, they created a war room. By locking all the principals in one room, by forcing those with the problem to confront one another—sales, marketing, promotion, manufacturing—they built up and tore down questions in front of one another, until they derived questions that made sense. These questions were ultimately the ones whose answers led to product formulation and promotional tactics that allowed Campbell to capture double-digit market share in this new market.

ONLY THREE PHONE CALLS AWAY . . .
SIX DEGREES OF PREPARATION

"I can find out anything within two to three phone calls." Gary Roush has been saying this for nearly two decades. As if to prove his point that anyone looking—truly looking—for vital information can find it, anywhere in the world, he told a story that occurred a few years ago. It all started with an insignia ring.[3]

Gary Roush, formerly of Corning, spent nearly a decade teaching analysts, product managers, marketers, and engineers throughout Corning this most elemental of intelligence facts: You are only a few steps away from any answer you seek.

Roush learned the "secrets" of Schott Glas and other competitors by being able to locate just the right individuals with as few as three phone calls.

This sounded very simple, almost too simple. Roush wasn't trying to convince me or anyone else that any single individual would have the entire answer to a competitive question. Most of these questions often encompass dozens of smaller questions, each of which in turn require an answer. So what Gary Roush was trying to accomplish all those years at Corning was to teach his constituents, those engineers (and Corning has lots of engineers), that they needed to understand the power of global networks—people networks.

Gary Roush has worked hard during his entire career at Corning to fight off the creation of blind spots by constantly looking around, constantly double-checking his competitive landscape. He wanted others to understand that just as they could solve an engineering problem by working in groups, they could also work through a strategic question.

Gary's training for his job as head of Corning's intelligence effort seemed unusual or even at odds with the strategic analysis he had to perform. Aside from working in Corning's ceramics division and learning manufacturing techniques, he was also a helicopter pilot during the Vietnam War.

Roush did not necessarily come by this "360-degree" capability naturally. It was a habit that grew on him, a habit that emerged out of experiences he had during the Vietnam War. A helicopter pilot, according to Roush, has a difficult, mentally taxing job, even during peacetime. But during war, in combat conditions, he learned how important it was to look around.

"To fly helicopters you have to be a brooding kind of person and skeptical and always expect something to go wrong." Roush chose his words very carefully in describing the lessons he learned over three decades ago. "You're always looking around at what's happening to you. A helicopter is aerodynamically unstable, unlike a plane, which is dynamically stable . . . You can never relax."

Roush's discovery of Schott's pricing tactics (see chapter 2) resulted from his hypersensitive need to look around and see the entire competitive landscape, how the rival is behaving in various markets. Had he just examined the cooktop sector alone and not assessed the revenue and tactics in Schott's other business units, he would never have uncovered Schott's overall pricing strategy.

Rather than beat this point to death, he decided to tell a story, a remarkable story. His story was about a military ring, a keepsake lost to a family. The story covers thousands of miles and over three decades in time. Yet Gary solved the mystery with only three phone calls.

In the summer of 2001, a hiker found a military insignia ring on a dusty roadside in Nova Scotia, Canada. The finder, seeing the U.S. Army helicopter unit insignia, called the U.S. consulate in Halifax. The ring was inscribed with the name Joe Vad. No one by that name lived in Halifax.

Phone call 1: That same day, a navy lieutenant commander assigned to the consulate talked to the Web master of the U.S. Army Web site at the Pentagon. He told the commander to contact Gary Roush because Roush, a Vietnam helicopter pilot himself, maintains contact with former Vietnam helicopter pilots all over the world.

That day, Roush tried to locate Joe Vad. "I looked up Joe Vad in this database and saw that in 1968 a Joe Vad went to flight school and that he had a social security number. I also found that he was killed in Vietnam in 1969."

Phone call 2: Roush called the commander back the next day and told him that Joe Vad had died but that he would place his name on listservs, or Internet distribution lists. The following day, only two days and two contacts later, Gary received an e-mail saying a Hugh Mills wrote a book about Vietnam helicopter pilots; the book was dedicated to Joe Vad.

Phone call 3: Roush called the author, who told him that Joe Vad's wife and daughter were living in Halifax. Roush called the daughter, who informed him that her apartment had been burglarized a few months before. The ring, she said, was the only item not replaceable. She thanked him for his efforts.

This is the end of a story but the beginning of a lesson. Two days and five contacts (but only three phone calls for Gary) later, the connections were complete. Mystery solved. From Halifax to Vietnam to Washington, D.C., to Corning, back to Halifax. This is a powerful intelligence story. The lesson: No information can hide for long and when discovered is available to anyone.

Gary Roush's three-phone-call principle is really based on a 1967 study performed by Harvard and Yale sociologist Stanley Milgram. His experiment involved sending approximately three hundred letters to randomly selected residents in Omaha, Nebraska. He asked each recipient to use his or her personal network of friends and contacts to reach one individual identified in his letter who was located in Boston. Milgram discovered that of the sixty chains that ultimately reached the Boston target, it took approximately six steps. From this modest test, the six degrees of separation entered popular folklore. No one on earth, dictates this Harvard experiment, is more than six points of contact from anyone else.

The challenge is applying the six degrees of separation to the corporate intelligence process.

During one of my competitive intelligence courses, I discuss the power of an organized intelligence program. When in front of a U.S. audience, I typically ask the students at the course's outset, "How many of you directly know the president of the United States?" (Elsewhere in the world, I would ask a similar question about a prime minister or another head of state.) Almost no one answers yes. Yet when I ask, "How many of you know someone who knows the president?" I receive upward of one-third of the class answering in the affirmative. I challenge the students: Can you believe that so many of you are so close to the highest-ranking politician in the country?

There is a power in personal connections. Those who work full time in competitive intelligence viscerally know this but do not always act upon this very human dynamic. Swivel away from the computer and toward the telephone. Three phone calls may be far more effective than scores of clicks.

Roush had built a world-class intelligence process throughout the company in the late 1980s, long before competitive or business intelligence became a popular phrase. Roush is a builder, a developer of connections. Development seems to be in his blood. His past positions have involved product development, market development, business development, and development of the intelligence process at Corning.

He believes, much as Professor Milgram did, that everyone is connected to everyone else. Not just allowing serendipity to guide his efforts, Roush planned Corning's intelligence process. As Corning's intelligence chief, he knew he needed to create a catalyst to encourage the information flow.

Corning is geographically isolated. Roush has called Corning's rural location "Happy Valley," noting its physical isolation from the major cities. He knew that in his role as developer of an intelligence process at Corning, he would need to find ways to make these connections to the outside world. His motivating mantra of "just three phone calls" became the building blocks upon which he spread his intelligence habit around the entire corporation.

Nearly every day at Corning one could find Gary walking and talking to individuals throughout the company to gather different perspectives on a competitive issue. He would speak to people in purchasing, sales, and engineering. Although he helped create the corporate marketing·function, he did not see his position as wearing a tie and jacket and occupying a quiet office. He spent his career at Corning building information bridges to ensure he would always receive critical intelligence from every angle.

By the time Roush retired from Corning, he had imbued dozens of others at Corning with his "look around," just-three-calls-will-do-it habit.

THINK ABOUT MARS AND BEAN COUNTING

Two very different news items I saw recently spoke volumes of the need for even the greatest strategic thinker to see the competitive landscape from the ground up—and not exclusively from the rarefied atmosphere of the boardroom, staring at bar graphs on a screen.

In 2004, NASA successfully landed two robotic rovers on the surface of Mars. One of the main goals for these remote-controlled machines was to find evidence of life on Mars. As of this writing, the robots had turned over and drilled into Martian soil, examining each discovery closely with its sensors. The images returned to NASA gave ample evidence of erosion and sediment that could only be the product of a water-filled environment sometime in the geologic history of Mars.

But it was Dr. Christopher Chyba's comments that struck my intelligence chords. Dr. Chyba is an astrobiologist at the SETI Institute in California. SETI (Search for Extraterrestrial Intelligence) is the organization charged with finding life elsewhere in the universe.

"People have been talking about wet Mars for a long time," Dr. Chyba said. "There's nothing like actually having data. It's one thing to talk about it based on models and photographs. It's another thing to be on the surface and have evidence on the surface that Mars was wet. That's an exciting step."[4]

Hard evidence excites, it provokes, it confirms. As the scientist stated, information gathered from a distance is often scattered and based on too much speculation. The same analysis-from-a-distance can occur in boardroom discussions, where strategists may overanalyze speculative survey data on a market, sometimes using that data to explain very specific competitive activity. Using data collected from a distance can provoke great leaps of thought but may miss its mark in the real world. This was the first news item.

The second news report was entirely different. It had to do with coffee beans and a man who counts them in Brazil. Leon Yallouz, a former U.S. Department of Agriculture analyst, based out of Rio de Janeiro, is a leading authority on Brazil's coffee crop. A Cairo University–educated agronomist, his family moved to Brazil in the late 1950s where he soon began his work.

He drives over twenty thousand miles a year in his car, visiting coffee fields throughout the country. What does he look for? He examines the soil and looks for signs of frost and weevils. He counts the blossoms, the number of ripened beans, unripened beans, and those that are harvested, averaging the number per tree. By estimating the planting area and multiplying by his average yield, he derives total production numbers.

His estimates have moved markets quite dramatically. One assessment drove world coffee prices down by 7 percent. Another time, in 1975, he contradicted the official Brazilian government claim of widespread devastation to Brazil's coffee crops, which sent the price of coffee up approximately 500 percent. Through his regular information gathering of coffee crop data, he issued a public statement that contradicted Brazil's official estimates, nearly sparking an international incident.

One official, commenting on Brazil's attempts at improving its forecasting accuracy through the recent use of satellite photography, had this to say about Leon Yallouz and his penchant for looking at the ground-level details: "With luck, they'll get half as close to the truth as Leon."[5]

Bean counters—don't knock them. They are smart, street-savvy analysts whose ground-level information informs their ability to see the big, strategic picture.

Every company needs the bean counters who know and understand the information they collect. Not a pejorative in the least, a bean counter from an intelligence perspective is the lifeblood of management decision making. You can find bean counters in sales, finance, purchasing, customer service, and product management. It's less the function in which you find a bean counter that's important than it is how companies use the insight they bring that is critical.

One man, so much control. He exerts this control because his customers know he understands the market, down to each and every coffee bean. His bean counting, plus his knowing what the tabulations mean, make Mr. Yallouz an invaluable intelligence asset.

There is no substitute for direct contact with the data, and no one I spoke with exhibits this habit more than does T. Boone Pickens.

A few years ago, I had a conversation with T. Boone Pickens, the founder of Mesa Petroleum, onetime corporate raider by some accounts, investor's hero by other accounts. Born and raised in Texas, he is a geologist by training and an entrepreneur and risk taker by temperament. He, too, is a bean counter by nature and by practice.

T. Boone Pickens is a man of the field. He's a person who absorbs his competitive knowledge from the world outside his office. Pickens must experience his data, not receive it secondhand from printouts or analyst interpretations. He launched Mesa, an independent producer of natural gas and oil, in 1956 and grew the company to become one of the largest of its kind in the United States. In the 1980s, T. Boone Pickens took his knowledge of the oil and gas industry and tried to acquire industry giants such as Diamond Shamrock and Phillips Petroleum.

No matter how big the business deal, Pickens needs to feel and smell his market opportunity. Even in his earliest days on the oil rigs, gathering critical information on a rival's rig meant observation, firsthand observation. As you read in chapter 1, Pickens continues to apply the lessons he learned in his early days of watching the number of joints of drill pipe his competitor sank into a prospective well, thereby estimating the rival's drilling costs.

Like Leon Yallouz, T. Boone Pickens was always counting. Even when he was assessing the depressed petroleum industry in the early 1980s, he used his counting to draw vast market conclusions and gain competitive advantage. At one investor conference, he predicted a slow industry recovery. This time, he based his assessment not on the length of drill pipe but on the number of rigs.

"With the rig count down to 2,107 rigs this week from 4,531 rigs in December 1981," he reviewed, "drilling activities have slowed." He directly (and correctly) gauged slow economic recovery on the available rig count and the cost of finding oil. The remainder of the talk heard him itemize specific investments in oil exploration, the costs involved in each well.[6]

Oil rigs. Beans. It's all the same.

Now in his midseventies, Mr. Pickens is still in business—in as many as a half-dozen businesses—and still has interest in acquisitions in the energy sector. In recent years, after he was forced out of Mesa, the company he owned and from which he conducted his aggressive acquisition strategies in the 1980s, he has far from retired. He owns water rights in Texas, runs a quail farm, buys and operates a number of ranches, owns and runs a natural gas fuel business on the West Coast, runs a restaurant services business, and even participates in drilling a few oil wells.

In his water business, he is again counting and cajoling. Mesa Water is his venture to tap into the Ogallala Aquifer, located near his ranch and one of the world's largest underground reservoirs, and deliver water to cities such as Dallas, San Antonio, and El Paso. Again, he is on the ground negotiating with ranchers and landowners for rights to tap into the water table and run pipes from beneath their properties. At last count, he has permits for drilling 124 wells.

Pickens has a strong and proven instinct. What he sees on the ground he translates into business opportunity, often far ahead of market demand. Water is the next big market opportunity, claims Pickens. He can feel it because he's on the ground, sniffing around.

"When I went to Canada in 1957, I saw all these wonderful prospects. I saw wells that had been drilled and plugged—no market. And I said, 'Well, by golly, if I can find the gas, surely I can find the market.' And here I think it's the same thing. You've got the water. There is a market and you are going to get it to them."[7]

With Mesa, he recognized a pent-up demand for natural gas. He sees the same market prospects for water buried far beneath the ground.

Beans, rigs, and wells. It's all the same to Pickens. It's all ground-level data, the source of intelligence. He can see the market far more clearly at this level than most businesspeople can at any altitude.

LET THE DATA COOK

I walked into the Massachusetts General Hospital intent on donating blood for a friend who needed a transfusion. The receptionist in the main lobby directed me to a room far to the rear of the central hospital corridor. I walked in and was told that the type of direct donation I wanted to give takes place in a different lab. The nurse pointed me to a room upstairs. Turning around, I took the elevator up a few flights and entered the other lab. It also was the wrong place, it turned out, and I was directed to yet another facility in the hospital. After nearly one hour, I finally located the right lab.

Exasperated over the poor information and apparent bureaucracy, I turned to the first nurse I saw and in a very tense tone of voice nearly commanded her to take my blood.

"Slow down," she calmly responded.

She shook her head as she applied a tourniquet to my arm to find the vein. "This is the microwave age. Everything has to happen so fast. Slow down," she admonished me.

Indeed she was right. She told me to slow down and not let the hyperspeed technology dictate how we act. Slow down your life, look around, and take a deep breath, she advised.

It sounds like sane, sensible, and altogether trite advice. Maybe so, but when it comes to absorbing thousands of pieces of data on a market and making sense out of that data set, a lot of people just don't have the patience. They rush to look for the answer, pushing aside much of the information in favor of the quick hit—a hit or answer that may never come.

The "microwave age" advice swims through my head even

today. Seeing the profound insights that is intelligence often takes time to form. You can't rush it. Trying to do so is usually self-defeating. Some of the most difficult assignments take hundreds of hours of concerted analytical effort before you can offer valid assessment.

Dale Fehringer is a patient man, thoughtful and methodical. With Dale you don't see a microwave; you see a broth slowly simmering in a pot over a low flame.

You would expect that the former vice president of marketing intelligence at Visa International, in charge of his company's strategic analysis efforts, to be a hard-charging, take-no-prisoners, type A personality. Dale is dedicated and focused but willing to bide his time until the answer emerges whole and intact, an answer that makes sense. He is willing to let the data stew and blend in his mind until the competitive logic appears.

During the mid-1990s, one of Visa's competitors had just launched a new credit card product in Asia. In trying to interpret the rival's rollout strategy, Dale and his team could not detect a pattern. It seemed like the rival's target market kept shifting, as did the features offered.

As a matter of habit, Dale printed out every press release, every news clipping on the rival and its Asian Pacific activity that he could find. Before long, he had filled a binder with hundreds of these news items.

As he had done many times before, he accumulated the information, expecting that at some point he would see a pattern, a strategic common link among all the news items. Then, one evening some weeks into the project, he dragged this fat binder home. He sat down at the dining-room table and reviewed each article, one by one, looking for that mysterious pattern.

Flipping through the pile a second time, he noticed an odd news report. "I had read a small item, a small mention in one clipping, originally dismissing it—knowing I had read it once before," he recalled. The article mentioned that the rival chose to shape its credit card differently for each country it entered in that region. "In fact that was the pattern, the shifting features . . . It was a small thing but I just ignored it the first time I read it. The changing features were the pattern I was looking for, originally."[8]

He then spent the next couple of hours around his dining-room table, starting from the beginning of the binder. Slowly, methodically, he picked out mentions of this approach from other news reports. Like dots in the Seurat impressionist painting, with each small piece of evidence littered throughout his binder, the competitor's logic and strategy took shape.

One news report out of Hong Kong, for example, described how the rival's marketing managers actually challenged people on the street to pull out their existing credit card, asking them who issued it to them and the card's interest rate. The marketing reps would then ask, "If you could design your own card, what features would you like? Low fee? Mileage?"

He now saw the rival's approach very clearly. He had his "aha!"

In today's credit card market, we almost expect credit card companies to customize cards to our particular lifestyle and needs. Back then it was a novelty.

Dale took his newfound insight and reviewed his findings with Visa's product managers. Visa redesigned its cards, adopting a similar approach to customizing the products for various markets and consumer segments.

Mix some data, let it simmer, and eventually intelligence will emerge. Don't rush it. Do not expect the intelligence to land in your lap, nice and neatly tied in a bow. His experience is a lesson for us all. Let it cook.

WATCH FOR THE COWBOYS!

T. Boone Pickens, Warren Buffett, and Dale Fehringer all need other sets of eyes and ears, other representatives to listen and see around the marketplace. At the same time, they need to ensure they collect the information in a legal and ethical manner. To do otherwise would place their entire enterprise in jeopardy. The individuals who manage and control their information gatherers are like orchestra conductors. Tom Berkel is one of those conductors. He, too, has lessons to teach us.

One of the greatest challenges in gathering information on a rival is knowing the difference between an activity that is simply aggressive and one that becomes unethical or illegal. In a short survey I conducted in 2001 on this topic, I learned that what is normal on one side of the ocean may be unethical on the other. For multinational companies that employ people from around the world, establishing any kind of intelligence norm can become quite a challenge.

"You are attending a trade show. You take off your badge that identifies you as a competitor," I challenged the survey participants, "and you then approach a booth at the exhibition. You tell the representative you have an interest in the product." I then asked each of the respondents to let me know whether or not such behavior was normal, aggressive, unethical, or illegal. They have four choices.

Nearly the same percentage of Europeans (56%) thought the behavior normal, while those from North America (50%) thought it leaned toward unethical. When I called some of the respondents after the survey, the Europeans explained that this was normal behavior for their industry for the types of trade shows they attend.[9]

Industry, I discovered, can make a big difference in how people feel about information gathering. Technology companies tend to encourage more aggressive tactics, while banks, as you might expect, promote more conservative, so-called safe approaches to collecting information.

The intelligence orchestra conductor needs to understand the quirkiness and subtleties that underlie any company information gathering effort. You want your salespeople to sell, but at the same time you want to hear what the market has to say and what the competitors are doing in that market. The same goes for your scientists, your marketing reps, and all other employees who are in touch with the market. At the same time, it's all a balancing act for the orchestra conductor.

Just imagine the repercussions for a company when information gathering spins out of control.

Every few years, a spectacular corporate intelligence "oops!" splashes onto the front pages of newspapers around the world. Long before the Enron, WorldCom, and Andersen accounting scandals of 2002, information and trade-secret theft earned a lot of front-page tabloid ink. In late 2001, Procter & Gamble (P&G)

allegedly confessed to Unilever that it had inappropriately (and possibly illegally) obtained information on its hair-care business during the spring of 2001. The case never made it to court, but P&G was suitably embarrassed and offered some undisclosed concessions to its rival for this legal-ethical breach.

"While P&G says the company broke no laws, a company spokeswoman says that activities undertaken by operatives hired by P&G 'violated our strict guidelines regarding our business policies,' " reported *Fortune* magazine.[10]

P&G may not have actually broken the letter of the law, but it certainly appeared to violate the spirit of the law. As soon as P&G's management discovered the activity, it ordered it stopped in April 2001. In fact, P&G settled the case out of court some weeks later, reportedly agreeing on a cash settlement. It turned over documents to Unilever, fired three employees, and agreed not to use the information in its business.[11]

These horror stories usually begin with an intelligence cowboy.

"I used to grade people," said Tom Berkel, a former brand controller at Best Foods (now owned by Unilever) and the person who managed the competitive intelligence activities for the company's mayonnaise, starches, and syrups. Berkel had built a network of contacts throughout the marketplace. These contacts included some Best Foods employees. He gave each a label, according to ability and disposition: "Occasionals" were those individuals who would give you something but not on a regular basis. "Bread and butter" types would want to pass along information on a fairly regular basis. "Cowboys" went off on their own, not telling you where they were going or what questions they would ask. Berkel was most nervous about using cowboys.[12]

"We tried to rein these people in," he said. He was nervous about these cowboys stepping over the line, literally trespassing or otherwise obtaining information under false pretense.

Overzealousness can be a problem. Berkel recalled one Best Foods employee who wanted to hang around a rival's plant for a couple of days, watching and waiting to see if certain exhaust fans would start up (implying production activity). He did this on his own time. "He waited to see if the exhaust fans started up," Berkel recalls. "He learned that the plant was not a continuous process and that they shut it down in the evenings."

The information had only marginal value to his strategy group, but had the employee trespassed, which was Berkel's chief concern, he could have placed Best Foods at risk for no good reason. This was Berkel's constant balancing act: Push and encourage them to gather, but make sure they also understand the limits.

Berkel said that most were harmless but nevertheless potentially dangerous—if only for the language they used. He recalls that another cowboy told him that he and his colleague did a "drive-by shooting." The cowboy reportedly drove the car while a colleague named Fred "took a couple of pictures." While Berkel realized that the cowboy and Fred had not truly violated anything, this kind of unchecked behavior and the language used in association with it could potentially lead to trouble.

Rogue information-interpreters are as dangerous as the collectors themselves. A chief corporate counsel for a Fortune 500 company once told me that one of his aggressive analysts decided to insert the words "surreptitious" and "dominate" into an intelligence assessment of a far smaller rival. That rival somehow received a copy of the report and filed suit against our client, claiming antitrust violation. For after all, said the plaintiff, the report does say "dominate" and "surreptitious." In truth, this was a well-researched report, containing hard-won but honestly obtained information. Yet it was the cowboylike words that sent the defendant into court for a few years until it proved its innocence.

Ashish Nanda, a professor who lectures on the management of professional services firms at the Harvard Business School, has his own definition of behavior employees must respect when collecting information on competition. He describes the distinction as the difference between crossing over "bright lines" and stepping outside a traditional box. Stepping outside these bright lines can present a "catastrophic risk" to a company, according to Nanda.[13]

He believes in the inherent value of competitive intelligence and believes management should encourage creative—albeit occasionally inefficient—information-gathering efforts. Once you see someone cross over one of these bright lines, you need to squelch it immediately. To do so will send a strong signal throughout the company that such behavior is wrong and detrimental to everyone.

The Tom Berkels of the world are always encouraging their managers to think outside the information box in which a company often finds itself. It is important to do so. It is also important to help your collectors to distinguish between what is creative and what is a legal boundary line. Educating those around you on the limits is critical. You need to harness the cowboy's ideas and energy but not let the cowboy loose to act as he sees fit—without any guidelines.

When I led a group at the Society of Competitive Intelligence Professionals, the largest professional group of its kind in the world, to design and present an excellence award in corporate intelligence, the one category in which most companies fell short was in their ethical and legal guidelines—and the communications of those guidelines. Most had guidelines, but they tended to be either poorly designed or poorly communicated. In other words, they existed, but employees did not know about them or how they affected their behavior in the outside world.

Rules of thumb, or guidelines, are the intelligence conductor's batons. Berkel and others have them.

Just the Facts is a quick reference guide I use with my analysts. It tells them what the bright lines are and how to stay within them. The guidelines also take into account that you cannot preordain every situation. When in doubt, I recommend the analyst go to a project manager to discuss the implications of how far an approach can be pushed.

The guidelines include such advice as to begin telephone calls by (1) asking your questions, and (2) when asked to identify yourself, give your full name. Never induce or pressure sources to disclose information they have specifically categorized as proprietary.... If you believe information has come into your hands illegally or through someone who was breaking a confidentiality agreement when disclosing the information, bring the information to the attention of your project manager.

One of the best and most effective pieces of bright-lines advice comes from Mike Sandman (see chapter 4). When he was chief operating officer of Dexter Corporation, a multinational textile company, management enforced what Mike calls the harm rule. Each year his management asked him to sign a simple letter that effectively said, "I will not do anything that if it were found

out in public might harm or embarrass my company in any way."
While this rule might sound vague, its message is very specific. If
you believe that what you are about to do might smear your company's reputation should anyone find out, don't do it.

The harm rule does not cover all the details—and, believe me,
intelligence is a business of details—but it does begin to paint the
boundaries. Once you have the boundaries, conductors, such as
Tom Berkel, can begin to fill in the important details.

———

SOME people come by their competitive intelligence skills naturally, like an athlete takes to a sport; others need to learn them.
Competition is what business is all about. You cannot compete
without competitive knowledge and insight. This starts with the
CEO but radiates all the way down to the heart of a company.
Every manager—you—needs to learn how to incorporate the
lessons of intelligence into your regular business life so as to better
see the competition around you. Transparency, six degrees of
preparation, bean counting, cooking, and cowboys: Remember
these intelligence life lessons and then stop reading this book.
Leave your desk and begin to examine and pick at the data dots
forming a competitive picture right outside your door.

Seeing your competition clearly means engaging with that
world, not hiding from it (and always remember that when you
begin a conversation, you must first remove the blinders of denial
and rationalization).

You need to practice improving your competitive vision, not
just think about it. Once you establish frameworks to give yourself
some structure, head outside. Making yourself into a pepperoni

means you have to walk the plant floor. Counting the length of pipe in an oil well means you need to be at the well site. Even distinguishing between good and bad information coursing through the Internet requires that you test the information with the world outside the Net—through interviews and *real* conversations. Confrontation and conversation, as war games are so effective at providing, are among the best ingredients you can add to your competitive information stew.

Eventually, and possibly when you least expect it, you will develop that competitive clarity somewhat differently than your neighbor. The salesperson will see his customers and their information in a new light. The purchasing manager may open his eyes to see an intelligence chain, not just a supply chain. You may begin to see the future in terms of scenarios and realize that you can anticipate competitive changes five or even ten years ahead.

Congratulations on your new spectacles, with 20/20 competitive vision. Enjoy the clarity and the better decisions you will make as a result.

CHAPTER 9

THE BIG UNANSWERED QUESTIONS

After more than a quarter century working in the area of competitive intelligence, I still have many questions I've been unable to answer satisfactorily for myself. Some are simple questions with seemingly simple answers; some are more complex. Still others sound almost silly—but they still nag at me because they act as impediments to broad, unfettered application of competitive intelligence concepts and tools.

Intelligence is a strange business. Successful companies have always thrived on it, even when they call it by another name—competitive assessment, industry analysis, or just research. Some companies, like Dell and Wal-Mart, may not have a name for it at all. They just do it.

In important respects, intelligence is an art. As such, its origin is unclear as is its place in the modern corporation. After all, where does an art department fit on an organization chart?

Maybe, just maybe, intelligence should never find a cozy, fixed place on a corporate organization chart. Coziness and neatness don't comfortably occupy the same sentence with "intelligence." Intelligence, when it's done right, is the product of many individuals from throughout the company, not just from one official, professional guru with a big CORPORATE INTELLIGENCE sign on his door. Its home is the corporation, the entire organization chart.

Despite the serious message and the lessons I've tried to impart to you, despite the many CEOs and highly educated, down-to-their-boots professionals I've presented to you, despite all this I know you will encounter some weird, some serious, and some totally off-the-wall questions when you march ahead to create your next pointillist painting. Rather than let these questions go unasked and unanswered, I have decided to address them. No matter if it's your senior vice president who asks the question or if you catch yourself staring into the mirror thinking about these issues, here are some of the most subtle, most practical, and most ridiculous questions you will ever encounter about competitive intelligence.

By the way, these are all questions others have already asked. When I started scribbling them down on a piece of paper, they seemed to sort themselves out into four categories: (1) questions from family and friends, (2) questions from business colleagues, (3) questions from your management, and (4) questions you only ask yourself (and never admit to asking yourself in the first place).

Do yourself a favor and read them from start to finish. Consider them like one large dose of medicine you just swallowed to cure your cold. Take this elixir; you'll feel better by morning.

QUESTIONS FROM FAMILY AND FRIENDS

Will your friends and colleagues snicker when they hear you are "doing" competitive intelligence?

Probably some will snicker behind your back; the others will snort and chuckle in front of you. At parties, when the inevitable question "What do you do?" surfaces and you answer, "Part of my job is to develop intelligence on our competition," you can expect an awkward moment of silence. Then someone in your circle will ask, "Can you tell us any stories?" Believe me, whatever you tell them will not be lurid enough to satisfy their imaginations. The lesson, therefore, is to say you can't talk about it. In fact, this is the best answer. It has a dual effect: It keeps your audience guessing and allows you to maintain your confidentiality. The truly serious point I need to make here is that companies tend to be their own worst enemies when it comes to intelligence. It's not that the competitor has necessarily figured out your company's strategy; it's that an employee at a cocktail party gave it away.

Do you enjoy reading spy novels?

Answer whichever way you please; it makes no difference. Reading a spy novel doesn't help you become better at seeing through a competitor; only solid, diligent information gathering and analysis does that. (Yes, I enjoy a good spy novel, in case you're curious.)

Can you use competitive intelligence in other areas of life?

Yes, but it has its limits (something I should never admit, given that I'm a guru, an authority, an all-knowing author who is trying to pump up sales for his book). Nevertheless, the answer is as follows: The insight and analytical skills you have learned in this book about the Internet, war gaming, and even early warning can help your son or daughter hunt for the right college, shop for a car, look for a spouse—not necessarily in that order.

QUESTIONS FROM BUSINESS COLLEAGUES

When is enough intelligence enough?

Your response should immediately be "How much risk are you willing to assume?"

Certain organizations instill two deadly business dogmas that not only quash the use of good intelligence but also may in the end kill their business: (1) a sense of perfection and (2) a belief in "not invented here." Both dogmas are extremely risk averse. You can never supply these types of organizations with enough intelligence to satisfy them or to speed a possibly risky decision.

Science- or engineering-driven companies, such as biotechs or computer technology companies, often are run by managements that demand perfection. Engineering and technology cultures want every aspect of their company to be so perfect that they wish to eliminate virtually any risk. Since intelligence delivers a reasonable but not a perfect picture of a rival, a manager at such a risk-averse company will be unable to accept or act upon it.

The not-invented-here dogma belongs to companies that are established, mature players in a market. They've lived a successful existence for too long. General Motors is an example of just such a company. Although it had intelligence on Toyota's smaller cars and hybrid technology and on Volvo's safety features, management tended to react late and only when a sharp drop in market share became apparent.

You may find being the intelligence messenger in such companies a very lonely and perhaps risky job. How much professional risk are you willing to assume?

How many different ways can you use this art, skill, or however it's described known as intelligence?

I thought carefully about this question. It's an important one. Then I decided to flip through past assignment folders to gauge the range of questions our clients sent in our direction. There are literally thousands of different reasons why my clients have knocked on my door over the years. Here is a short list of assignments that will give you a sense of how wide-ranging and how powerful a concept intelligence can become.

> Understanding a competitor's core competency in R&D
> Determining exactly how a competitor was gaining market share
> Evaluating the success of e-commerce technology in the discount brokerage industry
> Assessing star talent defections and retaining top sales performers
> Analyzing a competitor's disruptive technology
> Determining which business process outsourcing strategic partnerships would have the most appeal to potential clients
> Using due diligence to identify the most likely acquisition candidates and potential spoilers that may quash the deal

> Anticipating new entrants and their strategies in a pharmaceuticals market
> Deciding how best to compete with a rival's unique distribution strategies
> Confirming channel expansion rumor to guide marketing efforts
> Exploring the best practices in mass customization to possibly change the business model
> Evaluating the global expansion plans for a major competitor
> Assessing the revenue and cost analysis of a European acquisition candidate
> Analyzing the impact of Citicorp/Travelers merger
> Determining how rivals are using contract manufacturing and contract design to improve efficiencies
> Examining to what extent competitors were using different parameters for supporting postsales servicing of equipment and the cost advantage they achieved
> Understanding who supplied the major component to a key competitor and at what price

QUESTIONS FROM YOUR MANAGEMENT

Should I call intelligence anything else? How do others, such as my employers, feel about the term?

Call it whatever you want, but just do it. Do it properly and do it well. That's all that really matters. In the ideal world, the process of developing intelligence should be part and parcel of everyone's job.

In its pure form, it is an activity, not a title. Just ask your top sales, marketing, and product management professionals. The people who pay their salaries and commissions in part pay them for their ability to assess competition and analyze a complex marketplace.

That said, corporations for a variety of reasons have chosen to label their intelligence efforts as industrial research, or competitive assessment. I have met managers who elected to disguise the concept because it didn't look good or because they believed it would impede their employees from collecting vital information, at a trade show, for example. That may be the case. Then again, it may not.

The professionals, those who work in this business full-time, may wish to call themselves competitive intelligence analysts. Labels can legitimately concentrate the issues and arguments that help develop a profession or ideas in a book, such as in this one. No doubt about it. Yet labels are just a means, a convenient way to focus an argument. In the end what you need are results, not labels.

When all is said and done, are you seeing through competitive smoke screens? Have you managed to accomplish this through honest and smart approaches—such as the ones I suggest in this book—that will allow you to sleep well at night? If the answer is yes, then what you call competitive intelligence is far less important than solving the competitive puzzle itself.

If I needed help, who would be really good at doing this kind of work? Whom should I look for within my company? Librarians? Ex-journalists? Crossword puzzle addicts?

I once polled a few dozen intelligence managers and asked

them what characteristic they looked for most, and it was "a good listener." I agree. As a class of employee, the best listeners I have come across over the years are the salespeople. Good selling means you need to probe your customer for their needs. Successful probing requires good listening.

Don't expect salespeople to just jump onto your lap or shake your hand at the mention of intelligence. If they are successful, they are incentive driven, particularly with respect to earning their commission. You can likely borrow some of their time, but you can't own them. Their livelihood depends on making that next sale.

Sophisticated librarians—I mean the ones with street smarts, not just the ones with database-searching skills—are invaluable. Include them in your initial information-seeking conversations. Let them become part of the brainstorming. You will find them extremely useful in leading you to experts and specialists.

Scientists—now there's a wow! Scientists and engineers are technical specialists. Many attend professional society meetings. Their promotion up the ranks depends on their expertise, which often begins by sharing information with colleagues at these conferences. Scientists have networks that are wide and deep. You need only alter their sights a bit when they attend such conferences. Include them on your competitive discussions so that next time they attend a technical congress they are looking for more than just the scientific poster presentations.

Crossword puzzles: This sounds like a wonderful test to give someone. I have met lots of managers who use such tests to filter out the intelligence winners from losers. Unfortunately, such simple tests rarely work. They do demonstrate the richness of vocabulary but little else. Street smarts, industry knowledge, persistence, and an ability to socialize and pick up on body language and social cues are valuable skills that cannot be assessed with a crossword puzzle test.

Hey, you want a test? Send your candidates to a shopping mall and have them interview a stranger or two to find out some very obscure information (favorite color, the salary they earn, and so on). I am serious. We run this exercise with my own analysts. The really with-it candidates will return with a raft of information and insights. These are the keepers.

Let's say I've come across or developed this great insight on our competitor's next moves. How can I convince anyone else that I'm not just a little loony or about to take the company down with me—especially if the insight involves actions on our part that are somewhat risky?

You're talking about almost every company I've ever encountered. By definition, intelligence is new, not something that's common knowledge. Often it challenges the status quo. It is fraught with risk, as I've said many times before.

In such a case, a straightforward report presented in a written document or even a PowerPoint slide deck is likely to fail to influence. If you submit a written document—even if it contains sophisticated graphs and well-designed clip art—you are begging for it to end up in someone's in-box where it will sit for a very long time.

I have found the most successful way to encourage managers

to act on especially aggressive advice is to involve them in the intelligence. I refer back to war gaming. War gaming or nearly any kind of strategic gaming will draw the decision makers into understanding the critical intelligence and its implications.

Don't expect managers to accept all vital intelligence. They won't. But get them to play the role of a rival, a supplier, or a customer, and suddenly your assessment becomes real. You can become the facilitator, not the decision maker, constantly fanning a dose of reality in front of them. Rather than sweep away what they can no longer ignore, they begin to act on it.

What is the return on investment (ROI)?

Ah, this is a magic question. Can you measure the ROI for competitive intelligence? This is also a common question, especially when companies find themselves in a recession or entering a cost-cutting phase.

The short answer (just so I don't keep you in too much suspense) is that I don't believe in such formulas. The "quants" (those who love numbers or ways to explain the world through numbers) will attempt to create a formula to address nearly every problem. You can certainly try. But the long and short of it is that there is no measure I would beg you to adopt.

I do have another anti-ROI argument for you. Not only is the company's investment intelligence relatively small, but the payoff can be enormous. So rather than try to measure an investment that may be insignificant (a few full-time salaries) in a multibillion-dollar company, concern yourself instead with the output. How many deals did management help close? Did they help the sales organization improve its win-loss rate on deals? Were they able to assist R&D in avoiding pursuing an expensive and time-consuming wasted research path (as we saw in the Novartis case in chapter 6)?

I can appreciate the need for ROI when you run a pharmaceutical company whose investment for one drug may be as high as $800 million.[1] Management certainly has a right to ask itself what the return on R&D will likely be and when to expect it. If you are ramping up your sales organization before a new product launch, you will absolutely need to know the expected revenue generated by each salesperson.

When you can identify the returns on intelligence, they are usually staggering. Max Downham, former CEO of NutraSweet, the artificial sweetener company, once claimed that his intelligence effort was responsible for revenue returns to NutraSweet of as much as $50 million a year.[2] I recall an assignment that cost an aerospace client about $150,000 to assess the bidding strategies of its chief competitors. Our assessment helped identify different ways it could bundle its technology with various services that would make it even more attractive to a vendor than the other bidders. This relatively small investment helped them win a $250 million contract. Looking at it another way, the ROI on this assignment was just under $1,700 to $1.

Metrics are important. You can't just hire or spend money without purpose. But intelligence being intelligence is still an art, not a machine. It is a process that sometimes yields great results, other times nothing. When it does deliver, however, the results usually exceed expectations, far beyond typical returns.

QUESTIONS YOU ONLY ASK
YOURSELF (AND NEVER ADMIT
TO ASKING YOURSELF IN THE
FIRST PLACE)

How do you know when you have X-ray vision, when you can see through or ahead of a competitor's tactics or strategy?

You will feel a real rush, a thrill. Being able to see how much it really costs a pepperoni company to produce its product took Mike Sandman nearly three months of painstaking discussions with the client, retrieval of government filings, and dozens of expert interviews. But when he assembled the first crude operating statement that pointed out the differences between his client's costs and those of the low-costs rival, he experienced a eureka moment. When I've walked the halls of my firm and bumped into an analyst who just completed a very successful interview that offered new insight on a company, I could see the clear-eyed thrill on his or her face.

X-ray vision describes the emotional and intellectual breakthrough you experience. At the beginning of an assignment, you are confronted with the frustration of the problem (how can their costs be lower or how do they manage to beat us to market?), a jumble of issues that truly blind you to reality. You'll find yourself filled with a bit of anxiety and lots of frustration at the start of nearly any intelligence assignment. The sudden revelation, the moment when all the informational pieces fit, is when you discover X-ray vision. That is when you feel the emotional rush intelligence brings.

Do people listen to you any more now because you offer intelligence instead of just information?

Watch out here! You enter the treacherous waters of managed expectations. For the consultants in my firm, this is probably at least as difficult a task as developing our chief product—the intelligence itself.

Never oversell. You have a sophisticated audience out there: CEOs, CFOs, directors of marketing, strategists. They all know the difference between the "aha!" intelligence versus the information you read along with millions of others in the *Wall Street Journal.*

Try to sell information in an intelligence wrapper and you have just defeated your purpose. One mistake I see all too often is some marketing manager or librarian summarizing news reports and publishing it in a newsletter format or on an intranet home page, masthead, logo, and all. He brands it with a title such as "The Intelligence Report" and expects readers to just gobble it up. What readers usually do is forget about it.

Intelligence by definition is unique and hard-won, not mass marketed. If it's information, call it that. Save the label of intelligence for a time-sensitive assessment that will direct someone to act.

Is intelligence the next Darwinian evolutionary step after market research? Are market researchers doomed to extinction? Will the survival of the fittest dictate that I, with my intelligence savvy, will come out on top?

Market research is here to stay and has a necessary place at the analysis table. Competitive intelligence is an addition to not a substitute for it. As I mentioned earlier, market research is all about the customer, while competitive intelligence concerns itself with the other four forces of Harvard professor Michael Porter's five forces model, including threat of new entrants, substitute products, the competitors, and key suppliers. Use them both.

Will your husband, wife, or Scout troop leader care about what you've learned here?

Nope. Just bring home the paycheck.

Can competitive intelligence make me into a Buffett or a Rothschild?

No amount of magic pixie dust can make us into anyone else, let alone a Warren Buffett or a Nathan Rothschild. When Roger Lowenstein, former reporter for the *Wall Street Journal*, wrote his book on Buffett, he included these opening comments:

> *In the annals of investing, Warren Buffett stands alone. Starting from scratch, simply by picking stocks and companies for investment, Buffett amassed one of the epochal fortunes of the twentieth century. Over a period of four decades—more than enough to iron out the effects of fortuitous rolls of the dice—Buffett outperformed the stock market, by a stunning margin and without taking undue risks or suffering a single losing year. This is a feat that market savants, Main Street brokers, and academic scholars had long proclaimed to be impossible. By virtue of this steady, superior compounding, Buffett acquired a magical-seeming net worth of $15 billion and counting."[3]*

Buffett has certainly employed numerous skills and talents illustrated throughout this book. But Buffett, as one example out of many, represents a unique talent that happens to also include an ability for knowing a company's strengths and weaknesses and acting swiftly on intelligence he acquires.

Imagine for a moment that you made one significant deal or Buffett-like investment using the intelligence available to you. You may not become Buffett, but you can benefit from the example he has set.

NOTES

DISRUPTIONS, DISTORTIONS, RUMORS, AND SMOKE SCREENS

1. The author recognizes the fact that the Factiva service over the years has added to the number of news sources it covers, which could account for some of the increase in the number of citations each year. At the same time, Factiva would likely have dropped a number of news sources or the publications themselves would have folded, canceling some of the effect created by the increase in the number of publications covered by Factiva. Even given this coverage growth, the nine thousand–plus articles cited in the press is evidence of a dramatic increase in awareness by the business press of competitive intelligence.

2. Reported on July 7, 2004, before the Select Committee on Intelligence, United States Senate, 108th Cong., 2nd Session.

3. http://groups.google.com/groups?hl...42db&seekm=323DAA09.3093%40 hbo.com, March 5, 2002.

CHAPTER 1. THE ART OF SMART

1. "Fuji's Joust with 'Kodak-San,'" *New York Times,* October 30, 1983, Section 3, Page 1.

2. Dewey Ballantine LLP, "Japanese Market Barriers in Consumer Photographic Film and Paper," May 1995, Vol. 1, Section I, 35.

3. The Hunts had speculated in the silver market beginning in the early 1970s. When the Hunts failed to meet a $100-million margin call from their broker, this set off a market crisis. Silver prices fell from $50 an ounce in early January 1980 to a low of $10.80 an ounce by late March. It was the Hunt brothers' initial failure to cover their losses that concerned the Federal Reserve and the Securities and Exchange Commission (SEC). At the time, experts made comparisons between the effects of the Hunt-induced silver collapse and the 1929 stock market crash. Karen W. Arenson, "Hunts Cited in Effort on Silver Curb," *New York Times,* April 17, 1980, D1.

4. "Fuji: Beyond Film," *Business Week,* November 22, 1999.

5. *Journey: 75 Years of Kodak Research* (Rochester, N.Y.: Eastman Kodak, 1989), 139.

6. Alecia Swasy, *Changing Focus* (New York: Times Books, 1997), 118–19.

7. Fatih Keenan and Cathy Schottenstein, "Kodak's Digital Dilemma," *Business Week,* March 24, 2003.

8. There was a great deal of evidence within Kodak that its management recognized the importance of digital imaging as early as the 1970s and early 1980s, including its pioneering work in charged couple device chips, the heart of a digital camera. Kodak kept amassing the patents but hesitated entering the consumer market for digital cameras until the late 1990s.

9. Leonard Fuld, interview with Robert Crandall, Factiva CI Center, 2001.

10. Leonard Fuld, interview with Jeff Taylor, Factiva CI Center, 2001.

11. Jon Bowen, "The Man Behind the Monster," *Arrive,* November/December 2001, 22.

12. Leonard Fuld, interview with Herb Baum, Factiva CI Center, 2001.

13. Leonard Fuld, interview with Daniel Vasella, Factiva CI Center, 2001.

14. Leonard Fuld, interview with T. Boone Pickens, Factiva CI Center, 2001.

CHAPTER 2. REALITY BITES

1. Overall African sales for Diageo, Guinness's parent, has risen dramatically in recent years with the exception of this reportedly brief mobile phone–caused sales dip, affecting the beer market overall in Africa. According to the Bloomberg.com news service, "African countries—Nigeria, Kenya, Cameroon, Ivory Coast and South Africa—account for five of the 10 largest markets by volume in the world for Guinness and 40 percent of worldwide profit." Bloomberg.com, August 23, 2003 (http://quote.bloomberg.com/apps/news?pid=nifea&&sid=ahg3j3Iw6f0w).

2. The EU directives officially prohibit any reference to alcohol as beneficial to your health or to your sex life.

3. "Nigerian Beer Market 2003," U.S. Consulate, Lagos, Nigeria. Foreign Agricultural Service, U.S. Department of Agriculture, July 22, 2003.

4. Carol Posthumus, "Mobile Africa: Leapfrogging the Digital Divide," *Feature,* July 5, 2001, www.thefeaturearchives.com/topic/Archive/Mobile_Africa_Leapfrogging_the_Digital_Divide.html. Feature.com was a Web site that existed from August 2000 through June 2005 and was sponsored by mobile

phone company Nokia. A similar drop in beer sales was reported by South African Breweries plc in its annual report for the fiscal year ending March 31, 1999. In the report, the company's chief executive explained the reason for the drop in consumption, which included an increase in mobile phone sales: "The proportion of disposable income which the average South African spends on food, beverages and tobacco has fallen steadily since 1992 . . . Mobile phones have also become very popular with the potential to further divert spending away from beer." A report in the *Financial Mail* (Tony Koenderman, "Wee Dram Holds Its Own," December 15, 2001), comments on the related liquor market in South Africa, which at that point had seen a decline in sales for three consecutive years. In addition to the weak economy, the article states, "Consumer disposable income remains weak, with continued erosion by other spending such as cell phones, gambling and lottery tickets."

5. "Cutting the Cord," *Economist,* October 7, 1999, http://www.economist.com/surveys/displaystory.cfm?story_id=246152.

6. "Simplewire Provides SMS Aggregation for Guinness Beer Promotion," September 1, 2004, http://www.prwebdirect.com/releases/2004/9/prweb/53921.htm.

7. Leonard Fuld, interview with Gary Roush, February 2002.

8. "The Softer Side of Due Diligence," *Competitive Intelligence* 6, no. 4, 2003, 45–46.

9. Ian Cookson, "M&A Issues Raise the Governance Bar," *Financial Executive Magazine,* October 2004.

10. "AOL and Time Warner Investors Are Starved for Facts," *Business Week,* June 22, 2000.

11. Leonard Fuld, interview with Chuck Rooney, March 2002.

CHAPTER 3. WILL GOOGLE BEAT MICROSOFT?

1. As of 2005, though, AOL sought to reduce its dependence on Google by expanding its reach globally and forming partnerships with other search companies, such as Norwegian-based Fast Search & Transfer Inc.

2. Yahoo! and Google share the same pedigree; both were founded by Stanford University students in the 1990s. Yahoo! started off its virtual life with a simpler, more catchy but less exciting name, "Jerry and David's Guide to the World Wide Web." Only later did its two founders, Jerry Yang and David Filo, rename it Yahoo! for *y*et *a*nother *h*ierarchical *o*fficious *o*racle.

3. John P. Hussman, "Google, iPods and George Foreman Grills," *Hussman Funds—Weekly Market Comment,* June 13, 2005, http://www.hussman.net/wmc/wmc050613.htm.

4. Michael E. Porter, *Competitive Strategy: Techniques for Analyzing Industries and Competitors* (New York: The Free Press, 1980).

5. Headlines are from *New York Times,* June 20, 2005; *Newsweek,* June 25, 2005; and *Financial Times,* May 15–16, 2005.

6. Timothy Roberts, "Internet Tax Remains Elusive $1.8 Billion Pot of Gold," *Silicon Valley / San Juan Business Journal,* July 3, 2005.

7. "Yahoo!'s Personality Crisis," *Economist,* August 11, 2005, 49.

8. Julia Angwin and Kevin J. Delaney, "AOL, Google Expand Partnership, With a Key Ad-Sales Provision," *Wall Street Journal,* December 21, 2005, B3A.

9. Leonard Fuld, interview with Michael E. Porter, June 26, 2002.

10. Dan Fost, "Mergers a Rite of Passage in Life of U.S. Companies," *San Francisco Chronicle,* December 19, 2004.

11. Joseph Menn, "For Oracle, Winning a War May Be Only Half the Battle; Even if the Software Maker Prevails, Melding with PeopleSoft Could Prove Difficult at Best," *Los Angeles Times,* November 22, 2004, C-1.

12. Leonard Fuld, interview with Youssef Squali, managing director, Jefferies & Company, New York, June 29, 2005.

CHAPTER 4. MAKE ME INTO A PEPPERONI

1. The Uniform Commercial Code (UCC) is a list of rules and guidelines used by forty-nine out of the fifty U.S. states (Louisiana being the exception) to harmonize commercial transactions among the states. One set of these guidelines involves a lending agency, such as a bank or leasing company, to report when a company borrows money or leases equipment. These filings usually list the equipment involved with the loan or the lease. Hence, a UCC filing can be an extremely useful source for identifying critical assets in a manufacturing plant.

CHAPTER 5. EARLY WARNING

1. Federal Reserve Bank of Philadelphia, "Credit Card Pricing Developments and Their Disclosure," January 2003.

2. Over 140 strategists from large corporations worldwide participated in a

survey conducted by the Fuld Gilad Herring Academy of Competitive Intelligence. Among the responses, 77 percent of respondents stated that although their companies should anticipate increased levels of business risk in the next two to three years, only 2.6 percent claimed to have a formal early warning process in place. Leonard M. Fuld, "Early Warning: Management Need . . . Management Failure," a Fuld & Company white paper, April 2003. Copyright © 2003, Fuld & Company.

3. Timothy Aeppel, Clare Ansberry, Milo Geyelin, and Robert L. Simison, "Road Signs: How Ford, Firestone Let the Warnings Slide By as Debacle Developed," *Wall Street Journal,* September 6, 2000, A1.

4. Leonard Fuld, interview with Melanie Wing, March 2002.

5. Jathon Sapsford and Paul Beckett, "Credit-Card Firms Still Need a Strong Hand in Web Game," *Wall Street Journal,* April 2, 2001, C1.

6. Leonard Fuld, interview with Dale Fehringer, February 2002 and January 2004; additional information for the Visa International early warning story gleaned from articles and public presentations by Dale Fehringer, including "Conducting 'Comfort Intelligence' with Scenario Analysis," by Dale Fehringer of Visa International at The Society of Competitive Intelligence Professionals Annual 2002 Conference, April 2002, Cincinnati, Ohio.

7. The early warning model described here is based in part on Ben Gilad's early warning model, and in part on scenario analysis work with clients at Fuld & Company. Ben Gilad, *Early Warning* (New York: AMACOM, 2003).

CHAPTER 6. THE INTERNET HOUSE OF MIRRORS

1. Harvard Business School intranet, http://intranet.hbs.edu/dept/operations/BLAC/history.html

2. Leonard Fuld, interview with Daniel Vasella, Factiva CI Center, 2001.

3. Leonard Fuld, interview with Mark Higgins, March 2002.

4. Philip J. Kaplan, *F'd Companies: Spectacular Dot-Com Flameouts* (New York: Simon & Schuster, 2002), 13.

5. http://comments.fuckedcompanies.com/fc/phparchives/search.php?search=Conxion, searched on November 28, 2005.

6. http://comments.fuckedcompanies.com/fc/phparchives/search.php?search=SwitchHouse, searched on November 28, 2005.

7. http://comments.fuckedcompanies.com/fc/phparchives/search.php?search=nextcard, searched on November 28, 2005.

8. http://www.cafepharma.com/ubbthreads/showflat.php?Cat=0&Board= genentech&Number=311593&page=5&fpart=all, searched on January 4, 2005.

9. www.hoovers.com/disney/--ID_11603--/free-co-factsheet.xhtml, searched on November 28, 2005.

10. http://transnationale.org, searched on May 14, 2002.

11. Chris Sherman and Gary Price, *The Invisible Web: Uncovering Information Sources Search Engines Can't See* (Medford, N.J.: Information Today, 2001).

12. Robert Hobbes Zakon, *Hobbes' Internet Timeline v7.0,* http://www.zakon .org/robert/internet/timeline/, searched on February 12, 2004.

13. Information published on the *Factiva* and LexisNexis corporate Web sites, http://www.factiva.com and http://www.lexisnexis.com.

14. Leonard Fuld, interview with Clare Hart, Princeton, N.J., April 2002.

15. Leonard Fuld, interview with Robert Crandall, excerpted from Factiva CI Center, 2000.

CHAPTER 7. COMPETITIVE FOG

1. Rothschild "interview" based on article: Leonard M. Fuld, "Intelligence Two Centuries Later," *Competitive Intelligence Magazine,* November–December 2002, 40–41.

2. Niall Ferguson, *The House of Rothschild,* vol. 1, *Money's Prophets: 1798– 1848* (New York: Viking Press, 1998), 234–35.

3. Ibid., 94.

4. Ibid., 410.

5. Leslie Miller, Associated Press, "Jordan's Furniture Sold to Warren Buffett's Berkshire Hathaway," Boston, October 11, 1999.

6. Roger Lowenstein, *Buffett: The Making of an American Capitalist* (New York: Broadway Books, 1995), 147.

7. Carol Sliwa, "Wal-Mart Takes 'Tough Love' Approach with RFID Directive," *Computerworld,* January 19, 2004.

8. Kim Girard, "How Levi's Got Its Jeans into Wal-Mart," *CIO,* July 15, 2003.

9. Steve Lohr, Andrew Ross Sorkin, and Gary Rivlin, "I.B.M.'s Sale of PC Unit Is Bridge Between Companies and Culture," *New York Times,* December 8, 2004, A1.

10. Dell Computer Corporation, "The Core Areas of Dell Business Run on Dell," October 2002, http://www.dell.com/downloads/global/casestudies/dell_on.pdf.

11. "Customer Experience Forum for Consumers," 2003 Consumer Electronics Show, Las Vegas, Nev., January 9, 2003.

12. Richard Branson, *Losing My Virginity: How I've Survived, Had Fun, and Made a Fortune Doing Business My Way* (New York: Three Rivers Press, 1998), 251.

CHAPTER 8. DAY TO DAY

1. Mintel International Group, "Pasta Sauce Market—US Report," Chicago, January 1, 2003.

2. Leonard Fuld, interview with Tony Adams, March 2002.

3. Leonard Fuld, interview with Gary Roush, February 2002.

4. Kenneth Chang, "New Signs of Water Mean Mars May Once Have Supported Life," *New York Times,* March 3, 2004, A1.

5. Peter Fritsch, "Leon Yallouz Knows There's an Awful Lot of Coffee in Brazil," *Wall Street Journal,* June 14, 1998, 1.

6. "Restructuring in the Petroleum Industry: The Free Enterprise System at Work." Remarks made by T. Boone Pickens, Institutional Equity Corporation, April 19, 1984, Dallas, Tex.

7. John Burnett, "Profile: Controversial Efforts to Pump Water and Sell It in Texas," NPR News, October 15, 2002.

8. Leonard Fuld, interview with Dale Fehringer, February 2002 and January 2004.

9. Fuld & Company, "Intelligence Gathering on Gut Instinct Rather Than on Knowledge: Survey on Ethical and Legal Intelligence Gathering Shows US-Europe Cultural Bias," Cambridge, Massachusetts, May 15, 2001.

10. "Fortune Reveals Case of Corporate Espionage by Procter & Gamble Against Competitors," *Fortune* press release, August 30, 2001.

11. Ameet Sachdev, "P&G Admits Unilever Garbage Search—Regrets Voiced About Spying on Haircare Unit," *Chicago Tribune,* September 1, 2001, N1.

12. Leonard Fuld, interview with Tom Berkel, March 2002.

13. Leonard Fuld, interview with Ashish Nanda, July 2002.

CHAPTER 9. THE BIG UNANSWERED QUESTIONS

1. Merrill, Goozner, *The $800 Million Pill: The Truth Behind the Cost of New Drugs*, Berkeley, Calif.: University of California Press, 2004.
2. Gary H. Anthes, "Competitive Intelligence: It Is Helping Companies Dig Up Vital Information on Their Archenemies," *Computerworld*, July 6, 1998.
3. Roger Lowenstein, *Buffett: The Making of an American Capitalist* (New York: Broadway Books, 1995), xiii.

ACKNOWLEDGMENTS

Competitive intelligence is not one of those subjects you just invent. I have spent the past three decades shaping and molding it, helping to educate a worldwide corporate audience of its value. But mostly I see myself as a conduit or translator of many people's ideas. I truly owe a lot to lots of individuals, some of whom never labeled what they do or did as "intelligence." I owe them a great deal of thanks. That's what this note is about; it's one big grateful thank-you.

I would never look at a sausage, a Google printout, or a strategic framework quite the same way had I never met these folks. My friends and colleagues can take common, everyday objects, such as a patent filing or a database printout, and turn them into a pair of competitive spectacles. With these intelligence glasses, I have learned techniques and approaches for lifting most competitive veils.

I thank my partner, Mike Sandman, who has made intelligence concepts come alive through his insatiable curiosity about any and all industries and how they work. His natural desire to intellectually tinker with a paucity of information and then assemble it into a reasonable competitive image is fun to watch.

In addition, I would like to directly thank Lenore Scanlon, who has patiently argued with me about ideas over the years, reasonably bringing many of them back to reality. Her editing and insights have provided me with a critical intellectual anchor.

Then there is my organization, a bright and inquisitive bunch who never fail to send me notes or call with insights learned from recent assignments. In particular, I want to acknowledge members of my senior staff, including Marcia Crumley, Mark Chodnowsky, Cindy Gerber Tomlinson, Tony Nagle, and Spencer Jones, who are my eyes and ears and guideposts for the many markets they serve. I would also like to thank my local Internet guru, Helene Kassler, the head of our information services, for teaching me so many searching tricks and tips. She has saved me from joining the "million hits" club time and time again. In addition to Helene, I want to thank Cynthia Correia and Frederique Feron, two wonderfully talented librarians, for educating me on the Internet's cultural and language overtones.

Most people are fortunate if they are able to earn a living while enjoying a single career. My first career is consulting, but I have also been privileged to enjoy a second simultaneous career as a teacher. In classrooms and executive suites around the world, I have had the pleasure of showing thousands of businesspeople how to apply intelligence to improve their competitive position. I have done all this teaching alongside some of the best. Thank you, Ben Gilad and Jan Herring, two very different but wonderful friends and colleagues at our academy. They bring with them a joy in getting others to say "Wow!" To Ben, both a mentor and a great debater, thanks for your lessons in early warning and overall insights. To Jan, never would I have thought that an ex-CIA guy and a boy from the Bronx would have so much in common. To all my students at the Academy of Competitive Intelligence, thanks for all the scores of conversations and for passing along to me your wonderful stories, examples, and techniques. I have learned a lot from you.

Attempting to achieve global appeal for this book, I had to speak with many industry experts, leaders in their respective markets. They may not be gurus in competitive intelligence, but they do use intelligence or are the chief consumers of such products. It was an honor and a privilege to speak with each and every one of them. I owe special thanks to Clare Hart, CEO of Factiva, the Dow Jones–Reuters joint venture, not only for taking the time to offer her observations on the Internet and the direction the online world is taking, but also for providing me with the platform to interview many industry leaders. Through our jointly run Competitive Intelligence Center, I found the wonderful excuse to tap into the intelligence insights of Robert Crandall, T. Boone Pickens, Daniel Vassela, Herb Baum, and Jeff Taylor, among others.

Then there are the corporate foot soldiers. These are the people who have pioneered or experimented with competitive intelligence, sometimes risking safer career choices. Thank you to Melanie Wing, Gary Roush, Tony Adams, Chuck Rooney, Dale Fehringer, and Tom Berkel for the time they spent speaking with me.

Thanks to Professor Michael Porter at Harvard Business School, whose conversations over the years have always been informative and very helpful. It's been an honor and a privilege. To Ashish Nanda of Harvard, thank you for helping me articulate my thoughts on ethical boundaries in this business. To MIT's Jack Rockart, arguably the father of executive information systems, I appreciate your observations, particularly the ones that focused on technology's information limits, how in the world of information there are areas where machines stop and people begin. Thank you also to John Prescott, who has had many conversations with me over the years on this quirky profession of ours.

There are whole hosts of people whom I have never met but to whom I also owe a great deal. These are the business greats who have mesmerized us with their investment wisdom and business derring-do. Their actions, while not designed to teach approaches to developing our ability to see through rivals' smoke screens or market disruptions, taught us lessons anyway. The lessons I have learned from Warren Buffett, Nathan Rothschild, Richard Branson, Sam Walton, and Michael Dell are lessons I will remember for a long time to come. They have all taught me the fine balance between the value of appraising risk and acting on intelligence.

I owe a great deal to David Gumpert, who is officially the person I go to for public relations efforts, but who unofficially serves as a sensible, business-savvy sounding board. Ideas can rattle around in an author's head until they achieve a certain wonderful level of noise—but in truth need a lot of reshaping. David has acted as my outside critic and wonderfully so.

My editor John Mahaney, whom I have followed from publishing house to publishing house, believed in my message and helped me refine that message through his gentle prodding and fine sense of what business readers want and need. Thank you, John. It's been a pleasure.

Most of all, I would like to thank my family for grounding me in the important matters in life. Finally, to my wife, Suzi, thank you for always believing in me and for allowing me to share my life with you.

INDEX

302

About the Author

LEONARD M. FULD is the founder and president of Fuld & Company and cofounder of the Fuld Gilad Herring Academy of Competitive Intelligence. He is a leader in the field of competitive intelligence and has created many of the techniques currently used by corporations around the globe. He and his firm have been profiled in many publications, including *Harvard Business Review, The Economist,* the *New York Times, Wall Street Journal, Investor's Business Daily, Newsweek,* and *Fast Company.* He has also been featured on the *Today* show, *CNNfn,* and *Marketplace.* His articles have appeared in leading business publications, including the *Wall Street Journal, Harvard Business Review, Pharmaceutical Executive,* and *Journal of Business Strategy.*

Mr. Fuld has lectured at major corporations worldwide and at numerous professional conferences, including the American Marketing Association, the Conference Boards of New York and Canada, the United Nations Industrial Development Organization (UNIDO), and Management Centre Europe.

In addition to this book, Mr. Fuld has previously authored *The New Competitor Intelligence* (Wiley, 1995), *Competitor Intelligence: How to Get It—How to Use It* (Wiley, 1985), *Monitoring the Competition: Find Out What's Really Going On Over There* (Wiley, 1988), as well as *The Fuld War Room* (Ironhorse Multimedia, 1998), a distance learning program for corporate training in competitive intelligence.